Pentecostals in America

The Columbia Contemporary American Religion Series

Columbia Contemporary American Religion Series

The spiritual landscape of contemporary America is as varied and complex as that of any country in the world. The books in this series, written by leading scholars for students and general readers alike, fall into two categories: Some titles are portraits of the country's major religious groups. They describe and explain particular religious practices and rituals, beliefs, and major challenges facing a given community today. Others explore current themes and topics in American religion that cut across denominational lines. The texts are supplemented with carefully selected photographs and artwork, and annotated bibliographies.

—

Roman Catholicism in America
CHESTER GILLIS

Islam in America
JANE I. SMITH

Buddhism in America
RICHARD HUGHES SEAGER

Protestantism in America
RANDALL BALMER AND LAUREN F. WINNER

Judaism in America
MARC LEE RAPHAEL

The Quakers in America
THOMAS D. HAMM

New Age and Neopagan Religions in America
SARAH PIKE

Baptists in America
BILL J. LEONARD

Islam in America, Second Edition
JANE I. SMITH

Buddhism in America, Revised and Expanded Edition
RICHARD HUGHES SEAGER

PENTECOSTALS
in America

Arlene M. Sánchez Walsh

COLUMBIA UNIVERSITY PRESS
NEW YORK

COLUMBIA UNIVERSITY PRESS
Publishers Since 1893
New York   Chichester, West Sussex
cup.columbia.edu

Copyright © 2018 Columbia University Press
All rights reserved

Library of Congress Cataloging-in-Publication Data

Names: Sanchez-Walsh, Arlene M., author.
Title: Pentecostals in America / Arlene M. Sanchez Walsh.
Description: New York : Columbia University Press, [2018] | Series: Columbia contemporary American religion series | Includes bibliographical references and index.
Identifiers: LCCN 2017051840 | ISBN 9780231141826 (cloth) | ISBN 9780231141833 (pbk.) | ISBN 9780231512220 (e-book)
Subjects: LCSH: Pentecostalism—United States.
Classification: LCC BR1644.5.U6 S264 2018 | DDC 277.3/083—dc23
LC record available at https://lccn.loc.gov/2017051840

Cover image: Photo courtesy of the Dixon Pentecostal Research Center, Cleveland, Tennessee

Dedicated to:
My parents
Miguel & Cora Sánchez
My mentor, oracle, inspiration and friend:
Dr. Vicki L. Ruiz
And the young women I've been honored to help raise as my smart and beautiful daughters with my patient and supportive spouse, Tim
Love forever,
Siobhán & Soledad

CONTENTS

Acknowledgments	ix
INTRODUCTION	xi
CHAPTER ONE Pentecostal Faith and Practice	1
CHAPTER TWO Pentecostal Innovators	14
CHAPTER THREE Gender, Sexualities, and Pentecostalism	34
CHAPTER FOUR Pentecostalism and Popular Culture	52
CHAPTER FIVE Race, Ethnicity, and the Construction of an American Pentecostal Identity	69
CHAPTER SIX Outliers in American Pentecostalism	87
EPILOGUE A Whole New Thing—The Future of Pentecostalism in America	103
Notes	113
Bibliography	135
Index	147

ACKNOWLEDGMENTS

I began writing this book while I was pregnant with my second child. I finished it as she was about to turn ten years old. I am grateful to the professionals at Columbia University Press, especially my editor, Wendy Lochner, who shepherded my first book and patiently waited for me to complete this book. Wendy is the kind of editor so many of us need. I have lost count of the emails I've sent her over the years, humbly excusing my lateness with this project: difficult pregnancy, recovery from a C-section, my family health issues, and my own health problems—life. Wendy offered nothing but comfort and understanding. Such understanding served as an antidote to the harsh realities of the academic life for working women, where work/life balance is more aspiration than reality.

Thanks to Michael Wilkinson and Philip Sinitiere, who read the early drafts and made insightful comments and critiques. Paul Harvey and Phil read the nearly final draft, and both are the reason the book has finally seen the publishing light. The best colleagues are also friends, and I am especially indebted to Angela Tarango, Anthea Butler, Benji Rlsky, David McConeghy, Leah Payne, Kim Alexander, Jackie Hidalgo, Edwin David Aponte, Justin Doran, Clayton Drees, and Lloyd Barba, who shared their experiences, wisdom, and advice throughout this process. My colleague Lynn Losie, now retired but never far away thanks to Facebook, was and still is the senior scholar who every mid-career person needs to help navigate this business.

Faculty research grants from Azusa Pacific University have helped me take time off during several summers to interview people, gather information in archives, and do what I do for a living, sit in churches. I am especially grateful to Provost Mark Stanton, Dr. Donald Isaak, and Dean Bobby Duke for the chance to spend a week doing nothing but writing, overlooking the exquisite California coast in Malibu, nearly every year since I have been at APU—you don't know how rare it is to dedicate that much time to writing unhindered by distractions. Thanks also to the Perkins School of Theology, where I spent my sabbatical year 2012–2013 finishing the middle chapters of this book and teaching fabulous students, many whom are now friends. The financial and material support from Perkins was essential to pushing this book from a few formless ideas to reasonably well-formed chapters. To the many Pentecostal archivists, church members, and personalities who have done researchers a great service by putting their sermons, pictures, and magazines online, many thanks. And to those few Pentecostal pastors who offered insights into their lives and helped me think about how Pentecostals experience their lives I am very grateful.

Thank you to Tim Walsh—you're a supportive spouse, a wonderful partner, and my best friend, and I'm so glad you're still willing to listen to all my stories. To my daughters, who sat with me on many late nights, asking me what I was doing or why I was up so late. Especially Siobhan, who stayed up with me so I wouldn't feel "lonely," you are wonderful. Yes, this academic work/life (im)balance impoverishes many of us, it is something I have tried very hard not to let affect you. Thank you, Soledad and Siobhán—you are intelligent, thoughtful, and beautiful young girls. Every aspect of my professional life pales compared to watching you grow up.

INTRODUCTION

Pentecostals tell great stories. Resurrections. Healings. Prophecies. People who are brought back from the edge of despair, limbs that grow back, marriages that are restored, children who are lost and found. There is a story for every existential ill that befalls humanity. This volume encapsulates my readings, musings, interviews, observations, and experiences while traveling through this subculture for twenty years. As such, it is not an exhaustive linear history of Pentecostalism in America. Rather, it is a thematic exploration of what I believe Pentecostalism represents to its followers and to the general public; it is an exploration of its stories. Of course, the standard history of Pentecostalism—its names, dates, and spiritual genealogies—matters, but it does not do the story of American Pentecostalism justice.

The early years of Pentecostalism—its divisiveness, its remarkable growth and geographic vastness, and its personalities—created a bewildering array of narratives and counter-narratives all in search of one coherent story of triumph, of faithfulness, and of holiness in the face of the weight of worldliness. It is a scattershot of spiritual lineages that try to trace their origins back to the movement's most respected pioneers—Seymour, Parham, Haywood, Cashwell, Llorente, Nava, Ewart, Goss, Opperman, Urshan, Durham, Sinclair, Argue, Bell, Francescon, Sungren, Fisher, Smale, Mason, Farrow, Taylor, King, Flower, Copley, Tomlinson, Lopez, Olazábal, Cook, Barratt, Boddy, Lawson, Lake, and literally hundreds of others, all of whom vie for the prized title of "founder."

One can look through the hundreds of books, dissertations, and articles, especially from confessional Pentecostals, and find attempts at uncovering the linkages to these spiritual lineages: who ordained whom, who broke away from what church, who mentioned whom in a diary, who left his or her book of sermons to whom. Thousands of pages filled with timelines connect dot after metaphorical dot back to the mythical origins of the movement. Scholars of Pentecostalism and especially American religious historians should thank the legion of grassroots scholars, church historians, and laypeople who preserved their histories because, without them, we would not have these narratives. American religious history would be inaccurate and impoverished without this material. To be sure, these historians have unearthed mountains of information, including pictures, oral histories, and ephemera of all kinds, as well as digitizing and securing pages of early Pentecostal magazines and periodicals—quite a worthy task. But they have also created an imaginary consisting of hagiographic accounts of great men and women and often failed to interrogate Pentecostals' incredible claims. One reason for their unwillingness or inability to maintain some critical distance is that their subjects—the "pioneers of the faith"—were often their own brothers, sisters, parents, and grandparents. Pentecostal historiography has thus been more concerned with uncovering the genealogy of the movement than with its complexities, its weaknesses, and especially its place in the bigger picture of American religious movements, with which it surely shares some spiritual DNA.

American religious historians are not genealogists—we are not concerned with merely connecting the dots between who worshipped where and who followed whom in the pastorate. Collecting data is crucial; interpreting that data is our essential task. "Data," however, sounds too "scientific." Ever since the "linguistic turn" that history made with the help of literary theorists in the late 1960s and 1970s, we have eschewed the grand illusion that our methods are scientific or that our compilations of stories describe what "really happened." Theorists such as Hayden White and others have freed us from such unattainable goals, and many of us, though certainly not all, have been satisfied with writing about history the way we see it. That is, the only way we can really "report" what happened is to be self-reflexive about our own positionality. Why am I writing this history the way I am writing it?

For my part, I am writing this thematic history because I think this method allows voices that have not been heeded in Pentecostal histories to be heard. I believe a thematic approach allows for myriad narratives about conversions, healings, prophecies, revelations, and visions to be placed in their cultural and social context and, in effect, stripped of the hyperspiritualization found in narratives that support the theological preferences of the authors. Standing outside of its confessional corner, I find Pentecostalism fascinating in its mixture of ecstatic, almost magical expressions, metaphysical nuances, earnest pietism, and intense embodied spirituality. As one of the most significant Christian movements of the last century and one of the most populous worldwide, with 250–450 million adherents, it deserves to be studied critically. Too often, Pentecostalism has been viewed as a self-exculpatory triumph of what God is doing in the world or a distasteful backwater frenzy fit only for those willing to delude themselves. It is neither the triumphant last wave of the Holy Spirit as many of its followers claim, nor is it the cry of the dispossessed, the disinherited poor cousins of the more refined evangelical class. As Tanya Luhrmann observes in her exquisite book, *When God Talks Back*, Pentecostals believe, with passion, with faith, and with every fiber of who they are, that God speaks to them, listens to them, and acts on their petitions. Whether any of that is "true" is the domain of theology, where faith claims have been argued for millennia.

Borrowing methods from the sociology and the psychology of religion, this book also draws from studies of American religious history. American religious historians have begun to see the value in studying Pentecostalism as a part of a larger picture of the American religious landscape; they have created opportunities to extend that picture westward and to movements other than those begun in New England. In doing so here, I also go farther to argue that Pentecostalism's origins, its growth, its fractious nature, are all part of what is a quintessentially American religious experience. This experience includes the idea that religious competition requires vanquishing one's theological enemies, proving others to be theologically heterodox and one's own group to be more pious. Moreover, in Pentecostalism, the continual divisiveness over race, which is a genetic disposition of nearly all American religious traditions, is more pronounced because of its interracial beginnings. Likewise, the "limited liberty" of women in Pentecostal ranks mirrors the difficulties women had in religious bodies throughout the United States, while gender inequalities in Pentecostalism tend to mask both the discomfort male religious actors have with female sexuality and their own sexual proclivities.

While I tend not to rely on the obtuse language of theory, I do bring theoretical insights to bear on the faith lives of Pentecostals. By treating those faith lives critically rather than triumphantly, this book takes them seriously. The claims Pentecostals make in their narratives are astounding, but as I argue, their force derives from the narratives themselves, not the substance of the claims. Pentecostals tell great stories so that an unregenerate, unbelieving, lost world will follow them as they make the last call before the *eschaton*—the end of the age when Jesus returns. Since their first few years of existence in the early twentieth century, Pentecostals believed that the pouring out of the Spirit on all flesh, that they believed began in earnest at the Azusa Street Revival in 1906, signaled the end times before Jesus comes back to earth to claim the church.[1] It is this sense of urgency, this passion, that makes for compelling narratives.

Pentecostals may be upset with my characterization of testimonies as stories, of speaking in tongues as a dissociative state, and of prophecy as driven by personal, social, and political considerations. But these are the kinds of positions scholars take with regard to this movement. Some might also ask: Does one have to be in a trance to speak in tongues? What part of the brain needs to be stimulated in order for this process to be considered "real" considered "real"? It is part of my task in this book to suggest that the issue is not whether such phenomena are "real"; it is that they are taken as real by the people who describe them as part of their everyday faith lives. The testimonies do not have to be "realistic" any more than the grand narratives of early church martyrs or the stories of miracles in the annals of medieval Christianity.

Pentecostalism is part of a stream of narratives in which the miraculous makes faith real for novices, so much so that they decide to convert, to receive prayer for healing, to get up in church and utter prophecies about the impending doom befalling a benighted America. They become Pentecostal first by hearing then by doing. It is a script as old as Christianity itself.

What is distinctive about Pentecostalism is its ability to grab an audience, its personalities, its showmanship, its preening paternalism. Though quite off-putting for some, this is what makes it tick. While other forms of Protestantism have lost many followers, Pentecostalism remains powerful, due in part to its constant remaking of its mythic origins and narratives of triumph over darkness. Thus, the figures I have chosen to highlight particular themes in this book are, in fact, signifiers whose meaning has changed over time, according to who has told their story. Similarly, their stories of triumph, of healing, and of the miraculous change depend on who chooses to tell them and why they want to tell them.

Pentecostalism in America is about how "competitive spirits" go about selling their wares, remaking their stories, giving in to their prejudices, and hoping to maintain their zealous certainty that they are the last wave before Jesus comes. In the face of both the scandals of past and the reality that they have been waiting probably one hundred years more than they thought they would have to, Pentecostals remain steadfast. Individually, they change, they accommodate, they forgive. Collectively, they insist that their movement has never changed, never adapted, and that all the theological heterodoxies that have darkened its doors have been ferreted out. It is these mythic narratives that hold the power of Pentecostalism to succeed.

What this book seeks to do is to ask questions about geography and how Pentecostalism works in various American spaces. It also examines ideas about healing, broadly construed, since healing is Pentecostalism's calling card. And it traces Pentecostalism's many lineages—in African and African American spiritualties, nineteenth-century New Thought, and midwestern and southern adaptations of German and British pietism—and looks at some of the remarkable people who found themselves enraptured by the Holy Spirit, so much so that they made that experience the cornerstone of their faith lives. Though colorful, these "great men and women" of Pentecostal hagiography were ordinary; like anyone else, Charles Parham, Aimee Semple McPherson, Maria Atkinson, Joyce Meyer, Maria Tate, Carleton Pearson, and Joel Osteen were all subject to egotistical flights of fancy, lacking self-reflective abilities to see their own faults and exhibiting racism, sexism, and all manner of debilitating pathologies that exact severe personal costs. It is the ordinariness, the normalcy of these figures that is most interesting to me. Seen without a hagiographic gloss, they become real, and their faith trajectories all the more enticing, heroic, and sometimes tragic. If we take off the gloss, we also can see that the Pentecostal focus on spiritual and geographic lineage is not unique to the movement and more often than not, the way many religious movements attempt to lay claims to authenticity.

The best parallel I can think of for how early Pentecostalism worked is to go outside of the Christian tradition completely and look to the way that Buddhists train their leaders, how they transmit their dharma, how novice Tibetan Buddhists seek out their root lama in hopes of finding the quickest bodhisattva path. Similarly, in Pentecostalism, teachers are valued for the purity of their teaching. "They teach from the Bible" is shorthand for theological purity and maintaining Holiness standards where others have gone the way of the world. There is a move of God here (in Chicago or Los Angeles or North Carolina), and we need to experience that since this is the last wave before Jesus comes back. Finding the right root lama, the right teacher, pastor, the right move of the Spirit, then becomes the precursor to the climactic final age when the biblical prophecies Pentecostals urgently await unfolding start coming to pass. Having the right teacher in Buddhism often means you are one step closer to enlightenment. For Pentecostals, the practice of Baptism in the Holy Spirit, evidenced by speaking in unknown languages, begins their dharma transmission, where they seek to promote that same experience, promote the same teachings, and extoll the virtues of their lineage. As in various forms of Buddhism, what lineage you come from determines your path. Pentecostal faithful like to portray their various paths as singular, unified, and infused with the Spirit, which is their right and forms the basis of their beliefs. This book does not argue that this theological positioning is wrong, but it does argue that history told from this perspective is skewed and that a different approach is required in order to get at the multiplicity of paths, the disunity, and the diversity of stories told by ordinary Pentecostals in their writings and their diaries, through their ephemera and in person. These Pentecostal friends, acquaintances, and raconteurs often started their stories the same way many of us do when asked to describe our histories—they told me where they were from.

Pentecostalism, and I would argue just about any form of Christianity born in Palestine, wants to find its spiritual lineage in that land. If it cannot find its historic roots there or in family trees of bishops who trace their ancestry back to St. Mark in Alexandria; St. Peter in Rome; St. Paul in Rome, Jerusalem, and Antioch; or St. Thomas in India, its adherents struggle mightily to place their spiritual lineage back as far as they can. For Pentecostals, indeed for the hundreds of Pentecostals I have spoken to over the course of twenty years, they implicitly, if not explicitly, locate their origins in the times of the New Testament, claiming that the tongues of fire that fell on the Apostles depicted in the Book of Acts is the exact same event, and it occurs in their churches today.

This timeline is not meant to be taken literally, since Pentecostal notions of their history begin at about 33 A.D. and then jump over almost two millennia to the beginning of the twentieth century. Insofar as such a mythic timeline is itself a narrative construction meant to validate Pentecostalism's experience and theological supremacy, it is no different from the kinds of narratives other Christian movements and denominations have always been putting forth—the idea being that if you can trace your origins back far enough, you have the upper hand against the myriad of competing Christian groups that seek to make the same claim. But for Pentecostals, their specific timeline further establishes a spiritual lineage through which they can remedy their chronological distance not only from the Book of Acts, but also from the early church. Pentecostalism started at Pentecost, was forgotten for a time, and reappeared sometime at the end of the nineteenth century. But such a historical trajectory is itself constructed to portray Pentecostalism's spiritual lineage as unbroken since the Apostolic era—as nearly every Christian movement does in promoting itself. While the seemingly endless attempts to locate the genesis of American Pentecostalism at Azusa Street in Los Angeles, or in Chicago, North Carolina, or Indianapolis can be interesting insofar as they tell us something about how socio-geographic factors shaped Pentecostalism, they are far less interesting if they amount to trying to identify which site had a Pentecostal revival first. Arguments over "firsts" are another weakness in Pentecostal historiography that this volume seeks to go a way toward correcting. It is not about who came first, how many were healed, who followed whom in the pulpit.

When it comes to the sacred sites of Pentecostalism's origins, many want to continue to make cases for North Carolina, Arkansas, Kansas, Indianapolis, Chicago, Portland, or Los Angeles. Moreover, scholars who have studied the global origins of this movement would like American religious historians to gain a little perspective and broaden our views to include Wales, Korea, India, and at least a dozen other sacred sites. Once scholars choose the one they find most compelling, believing there is more evidence for claiming that particular site than another, the historical arguments that ensue can go on for quite a while. So do arguments about founders of the movement, which tend to go along the lines of the Abbott and Costello skit about "Who's on first?" The candidates here are endless, and if this were a conventional history of the "great men and women" of the movement, they would all figure centrally. Some of their feats are extraordinary, some of their theology is path-breaking, and some of their personal stories are heroic. But this is not a conventional history that privileges the lives of the "greats" over those of the commoners. It is a thematic history in which some of those renowned figures appear in case studies, along with others who would not be considered "great" by any self-respecting Pentecostal. This, for me, is exactly the right balance. Before outlining the beginnings of the movement, this book will be divided in the following manner: This book examines Pentecostalism in America through various lenses—faith and practice in chapter 1; innovators in chapter 2; gender and sexualities in chapter 3; popular culture in chapter 4; race, ethnicity, and the construction of an American Pentecostal identity in chapter 5; and finally Pentecostal outliers in chapter 6. The epilogue offers some speculations on the future of the movement in the United States from the point of view of a Church of God in Christ (COGIC) family from Texas.

The book covers some of the important figures in the movement, but it cannot cover every important figure that every denomination (in the thousands) wishes to see in print. That is not its purpose; there are fine books that take a linear approach to history and more that include biographical information on many of the movement's leaders. Rather, starting with the premise that "history as it really happened" is illusory, I think that in studying Pentecostalism we must examine the social and cultural contexts that shaped its theological bent and continue to influence it today.

Chapter 1 examines the faith and practices of Pentecostals and, like most of the book, includes stories that have had the power to shape those beliefs and practices. In considering such phenomena as speaking in tongues, healing, and prophecy, the chapter uses sociological concepts borrowed from sociologists Peter Berger and Thomas Luckmann, namely the idea of "plausibility structure," which argues one needs to be predisposed to belief as plausible before one can accept the belief and its practices.[2]

Chapter 2 examines the lives of John Alexander Dowie, Charles Parham, Aimee Semple McPherson, and A. A. Allen. Their particular innovative theologies, ministries, and legacies demonstrate my contention that despite the claims of its adherents, Pentecostalism is a fluid process of reinvention of stories, biographies, and theologies.

Chapter 3 examines gender and sexuality in Pentecostalism by focusing on two institutions. One is educational, and here I look at Pentecostal bible colleges and universities and the standards of holiness and piety they teach and expect of their students. Since Pentecostalism has no rite of passage for young adults, one way to understand Pentecostal views of gender and sexuality is through these institutions. The other focus is on marriage both as a public spectacle (along with divorce) and as an idealized imaginary for promoting acceptable gender roles among Pentecostal adherents.

Chapter 4 considers expressions of Pentecostalism through music, literature, and media broadcasting. Since each of these areas of popular culture deserves its own extended study, this chapter narrows the field to focus on healing as a metaphor for the public faith lives of Elvis Presley, Agnes Sanford, Marvin Gaye, and Joel Osteen.

Chapter 5 concerns race and ethnicity, as well as how Pentecostals adopted, revised, and reshaped their identities to fit particular contexts. After a brief history of the African American Pentecostal experience, the chapter presents three additional case studies that demonstrate what has largely been the modus operandi for white Pentecostals—namely, their efforts to assimilate Pentecostals of color into the larger white world of American Pentecostalism. It also demonstrates what many Pentecostals have probably suspected but have been reluctant to admit—that their earnest desire to evangelize is culturally and socially constructed and that appeals to take the Gospel to the whole world usually mean taking it to mostly suburban and rural areas of the United States, where there is little or no diversity and where the church is more comfortable.

Chapter 6 examines public figures who are outliers in a Pentecostal movement that eschews that label and attempts valiantly, yet futilely, to promulgate the idea that Pentecostalism offers some universalizing script to which all Pentecostals must adhere. The careers of Kathryn Kuhlman, Joyce Meyer, Carlton Pearson, and Jay Bakker, however, demonstrate that that is not the case. Rather, while each of these figures represents certain strains of Pentecostalism, including charismatic healing, the prosperity gospel, and so on, they do not fit Pentecostal stereotypes or ideals for a variety of reasons and to various degrees. Considering how Pentecostals themselves construct insider/outsider categories, the chapter also looks to what many young Pentecostals hope is the future for their religion—theologically liberal, culturally connected, and painfully aware of its own flaws.

Pentecostals write their history by focusing on their pioneer generation, usually vaunting the stories of triumph over all manner of obstacles: social location, race, gender, and illness. These stories demonstrate that Pentecostalism offers remedies for all these human ills. Because it is a faith for the ages, specifically for the last age when the stars fall from the skies, Pentecostalism gathers the faithful for the end times. Historians of the movement, on the other hand, rightly point to the other side of those triumphant stories, to the realities of schism, racism, sexism, and yes, even fanaticism. They note that yesterday's pioneer is today's heretic. And they observe that, despite the earnest desire of some in the early years, Pentecostalism's surrender to the racism of the time meant that as valiant a person as Azusa Street founder William C. Seymour was, his attempts at building a multiracial, multiethnic church never materialized. Pentecostalism was divided by race for decades, and no amount of interracial worship service can obliterate that historical reality. As much as Pentecostals like to see their movement as an Apostolic one, they are faced with the stark reality that currently there are over 23,000 Christian denominations and among them are thousands that are Pentecostal or charismatic. The historical reality is that whether we look at Chicago, Indianapolis, Arkansas, or Los Angeles, Pentecostalism is a fractious, unwieldy, messy business filled with countless breakups over polity, piety, and belief. Telling the easy story that all this was worked out, and that the right people won out, does a disservice to those historical figures who left or were locked out of their churches because they continued to teach their "heresies" or refused to teach someone else's. It may be instructive to delve into a brief history of these origin stories to try and tell the story of American Pentecostalism's beginning.

Beginnings

That Pentecostalism is a southern and midwestern tradition with deep roots in the late nineteenth-century Holiness movement (a movement rooted in reasserting personal piety) may be what people vaguely familiar with the movement know about its genesis. Early stirrings of Holiness doctrine infused with a sprinkling of Pentecostal practice occurred in Benjamin Irwin's Fire Baptized Holiness Church in Iowa, where Irwin taught conversion, Holiness-inspired sanctification, and a few other "baptisms," the most intriguing being the baptism by dynamite. One of the most significant denominations, began as a black Holiness church, before becoming the largest black Pentecostal denominations in the United States. The first black Holiness Pentecostal denomination was organized in 1897, when Charles H. Mason and Charles P. Jones founded the Church of God in Christ in Mississippi. But American Pentecostalism did not really kick into high gear until 1901, when Agnes Ozman experienced Spirit baptism at Charles Parham's Topeka, Kansas, ministry and appeared to be able to speak Chinese. This event, in turn, was interpreted as ushering in the last age of global evangelism before the *eschaton*. Thereafter, the steady stream of formerly Holiness churches becoming Pentecostal picked up substantially, starting with the founding of the Church of God in North Carolina in 1902, founded as a Holiness group that soon became Pentecostal in 1906, re-naming themselves the Church of God, Cleveland, Tennessee.

The Azusa Street Revival began in April 1906, and nothing matches the mythic proportions of that event held in Los Angeles. Here Parham's brusque racist ambitions (more on Parham in chapter 2) to attempt a takeover of the Azusa Street Mission crashed into William Seymour's attempt to craft a multiracial and multiethnic revival in the midst of a social milieu that rejected such a revolutionary possibility. Individuals who experienced Spirit baptism in Los Angeles may have had their own racism broken on the wheel of this revival, but Pentecostalism's renowned powers of spiritual persuasion were powerless against the intransigent racist policies and institutions of the United States.

Subsequently, the movement continued to grow under the auspices of Methodist Holiness ministers like G. B. Cashwell, who evangelized the

South and brought many of his Holiness compatriots into the Pentecostal fold. American Pentecostals from various outposts, including Los Angeles, Chicago, and Indianapolis, helped spread the faith throughout Europe, Latin America, Asia, and Africa. Although the movement also came to be mired in fractious break-ups and theological divisions, efforts to stabilize it through denomination building predominated during the "Golden Age" of Pentecostalism, from 1910 through the end of the 1920s, when denominations like the Apostolic Faith Mission (Portland, Oregon), Assemblies of God (Hot Springs, Arkansas), Pentecostal Assemblies of the World (Indianapolis, Indiana), and the Church of the Foursquare Gospel (Los Angeles, California) were founded by women and men like Florence Crawford (Portland), G. T. Haywood (Indianapolis), and Aimee Semple McPherson (Los Angeles). However, even during the age of denomination building, Pentecostalism began to fracture over a variety of theological disputes. One of the most prominent breaks emerged over the intractable divisions between Holiness advocates, who believed the Holy Spirit sanctified believers for service and evangelism, but did not physically manifest in speaking in tongues, and those newer Pentecostal advocates who insisted that sanctification by the Holy Spirit could live alongside this new physical sign that God was revitalizing an ancient practice to imbue believers to evangelize and exhort an unbelieving world until the *eschaton.*

In 1897 Charles H. Mason and Charles P. Jones met to form a new group that stressed holiness above all. The first iteration of the Church of God in Christ Holiness would later see a split because Mason wanted to adapt the Pentecostal experience into the Holiness standards that his denomination made the cornerstone for what it meant to truly live a sanctified life. Indeed, one of the first of many theological issues that tore at the newly formed Pentecostal fabric had its roots in the late nineteenth century. Holiness advocates, with an eye toward reforming their home denominations, saw heightened pious behavior as the clearest way to live out a better formed Christian life. Sanctified Baptists, Presbyterians, and especially Methodists saw a series of splits over polity and Holiness piety. Holiness advocates stressed separation from worldly amusements such as dancing, drinking, and sports, promoted dress codes, and strictly regulated the behavior of adherents as a way to demonstrate their separation from the world and from other Christians, who, these advocates would say, had capitulated to the ways of the world.[3]

Like Pentecostalism, the Holiness movement has various different centers of origin—in New York (Phoebe Palmer), Boston (A. J. Gordon), Cincinnati (Martin Wells Knapp), and Los Angeles (Phineas Breese). Many of those movements resisted Pentecostalism's tantalizing gifts of the Spirit, but for the southern Holiness movement, especially the African American one lead by Mason and Jones, the split between Holiness and Pentecostal movements meant new denominations.

It was the exodus of African Americans from the South to the West Coast that brought Holiness and eventually Pentecostalism to Los Angeles. In Los Angeles, denominations like the African Methodist Episcopal (AME) Church were established with support from women like Biddy Mason (no relation to Charles). It was this at this AME church that Neely Terry, who had met William Seymour in Houston in 1903, when they were both exposed to Pentecostalism, invited him to Los Angeles to preach. In Houston, a Methodist turned Pentecostal preacher Charles Parham fused together a physical experience of the Holy Spirit, that occurred after conversion, and claimed that this was a Spirit baptism, manifested with an initial evidence of speaking in tongues. The purpose of this baptism, Parham taught, was to evangelize the world before the second coming of Jesus. Los Angeles–based African American church leaders Richard and Ruth Asberry later invited Seymour to preach at their house on Bonnie Brae Street. Seymour's teaching and subsequent preaching now included the idea of Spirit baptism, being an effective and necessary partner with sanctification in the lives of regenerated believers.

The story of William J. Seymour[4] is familiar to all scholars of Pentecostalism, but to its followers, Seymour may be familiar only as a figure at Azusa Street, where he was instrumental in the leadership of the revival from 1906 to 1909. Rather than weighing in on the historical arguments over "who's on first," it may be more fruitful to say again that just as there are many geographic centers for the origins of Pentecostalism, so too there are as many founders. Is it important to choose? History that is captive to chronology does not analyze why certain people were first. It could be that those who advocate for Charles Parham to hold the founder's title are correct, but usually they do not say why this was important, aside from the fact that Parham and his followers helped establish the connection between the doctrine of Spirit baptism and speaking in tongues. If we look past timelines, the significance of Seymour lies in what he symbolized. Seymour's attempts to build a multiracial, multiethnic church in 1906 against a backdrop of the United States' entrenched racism was heroic. Nevertheless, that racism paralyzed most American Christianity and prevented it from grasping the most fundamental of ideas—that injustice toward large segments of marginalized people in the United States served the economic and political interests of a dominant culture for over a century. Seymour's desire for racial harmony, for Azusa Street to become a template for how the church and society ought to comport themselves, was a noble one, but, as it turned out, wholly unrealistic for early twentieth-century America.

Seymour's accomplishments—leading Azusa Street, sending out dozens of missionaries to promote Pentecostalism, beginning the newspaper *The Apostolic Faith*—and his unwavering commitment not only to the Pentecostal experience, but to other signs and wonders that followed, especially divine healing, certainly make him one of the most significant figures in Christianity in the twentieth century. Unfortunately, nearly as soon as Azusa Street began, the seeds of its own discord were already present. The Los Angeles media accounts that portrayed Pentecostals as crazy and the invective preached from fundamentalist pulpits in Los Angeles all pointed toward Pentecostalism as fanatical, extreme, and anti-Christian. With its disconcerting scenario of men and women worshiping together, not to mention mixed race and ethnic groups worshiping side by side, it was probably better that Pentecostalism break away into a thousand little pieces across the globe than remain in any of its centers of origin. Whether it was Los Angeles, Chicago, or anywhere else, Pentecostalism's entrepreneurial genius for adapting to the surroundings, for being whatever the believer wanted it to be, meant that maintaining a stable cultural and theological center would be impossible.

Some of the factors that led to the Azusa Street break-up included, a tantalizing story of purported theft, wrapped up in a potentially salacious love triangle. And, not nearly as interesting but as important, a series of theological disputes that further fractured the movement. First to the tabloid-like tale of Florence Crawford and her friend Clara Lum, who had met at Azusa Street. Crawford and Lum somehow got a hold of the mailing list of *The Apostolic Faith*, and they soon left Los Angeles and began their own church in Portland in 1909. The importance of this list is that this was how Azusa Street communicated news of its revival to supporters and potential financial backers. Depending on what story you want to believe, Lum's decision to leave Los Angeles was precipitated by her disappointment that Seymour had decided to marry Jenny Moore. Crawford's official story (more on her in a bit) was that she was given the list because it was no longer useful to the Azusa Street organizers.

Theologically, two fissures broke the nascent movement in several pieces. In Chicago, William Durham, a former Baptist minister turned Pentecostal, taught that after conversion all one needed was Spirit baptism, because that in effect was the "finished work" of Jesus. Detractors viewed him as cutting one of the foundational legs off of Pentecostalism, which treated sanctification as a central part of Christian life separate from Spirit baptism. Such teaching cut the ties to Pentecostalism's Holiness roots and the essential role of sanctification. But, perhaps the most contentious development was the rise of a non-Trinitarian branch of Pentecostalism called Oneness, which became a legitimate and strong competitor for the loyalty of Pentecostals.

The sheer extent of early Pentecostalism's squabbles can be baffling, so it may be useful to tell the story of the early years of movement in America through two figures who have not received enough press. One is Garfield T. Haywood, an accomplished illustrator who worked for the black press in Indianapolis before becoming a Pentecostal minister in 1909 and eventually shepherding the largest African American Oneness denomination, the Pentecostal Assemblies of the World (PAW). Focusing on Haywood spotlights a theological tension evident from the very beginnings of Pentecostalism—a movement whose characteristic fluidity makes it impossible to suggest any fixed theological certainties. The other story is Florence Crawford's, a twice-divorced woman who held that marriage was a trap that prevented women from pursuing their real callings. The incredible thing is that many Pentecostal women leaders did in fact decide to leave their husbands to fulfill their calling despite the enormous social stigma attached to divorce in the early twentieth century. Through Crawford, we can also gain insight both into Pentecostalism in the Northwest and the social geography that affected Crawford's brand of Pentecostalism.

Garfield T. Haywood

In the 1910s, after Garfield T. Haywood left his job as an illustrator and became a full-time minister, he assumed leadership of an interracial Oneness Pentecostal denomination, PAW, and moved its headquarters from the West Coast to Indianapolis. There, he maintained an interracial church at a time when such entities were rare (and in parts of the United States, illegal), until the realities of geographic growth faded those interracial dreams.[5]

Haywood's desire to maintain the interracial nature of the PAW fell apart because white ministers did not believe the movement would grow and, in fact, experienced a backlash in the South, where the movement grew most during the 1920s. White PAW ministers did not want black PAW ministers to sign their minister credentials. There was also a deeply seated fear that PAW interracial churches performed interracial marriages. Persian minister and Oneness pioneer Andrew Urshan advocated breaking up the interracial PAW because it was necessary to the proclaiming of the Gospel. This rationale would be used to explain the separation of the white ministers from the PAW fold, as it would be used to explain the separation of white ministers from Charles H. Mason's COGIC in 1923. Haywood's group, which became the largest black Oneness denomination, gave rise to several others, including R. C. Lawson's Church of Our Lord Jesus Christ, which broke away from Haywood due to differences over women's ordination and dress codes. And there were further breakaways into the 1950s and beyond. The continued segregation of Oneness groups today is a direct descendant of that fateful decision to refuse to confront the legal discrimination of the time and instead opt for preaching the gospel within their own communities.

Pentecostalism never had the boldness theologically or politically to confront the intractable systemic evil of racism. If, as Iain MacRobert has aptly noted, the "color line was re-drawn" with the Haywood affair, then subsequently it was never erased. Different racial groups in church may equal diverse audiences, but it does not signal racial justice. Those efforts require much more sustained political effort than Pentecostals like Haywood, Lawson, and Seymour could muster at the time. None of these men had the political tools to move beyond their communities' racial composition.

At the time that Haywood rose to prominence in Indianapolis, the city was a bastion of Ku Klux Klan activity. There is little doubt that having interracial churches there in the early 1900s was heroic. So why did the passion for interracial ministry not extend to political action? Did Haywood ever entertain aspirations beyond his church? The answer lies in Pentecostalism's fervent premillennialism and its near-paralyzing fear of being tainted by the world, which rendered whatever political aspirations members had inert. Pentecostals, from the beginning, loved to argue—about sanctification, Spirit baptism, women in ministry, dress codes, and whether to attend sporting events, listen to the radio, become involved in politics, go to doctors, or go to war. Such constant arguing over matters that they found to be crucial to their theological purity meant pitting group against group, faction against faction, and leader against leader for decades. What many Pentecostal leaders did not argue about nearly enough was the near universal belief that their time on earth was short. With the urgency to preach the gospel trumping worldly political issues, and in one of the movement's many ironies, leaders argued incessantly over shirts, ties, skirt length, make-up, movies, sports, dancing, drinking, and jewelry. They argued about the things of this world to the exclusion of perhaps the most pressing issue of their time: soul-crushing racial inequality that somehow did not matter as much as whether one could wear a wristwatch or not.

Florence Crawford

Born in Coos Bay, Oregon, Crawford found God in the midst of a dysfunctional and atheist home, turned to Methodism first, then to Pentecostalism, and moved to Los Angeles, where she joined Seymour's Azusa Street Mission. Subsequently, she and her friend Clara Lum allegedly absconded with the mailing list that kept Azusa Street linked to its international constituency and used the list to found their own denomination, the Apostolic Faith Church, though the circumstances surrounding the supposed theft remain somewhat uncertain.

Depending on what source one privileges, Crawford grew tired of Seymour's leadership and felt called to go back home and begin the Apostolic Faith Church (AFC) in Portland, Oregon.[6] The other story, admittedly more interesting, has fellow Azusa Street member Clara Lum, a white woman from Wisconsin, feeling jilted because Seymour communicated his intentions to marry another woman and, in revenge, made off with Azusa Street's only copy of their international mailing list. At a time when the mail was not only the main communication outlet, but also a financial lifeline, losing this list eroded Azusa Street's capacity to communicate its successes and, more importantly, ask for funding to continue its work.

Armed with the list, former Azusa Street compatriots Lum and Crawford left Los Angeles and moved to Portland to start the Apostolic Faith Church. This was not the first Pentecostal work in Portland, but since Pentecostalism in the Northwest has not received nearly as much press as in California, Crawford's role in forging a new path of Pentecostalism is worth highlighting. While the sources for her story are many—they include her own work, the collected sermons the church published, and a dozen or so scholarly monographs, articles, and dissertations—the church's own version, which it published on its website a few years ago to celebrate its one hundredth anniversary, is particularly illuminating in showing us how denominations' spiritual life stories, like those of individuals, are composed of what they would like their people and others to know about them.

The AFC, according to their timeline, began during the time of the Apostles and skips over 1,900 years of history with the next dot on the timeline at 1900 and Charles Parham. On page 26 of their e-book, the authors make the claim that the faith of the Apostles was "lost during the Middle Ages," though there is no explanation of what that means. The next few sections mention Crawford's work as an assistant at Azusa Street Mission, where she helped publish the mission's newspaper, *The Apostolic Faith*.[7]

According to the church's biography, Crawford's atheist family is no match for her burgeoning conversion. She sings and changes their disposition. Describing Crawford's work with local Methodists and the poor and dispossessed of Portland, the story moves on to the Azusa Street Mission, where her life is represented as being filled with theological crisis.

The rationale for placing Crawford's pending break with Azusa Street in wholly theological terms is two-fold. One is that Pentecostals were deeply concerned with doctrinal purity, and something like the "Finished Work" controversy (the idea that Spirit baptism completed the work of sanctification, negating the need for a separate sanctifying experience after conversion) caused great consternation. The other has to do with the church seeking to control the narrative that Crawford did not "steal" the mailing list from Azusa Street (there is no mention of such actions in the history); nor did she consciously break away from Azusa Street in a fit of anger or divisiveness and cause the mission permanent harm. Rather, Crawford was "called." The narrative is then framed so that the growing popularity of the "Finished Work" theology had on Azusa Street led to Crawford's leaving; even if she took the mailing list with her, there was a larger spiritual issue that made that action justifiable.

By 1908, the Portland church, growing and actively engaged in camp meetings, also experienced outbreaks of miracles. At one meeting, on Mount Tabor, a vision of Jesus and an angel moved over the campground tents, and a person with smallpox was healed. And not only that—it was also reported that one of the most contagious diseases in human history had stopped spreading.

That Pentecostals saw and still see themselves as part of various scriptural stories is not surprising. As anthropologist Tanya Luhrmann notes, placing yourself in the scripture is crucial to making the text "real." From there, to speak of healing, prophecy, and the eventual defeat of the powers of darkness is to join the lineage of the faithful.[8] This is why timelines can be placed back as far as the meeting of the Apostles in the Upper Room with a certainty that the experience described in Acts is the same one that occurs today. Chronological timelines subsumed to spiritual timelines marked the life of the church. But tying the AFC to an apostolic lineage is not the only goal of the church's e-book. While one cannot blame religious groups for wanting to be part of the origins of their respective movements, a far more temporal rationale helps explain why they exclude historical and biographical details. For the

AFC, not mentioning Crawford's two dissolved marriages and her racial prejudice is a way to solidify Crawford's status as a pioneering Pentecostal woman.

Crawford married young, before 1890, which was the year she left Portland for Los Angeles both for her health and to escape marriage to a rancher. Then in 1891, she married Frank Crawford, a Los Angeles businessman specializing in real estate, and in the following decade she worked in Los Angeles' prisons. By 1906, after her visit to Azusa Street, her demeanor changed; she gave away her jewelry and began to dress modestly, and it was probably at this time that she left her husband, though those details are murky. Becoming one of Seymour's top assistants, the restless Crawford sought a way out from under male church leadership within a year.

In 1907, Crawford attempted to take over a revival being held under the auspices of the Azusa Street Mission in the nearby Arroyo Seco area near Pasadena by teaming up with a mysterious "Mr. Trotter." They failed. Nevertheless, Crawford attempted to undermine Seymour again a year later, and this time, she was successful. The reasons for the attempt, however, differ depending on the source. According to Edwin Williams, an Azusa Street witness, it was not just that she chafed under male leadership. Crawford also had little respect for African Americans and thought they should be "servants." Thus, what bothered her was Seymour's maleness and blackness.[9] Contentions that Crawford's split was based on theological disagreements over the "Finished Work" controversy have limited credibility. Though the AFC would prefer to have that portrait of its founder be the official story, as I have asserted throughout this chapter and will continue to do throughout this work, Pentecostalism, its adherents, and many of its historians have participated in the ongoing work of shaping and re-purposing their narratives.

Crawford, according to Williams, was a strong-willed dominating personality, who was "dead set against the institution of marriage." Freed from Seymour's leadership and her second husband, she began to shape the AFC in her image. Potential ministers lived in her house while she trained them; if they married, she kicked them out of the house and out of her ministry. Crawford advocated celibacy for her ministers and was upset that her children chose to abandon their chaste lives in favor of marriage. Crawford's actions, to outsiders may seem extreme. Her racialist attitudes are enough for most to dismiss her. Why do so many of her fellow Pentecostals not see her as extreme on either instance? Because what matters to Crawford's followers is that she was willing to sacrifice it all for her ministry. Being able to dismiss purported theft, racism, and stringent practices regarding marriage becomes part of what kind of narrative Pentecostals tell themselves matters about their leaders—what story they choose to tell becomes the story they repeat and hope others will believe. How Pentecostals use belief and practice to create these spiritual life stories is the subject of chapter 1.

Pentecostals in America

CHAPTER ONE

Pentecostal Faith and Practice

Pentecostalism is a movement within Christianity that emphasizes an active presence of the Holy Spirit in the lives of its adherents. Theologically, Pentecostalism in America can be characterized as evangelical in outlook, but with practical emphases that set it apart from mainstream evangelicals and other Protestants. Pentecostals, like evangelicals, believe that the Bible is the infallible word of God and the sole authority for theological doctrines. More than other evangelicals though, Pentecostals focus on the making of what folklorist Elaine Lawless calls "spiritual life stories" as a way of promoting an addition to biblical narratives.[1] The role of testimonies takes on a sacred nature because they are stories told and retold to validate the ongoing work of the Holy Spirit, although by no means do testimonies supersede the Bible as the source of religious authority.

Within Pentecostalism, there are two major branches: the Trinitarian and the Oneness, the latter of which broke away from the Trinitarian branch in the wake of a prophecy uttered at a healing revival in 1913 in Pasadena, California. That one of Pentecostalism's first schisms came because of a prophecy is not exceptional; rather, it is a common device for moving the faith in different directions. Prophecy, healing, speaking in tongues, interpreting tongues, words of wisdom, words of knowledge, and faith are all gifts that Pentecostals claim for themselves and others willing to seek them. Some gifts, such as healing, speaking in tongues, interpretation, and faith, are self-explanatory. Less clear are prophecy, words of wisdom, and words of knowledge, which often become conflated to represent one thing. All three spiritual gifts are synonymous for prophecy. For the sake of clarity, prophecy will be used to discuss words of knowledge as well. Words of wisdom, usually about scripture, and the gift of faith function together to deepen a person's understanding of faith. Though Pentecostals partake of several of these gifts throughout their lives, the most popular—healing, prophecy, and speaking in tongues—require explanation in depth.

Speaking in Tongues

I never did get used to living in Chicago. I am a Southern California native, and years of snow and bitter cold were about all I could stand before I moved back home. Before I left Chicago, I visited a suburban Church of God in Christ (COGIC) church. It was my first experience with COGIC services and the speaking in tongues phenomenon. I knew it was faked, even coerced, and yet saw that it seemingly benefited the entire audience's relationship to the pastor.

The pastor called people up to help him pray for the young children at that church, in the hope that they receive the baptism of the Holy Spirit as evidenced by speaking in tongues and that they renew their faith at the revival meeting. I watched as the pastor prayed fervently, as he laid hands on them, as the crowd began to surround these kids and people began praying in tongues on their behalf. The pastor tried very hard to push a young woman down, so she would either fall to the ground or fall back onto her chair, but she did not move; she exhibited a bit of emotion, but nothing that passed for very excited Pentecostal emotion. After a few more minutes, the pastor thanked the people, thanked God, and the service continued. The kids managed to mutter a few unintelligible words; there was no great breakthrough, there was no great rush of emotion, and no one was on the floor. The kids knew what they had to do to get out of what seemed like an endless ordeal for them. It must have been embarrassing. I felt bad for them.

So, what went on here? Skeptics would say, "Exactly what I thought, it is all fake!" "How tragic to involve children in such a charade!" Adherents would possibly charge the pastor with a lack of discretion, a lack of being sensitive to the Spirit in carrying this prayer on way too long. However, they would have no problem with the doctrinal confession of the baptism of the Holy Spirit or the initial evidence of speaking in tongues, and they would not begrudge those young people the attempt to be open to the Spirit. You are never too young to be touched by the Spirit, and you are never too old. Speaking in tongues, then, seems to be the process by which you lay your most deeply personal and overwhelming burdens onto God so that they can be the subject of God's countenance. This is what makes this practice so central and, even though globally less than half of Pentecostals speak in tongues,[2] it remains a deeply held doctrinal belief.

Spirit baptism narratives sacralize the practice by which most people become Pentecostal. When someone speaks in tongues, he or she becomes part of an ongoing narrative, assuring that others will hear a similar story and want to seek the same experience.

Just what speaking in tongues is has been open to interpretation since the beginning of the organized Christian church. For some, it is nonsensical babble brought on by a psychological prompt. Or it is a neuropsychological chemical reaction that releases good feelings, like a piece of chocolate does for some by releasing serotonin.[3] Others view it as a life-changing experience that marks a person's entry into the Pentecostal world and offers him or her the ability to communicate with God. Doctrinally, there are myriad positions about the practice. Is it required? Optional? Or even possible? To understand Pentecostalism in America, it is necessary to understand the importance of speaking in tongues since it demarcates the entryway to the faith, and though it has lost some of its luster, it is still the practice that sets Pentecostals apart.

Pentecostals would like to claim that their spiritual and indeed their geographic lineage goes all the way back to the experience related in the New Testament Book of Acts, in which tongues of fire appeared over the heads of the Apostles fifty days after the resurrection of Jesus (Acts 2:4). *Glossolalia* may involve existing languages or it can be an unintelligible language that allows the practitioner to speak to God. Contemporary research of this phenomenon suggests that speaking in tongues affects the parts of the brain involved with speech. While people are conscious of speaking in tongues, they also seem to exhibit some dissociative state where that part of the brain is occupied with other activity. For practitioners, the brain is busy communicating something wholly nonscientific and irrational but heavenly, but for many outside Pentecostal circles speaking in tongues seems improbable. Why would someone need tongues to talk to God? As many of us were told since we were children, God is everywhere, so if there is a need to talk to God, why not use my real voice? Why take on the strange sounds of glossolalia? God hears people through a myriad of languages, right?

Why is this practice attractive? It has mainly to do with the outcome. Speaking in "tongues of angels" is a way for people to lay their deep burdens down or express joy. Divinity has a code that adherents know, and it's not used without permission. Only the Divine and you know its power. Tongues then are accessible if you allow yourself to be vulnerable so Spirit baptism may be possible.

Probably the most influential minister in crafting what speaking in tongues meant theologically was Charles Parham, who rethought what this experience was, what it signified, and who was allowed to practice it. At first, Parham believed, based on Agnes Ozman's New Year's Eve experience of having "spoken Chinese" (discussed in the introduction and more in chapter 2) that the tongues experience meant that people had the ability to speak in a foreign language. Parham wrote in "A Voice Crying in the Wilderness" that the act of Spirit baptism meant that believers became equipped with the ability to evangelize. Tongues, then, were prophecy expressed in a foreign language rather than in one's native speech. In both cases it was God speaking directly through the lips of Spirit-filled believers.[4] Parham assured his readers that: "In the close of the age, God proposes to send forth men and women preaching in languages they know not a word of . . ."[5] Pentecostals soon rejected the idea that they spoke known languages, because early Pentecostals reported back from mission trips overseas that they could not speak or understand the languages in such diverse places as Africa and Asia. Historian Douglas Jacobsen offers this interpretation of Parham's creation of the xenoglossic idea behind tongues-speech:

> He [Parham] was deeply immersed in apocalyptic speculation regarding the end of the world. . . . He believed that all Christians should experience a special baptism of the Holy Ghost. He was sure that a new wave of world evangelism was about to commence, and he believed that at least some people were specifically gifted by God with the miraculous ability to speak foreign languages without training to help them in that task.[6]

Parham himself seemed unsure of the role of tongues, and seemed caught unaware that this ethereal spiritual practice would be subject to a most human flaw—people faked it. Countering the common historical script that as the Holy Spirit worked its will at Azusa Street and harmony, unity, and peace broke out, Parham and Azusa Street leader William Seymour disagreed over exactly what speaking in tongues was and was not. Parham's critique of Azusa Street tongues-speech had deeper roots than the authenticity of the experience; Parham's dilemma was multifaceted. Five years earlier, Parham had posited the idea that tongues-speech enabled believers to speak actual languages in the service of the missions-oriented task of the church. Azusa Street's cacophony of sounds included some known human languages, but often it included languages of unknown origin. Parham posited the idea that when Catholic priests stepped off the boat in Asia, they had the ability to "speak in tongues" to their Asian charges—meaning they had the ability to speak Asian languages as missionaries. If the priests had that capability, Parham surmised, what would stop the Holy Spirit from giving people in the throes of the "last days" the instant ability to speak in "missionary tongues" to hasten the evangelization of the world? Parham failed to mention that it was probably the case that these Catholic priests had learned these languages the old-fashioned way.[7]

In Sarah Parham's biography of her husband, she recounted Parham's horror at the Azusa Street Revival breaking out into unknown tongues and worse, races mixing in worship: "I hurried to Los Angeles, and to my utter surprise and astonishment I found conditions even worse than I had anticipated. . . . Saw the manifestations of the flesh, spiritualistic controls, some people practicing hypnotism at the altar over candidates seeking the baptism."[8] Clearly for Parham, the loss of control over defining what this speech was signaled more than the introduction of suspect alternative practices such as hypnotism or forbidden alternative religious systems such as spiritualism. Parham's aggravation over what he not only heard but also *saw* at Azusa Street, namely, interracial worship, was for a devoted follower of the white supremacist doctrine of British Israelism (a notion that the lost Tribes of Israel could be found in the British people and royal family) simply too much. Parham's attempt to control the definition of tongues-speech seemed more than a familiar exercise for Pentecostals. It was an attempt to secure a boundary around orthodox belief, wresting away the right of others, particularly non-whites, to define tongues-speech for themselves. Broadening the definition of tongues to include language that had no human origin evinced African Americans' growing theological power.

It is not clear that there was ever any real consensus over the nature of speaking in tongues or if it is even necessary to a deeper faith life. Globally, most Pentecostals do not speak in tongues, and the informal, anecdotal evidence I have compiled in twenty years suggests that speaking in tongues is symbolically important, but waning in its active presence in everyday U.S. church life. It is a testament to denominational leaders' efforts to maintain some modicum of control over defining speaking in tongues that the debates over whether speaking in tongues is the first evidence of Spirit baptism still rage in certain quarters of the movement. As is the case with much organized religion, the institutional concerns of orthodoxy and correct practice are usually different than the popular expressions of religion that constantly stretch those boundaries.

While many Pentecostal leaders were busy preaching, defending, and defining tongues, there are literally hundreds of accounts of this practice in the pages of the earliest Pentecostal magazines. It would be too great a task to catalog them here, and indeed such a task would detract from the rest of the spiritual gifts in question. Suffice to say that people regularly described feelings of overwhelming emotion: crying, lying on floors of churches or homes for hours at time, and experiencing Spirit baptism. Some wrote of the intense pain and disappointment of not having had the manifestation; even though they had prayed for days, weeks, and months at a time, they never spoke in tongues. This gnawing sense that to be fully Christian, one had to speak in tongues, would often be the undoing of many young Pentecostals. Celebrity (ex-)Pentecostal Phil Jackson, for example, wrote of his intense disappointment and eventual disillusionment over never being able to speak in tongues, despite his South Dakota preacher parents exhorting him to keep "tarrying."[9] Although the incredible pressure certain people felt to speak in tongues was not the only reason some resorted to faking it, it cannot go unnoticed that an untold number of people, many sincere, some not, decided that they needed to fake speaking in tongues to become authentically Pentecostal. One wonders what those children at the COGIC church will remember about that night when they appeared to "get the Holy Ghost." Will the same sacred canopy of sights, sounds, and smells find its way to a formative spiritual experience? Or when asked about it by inquisitive academics years later, will they laugh?

But speaking in tongues, as well as the ability to interpret such language with a view toward speaking a word of prophecy or exhorting a congregation, is not the only gift that is central to what it means to be Pentecostal. Two other gifts of the Holy Spirit, healing and prophecy, are equally important, and they suggest that a supernatural relationship between humanity and God is not an abstract concept up for philosophical debate, but an everyday occurrence for Pentecostals.

Healing

Unsure about the medical nature of her problem, I did not know how to ask her what happened to her that had wrenched her body into such painful contortions. Her neck twisted back, and she had to use her hand to stabilize it enough for her to function. Though a member of the church for several months, church members did not have perhaps the nerve to suggest that she might want to receive prayer and ask God to heal her. Why the church waited so long will soon become apparent.

The young woman responded to the altar call for those who wanted to receive prayer for healing and her parents accompanied her. The circle closed in around her and began praying—hard. This was Pentecostal prayer at its most intense—loud, crying, pleading for God to touch the person in tongues intermingled with human speech. Finally, the person leading the prayer asked that as a sign that God was healing the young woman, would God allow her to straighten her neck? The second part of the prayer was pleading that God show her and show us all that healing in this instance was not just theoretically or even theologically possible, but empirically provable.

While at this church, I found out that this young woman had worked at another church as a part-time secretary. Her office space was small, with a desk, chair, and computer placed in such a way that she constantly had to turn her head. Consequently, the muscles in her neck became strained, and she sustained nerve damage. She told me that there was nothing medically that could be done, and not wanting to add to her obvious pain and self-consciousness, I never pressed her to investigate potential remedies like physical or chiropractic therapy or surgery. She seemed resigned to living life holding her head in her hand.

After the prayer was completed, those in the circle were visibly exhausted, emotionally drained, and though no one ever said anything, deeply disappointed. The young woman returned to her seat, no better off than before. No one said anything. No one openly questioned the viability of healing, the belief in healing, or the theological certainty of what they were doing—it just didn't happen. Why?

Rather than attempt to answer that question, since it gives rise to the eternal question of theodicy, it helps to note that even though the young woman was not healed, she kept attending services for a few months until she moved away with her family. Therefore, the sacred narrative accomplished its goals: it kept her faithful and hopeful that someday she would be healed.[10]

Probably no sacred narrative is more prized in the Pentecostal world than the testimony of healing. Such stories, whether recorded in early Pentecostal magazines or told in today's churches, share many characteristics and, overwhelmingly, follow a biblical script. Because one of the key elements of Pentecostal theology is the belief that the ongoing supernatural work of God exists as an unbroken continuum, healing solidifies Pentecostals' spiritual lineage. It connects them to the biblical narrative as no other narrative can.

Healing narratives, though, like most narratives, change. In those of many early Pentecostals, ill health is attributed to sinful behavior or an innate sinful nature. As such, medicine could be of little help. In fact, many early leaders of the movement were adamantly against going to doctors, and, much like their cohorts in spiritual healing, quite a few contemporary Pentecostals feel the same.[11] In terms of notable early Pentecostals, Parham as well as John Alexander Dowie (more on him in chapter 2) were adamantly against the use of medicine other than that provided by the "Great Physician." Parham viewed modern medicine as virtually useless: "The fact still remains however, that after 4,000 years of practice—humanity willingly laying herself upon the altar to be doped, blistered, bled and dissected, medical science has gained little more than has the Bible recorded of her."[12]

A more recent representative of the Pentecostal healing movement was Jack Coe, who was one of the most well-known healing evangelists of the post–World War II era. Raised in the throes of the Great Depression, Coe was shuffled from relative to relative in Oklahoma and Texas due to his father's acute alcoholism and gambling problem and was eventually placed in an orphanage. Later becoming an alcoholic himself, Coe reported being healed of that affliction and was ordained by the Assemblies of God (AG) in 1944. Coe, like many of his Pentecostal predecessors, viewed the use of medicine and doctors as ungodly. In the early 1950s, as the medical profession became a staple familiar to most Americans' lives, Coe was preaching in tent revivals across the country, and particularly in the Southwest, that medicine was not in God's plan. In 1953, Coe was expelled from the Assemblies of God for his views, and in 1956, he was arrested in Florida for practicing medicine without a license, which is what divine healing was called at that time.

Earlier that year, at a healing revival in Miami, Coe called up a three-year-old boy who had polio and asked that the boy's leg braces be removed, and they were. (Polio, it should be noted, was a large-scale threat for much of the country throughout the 1940s and 1950s, before inoculation became widespread and the oral dosage developed in the 1960s virtually wiped out the disease in the United States.[13]) When the boy was sent home and his mother noticed that his legs began to swell, she took him to the doctor, who ordered the braces to be put back on to prevent permanent disfigurement.[14] The mother, Ann Clark, took Coe to court, with the help of Joseph Lewis of the Freethinkers of America group. Although Coe was arrested, released on $5,000 bond, and tried, the case was dismissed because Coe was exercising his religious rights. Coe used his arrest in a sermon shortly thereafter entitled "Practicing Medicine without A License." In a YouTube video of Coe's sermon, Coe mentions that Miami does not recognize his license but the "the Son of God does."[15] It may be that the boy's persistent polio coupled with Coe's legal problems set the stage for his reluctance to seek medical attention for his own battle with polio.

Coe died in 1956 of bulbar polio, a rare and potentially fatal strain of the virus if it is not treated quickly. It may be a sad irony that a person who dedicated himself to healing died of a curable form of polio, but the fact is that Coe's family and followers are very reluctant to discuss Coe's death other than to say that he was taken ill due to physical exhaustion.[16] One reason for this reluctance may be that Coe's children followed him into healing ministries. Cursory examinations of other ministries and websites that trumpet Jack Coe's "fearless" healing ministry mostly concern themselves with his sermons, and snippets of television broadcasts of his tent revivals. Explaining how a famed healer died so young (he was thirty-eight years old) in the prime of his ministry proves to be difficult, if not impossible, for a movement built on its ability to tell a successful healing story with authenticity and efficacy. Dying of exhaustion allows Coe's followers to place Coe in that vaunted hall of heroes of the faith, who gave themselves to be living sacrifices. Speculations about whether Coe knew he was sick, whether he sought treatment, or even whether Coe would have taken the vaccine if it was available are beside the point for the faithful, many of whom would not be so enamored of Coe had he not died so young.

Historian Candy Gunther Brown notes that there is a difference between Pentecostals, who normally do not seek empirical proof of healing, and charismatics, like Kathryn Kuhlman (more on her in chapter 6), who sought medical evidence of healing as an "apologetic device." Classical Pentecostals like Coe and most of the Pentecostals I have met over the years believe that their narratives function as effectively as proof as do scientific studies.[17] Healing narratives, demonstrate not only the beneficence of God, but also that there is an ongoing relationship between the Divine and humanity. Early Pentecostal magazines chronicled the healing of physical ailments almost exclusively, though occasionally a cure of neurasthenia (nervous exhaustion, or mental fatigue) was also noted. Once Pentecostalism's focus broadened from physical to mental and emotional ills, the narratives of healing these types of ailments became as important as narratives of physical healing. Someone being healed of depression or even low self-esteem could be represented as emotionally as someone being healed of back pain. Certainly stories of people healed from terminal illness trump virtually any other kind of narrative, but Pentecostals have found ways to harness all manner of narratives to create "spiritual life stories" and to impart a sacred view of a world where God is always active, in all sorts of ways—from the most minor, such as finding lost luggage, to the most magnificent, such as healing terminal cancer. Pentecostalism holds that God cares about all of it, because God has a close, deeply personal relationship with humanity, and their narratives celebrate the sacred nature of that ongoing relationship.

Healing, when it takes place in prescribed settings and prescribed times, often has a defined ritual structure, as sociologist Meredith B. McGuire observes. When people are touched in a receiving line at a healing service, the expectation is that they will fall down; if they do not fall down, that signals deviant behavior. The same kind of expectations hold when healing does not occur in what McGuire calls "therapeutic failure." The process of defining failure is essential to confirming the idea of healing, and it favors the legitimating agency of the healer and the process while at the same time giving meaning to the failed healing itself.[18]

Prophecy

Riverside, California, used to be filled with orange groves. The easternmost reaches of the county are still rural, but as with most of Southern California, wide-open spaces are rare and housing tracts crowd the land. The house church I visited one weekend was in a neighborhood in Riverside proper, where Spanish-style houses with drought-resistant succulents planted in the small lawns are ubiquitous and replicated mile after mile. There, I did not expect to learn much about prophecy for this book, but as Pentecostals have been telling me for the last twenty years, the Spirit moves in mysterious ways.

There was an African American guest preacher from Arkansas on that particular Sunday, scheduled to hold a weeklong revival in this house church; this was the first of his appearances. After the worship time, he said that he felt God speaking to him about certain people in the church, which is a cue for the audience to get ready for prophecy time. Since I have attended these kinds of meetings for years, I thought I knew what to expect, and since my notebook and minimal involvement in the worship time tend to give me away, I don't generally receive prophecies the way that regular church members do. But this time, for some reason, I tried something new.

As the preacher was going through the congregation, offering all manner of prophetic words of knowledge about housing situations, marriage situations, children, jobs, I took my wedding band off and placed it in my pocket. Coming over to my side of the room, he called me up front. "I believe God has a godly husband waiting for you." I smiled politely and sat down. I think there were some faint "amens" from the group, but since the leadership knew who I was, and may have known that I was already married, there was little response from the pastoral staff. As I sat down, I did not think anything of the prophet, or his earnestness; I thought, this is what prophecies are supposed to do: they are encouragement and exhortation. Prophecy means whatever the hearer wants it to mean. In the form of prophecy, in Barthes's words, "the meaning leaves its contingency behind, it empties itself, it becomes impoverished, history evaporates, only the letter remains."[19]

There have been many different prophecies I have been subject to—prophecies that have more to do with wishful thinking than a divine utterance from God. I've been married off, come into money, been offered my dream job, and more than I could have imagined. In each case, strangers were coming up to me and purporting to tell me something about my private life, assured that whatever it was would come to pass because God has somehow let them in on the plan for your life. Such utterances require careful crafting; the surroundings must be right, and the person doing the prophesying has to have some skill.

These prophecies occur so often and are so rarely documented that by their very nature, they are anecdotes—things that people say but no one can prove. Still, it is worth considering how they work and even why they work, even though they often go unfulfilled. There are several types. Some do not involve any insight or foresight. These include prophecies exhorting the faithful to maintain steadfastness in the midst of trial; since we all have problems, these are intended to provide spiritual support. Other prophecies warn the faithful to steer clear of particular paths—not to marry a particular person or to take a particular job; whether these prophecies are valid or not depends on whether the receiver decides to follow the advice. In the case of the Irish rock group U2 who were warned by a female prophet from their Shalom charismatic group, not to continue their musical careers, the dire warnings were taken to heart by the guitarist, who was eventually talked out of leaving by the rest of the group, who dismissed the prophecy and the movement as "bullshit."[20]

Prophecies also take the form of those found in the Old Testament, especially those warning of calamity if God's commandments are disobeyed. But among Pentecostals, ranging from public figures like Pat Robertson to the local pastor, even the latest weather episode can be treated as a warning of impending judgment from God. Even though they are either incorrect or impossible to substantiate, these kinds of prophecies are very common.[21]

Prophecy as a highly specialized and individualized "word of knowledge" contributes much to Pentecostal spiritual life. It assures adherents that God cares about everything from the most mundane details of life, like what you watch on television, to the profound realities of existence: "You are suffering and in pain, but I love you." Prophetic words offer comfort; they respond to the insatiable desire to try to figure things out. They also add to the ever-growing pastiche of spiritual narratives that comprise the life of a believer. Prophetic words in the Pentecostal context have become internal conversations that adherents have with God, through mediators vetted through an initiatory process, this is how one become a prophet.

Prophetic services are rites for both the initiated and uninitiated alike. For the initiated, they demonstrate the benefit of continued pursuit of spiritual gifts, especially where prophecy is the most prized of spiritual gifts (1 Cor 14:5). For the uninitiated, they demonstrate God's reality, his desire to help people and answer questions people have regarding their lives. Here, the prophet is key. If the prophet is a church member in good standing, who has demonstrated loyalty and sacrifice, the veracity of his or her prophecies are more likely to be accepted. If the prophet is a not a church member but a reputable visitor, vouched for by the pastor, he or she will also have little problem convincing people of the validity of their claims. Prophecies that come from people who are unknown, who have not distinguished themselves in church, who have no one to vouch for their prophetic gift, will not receive the same welcome. These ordinary people, because of some perceived or actual spiritual quality, become capable, according to anthropologist Nils Holm, of speaking on behalf of God. The messages they give, Holm notes, "have a 'transcending' effect in the services—through an imagined switch of the 'transmitter' in the communication."[22] God then becomes responsible for the prophecy, and it "becomes an effective means of persuasion for those living within its norms."[23]

The prophecy itself and what people make of it are, of course, crucial too. Prophecy requires communication within a "plausibility structure,"[24] to borrow from sociologists Peter Berger and Thomas Luckmann, to stand much of a chance of being accepted as a prophetic word. Prophetic words of different stripes—the private revelation or the public pronouncement—work because they are spoken in a friendly atmosphere; where people share a common theological assumption, prophecy is possible. Within this friendly atmo-

sphere, people are insulated from the skepticism of a nonbelieving and hostile world. Prophecy in these contexts is a device to stir the believers to deeper faith, and to convince any unbelievers of the truth of Christianity. Prophecy, possibly more than Spirit baptism, has become the most common initiatory rite in Pentecostalism. Prophecy makes you an instant evangelist, capable of convincing nonbelievers of the veracity of faith. If someone is exercising a "prophetic gift," then, he or she is making a public declaration of the assurance that the Holy Spirit does operate prophetically. Tongues on the other hand, do not function in the same fashion, and according to the traditional reading of the New Testament, they are not supposed to.

One of the most utilized spiritual gifts for gaining insight into life is the word of knowledge, which many Pentecostals conflate with prophecy. Words of knowledge are given to people in need of direction or seeking answers to often vexing questions and are also intended to encourage them during trying times. These have nothing to do with forecasting events; rather, they are akin to the biblical example of Jeremiah, whose prophetic words were exhortations and warnings to the nation of Israel. In contemporary Pentecostalism, one way to find out God's purpose for your life is for another Pentecostal to offer you insight through a word of knowledge or wisdom. Words of wisdom are given to adherents so that they can receive a deeper knowledge of what the Bible says about a particular issue affecting their lives.

Prophecy in the Pentecostal world is not a fixed practice with secure outcomes. Its adherents often claim biblical authority for its authenticity, but such blanket endorsements of prophecy can often be very tenuous. Being someone who claims the power to be a prophet is often left to a select few who have some track record of being correct in their prophecies. Anecdotally, people have a hunch that they should say something, that they "feel like the Lord is telling them something." Prophets hint that there is more to their words than mere exhortation. That next step into full prophet mode often proves tough.

It may do us well to take these Pentecostal practices not as separate experiences, but as part of a whole Pentecostal identity that is always in flux. Some historical figures have been able to harness the power of these practices and wed them to social, cultural, and political circumstances of their times. As innovators of the faith, they have developed Pentecostalism's theological convictions and its spiritual exercises. It is to these innovators that we now turn.

CHAPTER TWO

Pentecostal Innovators

Pentecostalism's entrepreneurial spirit allows for constant rebranding of its most popular consumer favorites: healing and eschatology. While there are dozens of Pentecostals who have innovative theologies and ministries, the legacies of John Alexander Dowie, Charles Parham, Aimee Semple McPherson, and A. A. Allen are what shaped permanent brands of American Pentecostalism.

Dowie, a precursor to the "official" Pentecostal story that begins around 1906, was a pacifist and supporter of interracial relationships; he was also known for his antipathy toward allopathic medicine. However, because of Pentecostalism's conservative political trajectory in the early twentieth century, what remains of Dowie's legacy are not his progressive political and social views but his penchant for autocratic rule and the scandals that surrounded him. Not that Dowie was the first minister to have a scandalous life lay waste to his ministry, but the archetype of an autocratic ruler whose preening insistence on securing his flock's morality while ignoring his own has been played out countless times in Pentecostalism's relatively short history. Is it that Pentecostalism attracts the undisciplined? Is it the undisciplined who find solace in Pentecostalism's loose ecclesiology? Or is it the "bad apples" idea, that one should not link people like Dowie too tightly to Pentecostalism because he is the exception, not the rule? It may be coincidence, but scandal tainted these innovators, and some were destroyed by it. Is it the entrepreneurial spirit of Pentecostalism that attracts people, many whom who are looking for a broader play area for their own brands of Pentecostal experience?

Charles Parham is included here not only because of his influence in creating the linkage between speaking in tongues and Spirit baptism, but because his brand of autocratic, racist, premillennial dogmatism is what became the public face of the movement when the Assemblies of God became a denomination in 1914. While he, too, became embroiled in scandal—a ministry rival accused him of being with a male prostitute in San Antonio, Texas—unlike Dowie, Parham continues to have theological influence. Classical Pentecostal denominations (Assemblies of God, Church of God, and COGIC, among others) still describe speaking in tongues as the initial evidence of Spirit baptism. Parham's overtly racist eschatology may not be codified word for word in Pentecostal denominations, but I would argue that white Western superiority was the impetus for Pentecostal missions since their inception. Underlying both speaking in tongues and missions is an urgent premillennialism—an end time schema. According to Parham, the world waits for Pentecostalism to save as many as possible before succumbing to the powers of darkness.

Aimee Semple McPherson's innovations include making Pentecostalism fit into the mold of her adopted home of Los Angeles. That is, Pentecostalism as entertainment, as spectacle, is what truly made McPherson's brand. Breaking convention with Holiness forbearers, who viewed all forms of entertainment as demonic, McPherson reveled in acting, theater, props; she was born for the stage. The Foursquare denomination she founded nearly one hundred years ago remains tied to her brand. Indeed, it remains Sister Aimee's church, and it has protected her image as best as it can. Like Dowie and Parham, McPherson had her share of scandal, but her church has tenaciously defended her legacy. McPherson cemented a cult of personality and became the first Pentecostal icon.

For his part, A. A. Allen is known for his populist Pentecostalism, his theology advocating an early model of the prosperity gospel (the idea that God displays favor on believers by allowing them to live in material abundance as long as they have faith). Historian Kate Bowler notes that Allen also excelled at exhorting his followers in "faith building."[1] Despising the elites who led the Assemblies of God, Allen found his audience in common folks and preached constantly against losing the Pentecostal fire to elitist denominations or theological education. Like notable Pentecostals who promoted versions of the prosperity gospel, including Oral Roberts and Kenneth E. Hagin, Allen lived through the Great Depression, which undoubtedly contributed to the fetishizing of money as the symbol of God's providential blessing. Allen tied poverty to a demonic spirit and created a ministry that promoted an industry of blessing—water, oil, strips from old tents, were all offered as blessed "points of contact," available from the ministry for a "love offering." Allen is Pentecostalism's entrepreneurial spirit writ large. Freed from denominational accountability, Allen crafted his populist and prosperity messages under no supervision. It was this lack of supervision that also allowed Allen to racially integrate his worship team in the early 1960s, which was unheard of in most Pentecostal circles, but it also gave him a wide enough berth to self-destruct.

John Alexander Dowie

John Alexander Dowie was born in 1847 in Edinburgh, Scotland, and emigrated to Australia when he was a boy. There, he was ordained in the Congressional Church and had a ministry in Sydney, until he emigrated to the United States in 1888. Moving to Western Springs, Illinois, his healing ministry began in 1890, when he founded the International Divine Healing Association. Then, in 1894, he founded the Christian Catholic Apostolic Church in Zion, a suburban town north of Chicago. There, Dowie's empire included not only his church but the Zion Publishing House and Printing Works, a college, a bank, and a "Home of Hope for Erring Women."[2]

One of Dowie's most lasting legacies, though, was life-long antagonism to allopathic medicine. In 1895, armed police arrested him for practicing medicine without a license; Dowie called it the "Year of Persecution."[3] For him, healing was a command from God, as was countering the allopathic medical establishment. But to understand Dowie as a political radical with anti-establishment tendencies, one need look no farther than his support of African Americans and his establishing a utopian community in Zion City, Illinois.

Dowie considered African Americans to be a part of the Ethiopian nationality. This fit well with the premillennial eschatology that viewed Ethiopians as a part of the schema meant to fulfill end-time prophecy. But Dowie was also concerned with the plight of African Americans and devoted several issues of his magazine, *Leaves of Healing*, to this concern.

In one of the most interesting pieces in his magazine, entitled "The Flogging of Amos Dresser," Dowie attacked the churches that supported the racism of the day. "The same spirit that flogged Amos Dresser survives in the so-called churches which directly antagonize Christ by drawing a color line at the communion table on Him."[4] He also exhorted: "Let the Church of Christ in all her truth and purity arise, and cast the mantle of love and Brotherhood and Eternal Redemption around every man and woman whose blood was originally drawn from the veins of Ethiopia, from whom came forth so many of the earliest and greatest of the Christian army of martyrs for the Lord."[5]

Dowie's appeals for the fair treatment of African Americans certainly mark him as unique in the history of early Pentecostalism. Historian William Faupel may be too generous in suggesting that Dowie's concern for holy living translated directly to progressive causes and in making the case that Dowie tried to instill in every convert the conviction that God is the father of all and that all humankind are brothers and sisters.[6] But Faupel does note an incident when "one negro visitor . . . stated that Dr. Dowie must be the most courageous man in the nation." He also defended miscegenation as a means to regain the purity and strength of the human race.[7] Dowie also promoted pacifism and had a concept of united world government. Calling himself the "First Apostle," Dowie also began a series of sermons that focused on politics in 1904. He told his congregation to vote for Theodore Roosevelt. He viewed patriotism as intimately tied with Christian virtues, best displayed by the music of the Zion City band. Dowie eventually advocated theocratic rule, telling his followers "the masses are unfitted to rule themselves."[8]

At the same time, Dowie harbored considerable contempt for denominations. By 1895, he succeeded in alienating just about everyone who had wanted Dowie to join their ranks in Chicago's church leadership. Refusing to participate in Chicago's religious community, he moved on to Zion,[9] where he established a community in which only "born-again" Christians lived or did business. No liquor, tobacco, gambling, non-kosher foods, theaters, brothels, politicians, tax assessors, mortuaries, hospitals, or chain stores were allowed.[10] Zion, by most accounts, was an attempt at utopia that fell far short of its ethereal goals. Historian Grant Wacker makes note that Dowie's combative personality did not serve him well and that he made enemies very quickly. Dowie's sermons were nightly attacks on politicians, Masons, Roman Catholics, denominational clergy, and especially medical doctors.[11]

But he also became known for his healing ministry, a feature emphasized by his biographers, including noted healing advocate Gordon Lindsay, whose parents were members of Zion. One healing narrative Lindsey repeats concerns Dr. Lillian Yeomans, whose own healing and role as an allopathic doctor served several agendas at once. In her testimony, Dr. Yeomans admitted her own four-year addictions to morphine and chloral hydrate. "I asked again and again under what physician's care I might place myself, what sanitarium I might go to, but God never satisfactorily answered me."[12] The message, in effect, was that God did not approve of any doctors, and that her drug addiction would need divine intervention. This she sought at Zion, where Dowie said it was "required in the name of the Lord that she gives [*sic*] up the use of morphine and drugs of every kind before he would pray for her ... for there is not an atom of hope for the healing of anyone who will not first abandon that diabolical drug. We will nigh break our hearts and wasted time and strength until we learn that lesson."[13] Yeomans claimed her healing at Dowie's hands and continued her work as a healing evangelist in the early years of the Pentecostal movement.

So dogmatic were pronouncements against drugs and alcohol that the well-known story of the death of Dowie's daughter Esther bears repeating. As a student at the University of Chicago, her father warned her not to use alcohol in any form. While in her dorm room, her alcohol lamp fell and she suffered severe burns and died. Dowie took to the pages of his magazine shortly thereafter and used the story as a cautionary tale about how "Satan could infiltrate every part of a man's life."[14]

In his magazine, Dowie wrote a column replying to what were probably many letters regarding medical treatment and Christian faith. In a sermon delivered at Zion Tabernacle on July 11, 1897, Dowie wrote: "Neither in the Old Testament, nor in the New, from Genesis to Revelation, covering 4,100 years of human history of Divine Revelation in no part of that Bible is there one single word approving doctors, surgeons, or drugs."[15] So convinced that allopathic medicine was useless, Dowie condemned every aspect of traditional medicine:

> The druggist mourns: for his patent medicines and pills, his plasters and his poisons are in danger of becoming a drug on the market, instead of misery in the stomach of his victims. . . . Neither the allopath, nor the homeopath, the psychopath, nor the hydropath, nor any of the other well-trodden paths of pain to poverty, misery and despair shall see these sufferers anymore, for they have found the path to Divine Healing.[16]

In none of the biographies is there any mention of the riots in Mansfield, Ohio, in 1900, allegedly brought on by Dowie's followers' refusing to call a doctor when a child in their care lay dying, presumably of a treatable illness. The pages of Dowie's *Leaves of Healing* for that period is filled with stories about the events in Ohio; Dowie is unapologetic about his pastor's refusal to seek medical care and defiant about the pastor's subsequent persecution by Ohio officials.

Dowie's harsh stance against medicine mirrored his uncompromising attitudes towards other subjects. Lindsay's laudatory biography made note of Dowie's irascible personality: "Dowie's habit of thinking for himself did not lend itself to a sympathy for the formal unimaginative ministry of his day . . . he was perplexed and impatient with apathetic churches that seemed so unconcerned when all around were the dying thousands."[17] Lindsay excuses Dowie's lack of ecumenical spirit, and even excuses Dowie's most controversial assertion that he was the second coming of Elijah, uttered in a sermon at Zion in 1901. Lindsay simply says he does not want to judge him and instead blames Dowie's theological excesses on overwork and on the fact that Dowie's wife, who Lindsay calls his "spiritual reservoir," was not always there for him.[18] There is also little said in any of the three biographies about Dowie's eventual sexual infidelities and financial problems, which led to his rapid downfall and death in 1907.

Websites about Dowie's ministry still attract fans who believe his healing campaigns outshone his moral failure. It is this usable past that often becomes the narrative the faithful wish to promote, and, for a generation or more, it has been the narrative that has captivated the attention of many scholars, confessional or otherwise. It may be very useful to want to see Dowie as a forerunner for racial justice, an uncompromising advocate for divine healing and pacifism. He was also a theocrat, financially inept, and a sexual libertine. This archetype if you will—the flawed leader, the compromised spiritual hero, the pure servant of God felled by demonic forces—is common to Pentecostal narratives. Even if they don't end well, redemption is certain. From early biographers like Gordon Lindsay to the Dowie admirers who keep Zion alive on the Internet, Pentecostals need a spiritual narrative to make sense of the deeply flawed people they idealize. They need to have insulation that protects the message, that protects the claims of the faith to healing, that bifurcates the faith from its sometimes-flawed leaders. The innovators may be heroes; they may also be very ordinary.

Charles F. Parham

Parham was born in Muscatine, Iowa, in 1873 to a family that came from English and German descendants by way of Philadelphia. Growing up in poor health and losing his mother when he was twelve prompted the adult Parham to undertake a quest to find healing for himself and promote divine healing for others. In 1898, he and his wife opened the Bethel Divine Healing Home in Topeka, Kansas. This healing home also doubled as Parham's fledgling bible school, where he began to put some of his theological ideas about Spirit baptism into practice.

An event that took place on New Year's Eve, 1900, recounted countless times in histories of Pentecostalism as well as in Parham's own writing, passed into the realm of mythology.[19] It involved Parham's student Agnes Ozman speaking in tongues, purportedly Chinese. Thereafter, Parham became a fixture in the history of the movement. His career from that day onward, though, was checkered at best.

By July 1901, Parham's finances were depleted, possibly from traveling and preaching, without much financial reward. He sold the iconic building that housed his bible school, the "Stone Mansion." He continued holding revivals in the Midwest in a bid to shore up his waning ministry. A revival in Kansas in 1903 and the opening of a bible school in Houston, Texas, in 1905 helped keep his ministry afloat. Then, curiously, Parham decided that the best way to continue growing his ministry would be to take over other Pentecostal missions. His first attempt was to try and take over John Alexander Dowie's failing Zion empire in 1906. According to historian James Goff, Parham read about Dowie's crumbling empire in the local Kansas papers. Goff concludes that a hostile takeover of Dowie's empire, especially his global ministries, would give Parham something he longed for, but did not have the resources to acquire for himself—a network of ministers and churches that were ready for promoting his new doctrine that the evidence of Spirit baptism was speaking in tongues.[20] When Zion experienced an outbreak of speaking in tongues, Parham's takeover seemed assured, but by then Parham was thinking that a former student's revival in Los Angeles would be a much bigger catch.

The attempted takeover of William Seymour's Azusa Street Mission failed when Seymour's white leadership forced Parham to leave. Parham left, taking a few hundred white followers with him to his new church in Los Angeles. Why Parham felt the need to go on the offensive here is up for speculation. What is clear is that Parham was incensed that Seymour was the leader of a movement that Parham believed was his. Parham's racist views were always known, but never more crudely expressed than in his debasing views of Seymour.[21] After Parham failed, his life and ministry started falling apart.

Arrested in San Antonio in 1907 on charges of sodomy with a person named J. J. Jourdan, Parham never recovered, though the case was dropped apparently for lack of evidence. He spent the rest of his days publishing his essays and working on an unconventional eschatology that would be the culmination of his eclectic theological career.

A problem with Parham's treatment by historians is that there is little critical biography and only limited semi-critical attempts to assess his unconventional theology. Examining Parham's theological innovations, especially the idea of speaking in tongues as the evidence of Spirit baptism, requires more than exploring his writings or taking Parham's own self-described biblical study habits for granted. For example, Parham's claim that he grew up with "no preconceived ideas, with no knowledge of what creeds and doctrines meant, not having any traditional spectacles upon the eyes to see through . . . [so he could read the Bible] entirely unbiased" requires interrogation. The fact is, he was raised as a Quaker and later a Methodist, and more to the point, it is impossible for anyone to read the Bible entirely without bias. But then saying so is part of hermeneutical strategy that many evangelical preachers use to convince followers that the "truths" they had uncovered in the Bible were pure. For evangelicals, this type of reading of the Bible, based on the "inductive"[22] method popular in the nineteenth century, was meant to convey that the Bible could indeed be read "scientifically," thereby answering the Higher Criticism critics who simply did not see the Bible as a text capable of such empirical rendering.[23]

The two works that concern themselves with Parham's theological grounding, James Goff's biography *Fields White unto Harvest* and Douglas Jacobsen's work on the history of early Pentecostal theology, do not assess Parham's claims to being a spiritual tabula rasa. Theology, like anything else, is not created out of a vacuum, nor is it deployed for purely confessional reasons. One way to convince his followers that he had found the truth was to claim that his "new" reading of the Bible had led him to the astounding conclusion about Spirit baptism. Speaking in tongues was God's preferred mode for enabling ministers to communicate the Gospel for the last days on earth. As Jacobsen notes: "The ability to speak in other tongues was a special empowerment for end-time service, especially the end-time work of evangelism. . . . For Parham, the gift of tongues was an eschatological empowerment for mission. It was the ability to allow God to speak through you in whatever language God chose to speak."[24]

Parham rejected what most Pentecostals eventually accepted, that tongues were a heavenly unintelligible language, not a known language that people received for evangelism. For Parham, the Pentecostal movement was teetering on the brink of heresy, and his biting comments demonstrate his displeasure:

> By the Baptism with the Holy Spirit I do not mean all the chattering and jabbering, wind-sucking, holy-dancing-rollerism, going on all over the country, which is the result of hypnotic spiritualistic and fleshly controls, but a real sane reception of the Holy Spirit in baptismal power filling you with glory unspeakable.[25]

Perhaps the only explanation needed for Parham's bitterness is that his attempts to usurp other Pentecostal ministries ended in failure. But at least two other factors contributed to Parham's theology. His insistence that tongues be an actual language had more to do with his support of white supremacy, especially his ties to British Israelism. For Parham, denominations meant the end of the outpouring of the Spirit and ushered in the false gods of biblical criticism and the Social Gospel.

So what animated Parham's quest for how to best define Spirit baptism? Like many late nineteenth-century evangelical preachers, he was convinced of the rapidly descending fortunes of a lost world and preoccupied with America's place in the political as well as millennial scheme of things. He was also a racist who spent his final years fine-tuning an end-times theology that excluded African Americans from any kind of salvation scenario.[26] Parham's prejudices were intricately woven into his eschatological theology of Spirit baptism, which doubted that the salvific effects of the work of Jesus were sufficient to include people of color.[27] "The black race, the Brown race, the Red race, the Yellow race, in spite of missionary zeal and effort are nearly all heathen still," he said.[28] For Parham, as a British Israelism devotee, salvation was determined by one's racial/ethnic identity. White Europeans developed a more refined sense of salvation and therefore were burdened with taking the lead in attempting to evangelize even the most lost of racial groups. Parham explains: "The fact that the ten lost tribes of Israel constitute the present cultured world ruling Protestant nations should be brought from under cover so that the Scriptures bearing on Jacob's trouble and the ten-toed, ten-horned, ten-kinged powers might be understood and preparations made."[29] This in short was British Israelism, the replacing of Jews as the lost tribe with Northern European whites. The genealogy Parham cites in his booklet, "Voice Crying in the Wilderness," begins at Adam and moves forward to Queen Victoria, with a curious detour through the Celtic kings, who no doubt would have been loath to find their lineage linked to Anglo-Saxon Protestant lore.[30] For Parham, the schema was simple. God was going to use the superior Anglo-Saxon race, gifted with the ability to speak in any tongue necessary for evangelism, in order to bring about the end of the age. The reason God destroyed the world the first time around, the metaphoric flood of Noah's age, occurred, according to Parham, because: "God intended to destroy man whom He had created, with all the half-breeds resulting from inter-marriages."[31] Indeed, as first suggested by historian Leslie Callahan's work on Parham, scholars simply cannot divorce his Spirit baptism doctrine from white supremacy because, as Callahan interprets Parham's soteriology, people of color had no hope: "The damned have no eternity, rather they will be utterly destroyed, both body and soul."[32] The church, the so-called Bride of Christ, was equated with the Anglo-Saxon race, while the heathen and the Gentiles were not only "spiritual but also racial-ethnic classifications whose identity follows them through eternity."[33] Parham advocated a form of spiritual imperialism wherein reaching the "heathen" was futile. Echoing the arguments of European imperialist leaders like Cecil Rhodes, Parham believed only Anglo-Saxon rule of Asia, Australia, and Africa would save people of color. Why? Parham argued that the superior race had their general good will in mind.[34]

Parham developed the idea that because Jesus's return was imminent, the baptism of the Holy Spirit meant the ability to speak in a foreign language. Parham wrote: "In the close of age, God proposes to send forth men and women preaching in languages they know not a word of, which, when interpreted the hearers will know is truly a messages from God, spoken through lips of clay by the power of the Holy Ghost."[35] It should be noted that Parham's eschatological schema and its fusion with Spirit baptism were forged outside of denominational boundaries; though Parham never explicitly stated that his fusion theology was a reason for him never joining a denomination, it is clear from his writing that he was very distant from denominations, finding them stifling confines of "sectarian churchism."[36]

Parham also believed that the United States had a central role in the Book of Revelation. While Daniel's lion, for example, is Great Britain, the eagle's wings represent the United States, which "was the first nation to establish religious liberty, and the common brotherhood of mankind as the first principle of Civil Government."[37] These sentiments support the overall emphasis Parham gave to white Americans as exceptional in nearly every case, especially the role they played in ushering in the millennium. Like many preachers convinced they were living in the last days, Parham believed the United States was headed toward moral oblivion.

Parham practically begged preachers and church members to actively combat the evils of evolution, socialism, and allopathic medicine.[38] Parham echoed the sentiments of many of his co-religionists who viewed rapid social change and a loss of white Christian cultural currency as synonymous with moral decay. Parham's sermon on moral decay is aptly categorized under "Demonology": "We are facing the greatest attack upon the foundations of Christianity ever known, but we welcome the fight. Half the preachers, most all the newspapers, the moving pictures, high schools, colleges and universities, have arrayed themselves on the side of the anti-Christian movement."[39] What sounds very much like distant echoes of the nascent stages of the culture wars to some may also sound like a rallying cry to the common people; hence the desire by some historians to find populist stirrings within the early Pentecostal movement as a way to explain the racism and the appeal to the grassroots.

Biographer James Goff sees Parham's populism in this light: "For some [including Parham] the explanation was undoubtedly that human efforts for justice are futile; only God could restore order on behalf of the weak and oppressed. . . . It was from this insecure world that Charles Parham drew his formative thoughts."[40] What neither Goff nor Jacobsen do effectively is examine populism's ties to race, especially in the Plains states. In this part of the United States, anxiety on the part of poor whites stemmed from the conspiratorial idea that hidden forces were robbing them of their futures by manipulating and controlling financial resources that they had no access to and were powerless to change.

An alternative interpretation from historian Jarod Roll examines this rural populism with an eye towards radical political action. Roll writes: "Early Pentecostalism, like rural socialism, provided a means to resuscitate community institutions for migrants ripped from their homes, facilitated social interaction and entertainment for the rural poor, created a social space friendly to the working class, gave much needed spiritual sustenance in a changing world, and empowered the socially and economically marginal by offering a radical critique of their situation."[41] It is one of the more understudied aspects of American Pentecostalism, but there was once a progressive populist movement advocating for socialism in places like Oklahoma and agitating for labor organizing in Kansas. For Roll, Pentecostalism simply made the wrong choice: "These two streams of early Pentecostalism—Parham's conservative, segregationist variety and Seymour's interracial emotionalism—polarized the early movement, casting a long shadow over the development of Pentecostalism."[42] As such, institutions such as the Assemblies of God are the descendants of Parham's white supremacy. One could extend Roll's assertion out further and note that Parham represented the triumph of a segregated American Pentecostalism wholly taken captive by its premillennial imagination, and with few exceptions, certain sectors of today's American Pentecostal church resemble Parham more than they resemble Seymour.

Aimee Semple McPherson

A drive past Angelus Temple today is testament to the contemporary Foursquare denomination's ties to its founder. Though the denomination has a worldwide presence, its beginnings in Los Angeles are still celebrated as part of the legacy of Aimee Semple McPherson.[43] The first woman to lead a Pentecostal denomination, she was also one of the first to own a radio station on the West Coast, and she led the remarkable healing and evangelistic campaigns that made her one of the most significant religious icons of the early twentieth century.

Born in the village of Salford, Ontario, in 1890, "Sister" Aimee began her religious trajectory as a worker for the Salvation Army. She converted to Pentecostalism in high school, and by 1907 was married to Robert James Semple, an Irish missionary; both had desires to go to China. It was this fateful trip that resulted in the couple contracting malaria, which eventually claimed Robert's life in 1910 in Hong Kong. Aimee resettled with her mother in New York and began to work again with the Salvation Army. The desire to minister was never far away from her plans. Shortly after her Salvation Army time in New York, she married Harold Stewart McPherson, who initially was cool to the idea of the life of itinerant ministry. Aside from a brief time when Harold was content with ministry life, the unsettled life of ministry was not for him. In 1918, he filed for divorce. Aimee, seeing this as an opportunity to begin her own ministry, moved to the West Coast and founded Angelus Temple in 1923, a 10,000-seat church that would become one of the first megachurches in the United States. As her ministry grew, McPherson's life as a single mother, a divorced woman, and a woman running a business (badly, by most accounts) took a physical and mental toll.

In the spring of 1926, McPherson disappeared in Venice, California, and reappeared a month later in a beach town by the Mexican/U.S. border. She claimed to have been kidnapped. She was allegedly abducted and taken to Mexico. This was a common urban legend, since Mexico has played a kind of double role for Anglos living in Southern California—both exotic playground and dangerous hideout. At once it was a vacation spot, a dangerous den of vice and a harbor for an "indigestible mass" of immigrants.[44]

After her supposed kidnapping, she was found alive and not too worse for wear in Agua Prieta, Sonora, just south of Douglas, Arizona. Alternatives of this narrative have McPherson seen with her lover vacationing in Carmel, California, a tony hamlet on the coast of Central California that since the 1920s served as an artist/writing colony as well as a quick get-away for Los Angeles' celebrity class. The point of this brief excursion to McPherson's scandalous kidnapping is not to try make a case either way. A Los Angeles County grand jury convened to investigate the alleged kidnapping, but those findings eventually led to a standstill. But it is celebrity that McPherson was selling most of the time, presenting herself as an agent of change in the tumult of the Great Depression and her church as a haven from the coming apocalypse (hastened by America's descent into loose morals and communism). Her role as a healer and evangelist extraordinaire required more than the typical showmanship. McPherson needed to make herself bigger than life; she needed to become what much of Los Angeles was becoming known for—being famous.

Sensing that it was inappropriate for her to be single and involved in ministry, and suffering from a life-long sense of loneliness, McPherson became involved with actor/musician David Hutton and the two were married in 1931. This marriage immediately caused problems. The Foursquare denomination's bylaws forbade ministers to remarry if spouses were still alive. McPherson avoided scandal with her marriage to Hutton because within two years, the marriage was over. It seems that Hutton was keen to profit off his notoriety as "Aimee's Man," to further his cabaret act, an act that included lots of pictures of Hutton with scantily clad women.

The McPherson of the newsreels was also a single mother, a divorcee, and a bad business manager. What matters to the faithful, if the current Foursquare headquarters website is any indication, is that McPherson's evangelistic skills and her devotion be remembered by today's Foursquare adherents. There is no mention of the scandal, or of ensuing court battles over control of the ministry. Nor does the church mention that McPherson died of kidney failure, possibly caused by an overdose of Seconal. However, there should be no doubt, Sister Aimee was Hollywood as Hollywood was being born; feeding off its insatiable need for spectacle, Aimee was a star and probably died like one.

McPherson, as Richard Rayner notes in his admirable book about Los Angeles in the 1930s, was part of a rich religious amalgam of faith-cure salespeople, Eastern/esoteric/metaphysical groups, and a brimming fundamentalist bastion. What is interesting in this context of gender, is how Rayner describes McPherson as a woman practically pushing men off the edge of their piety chairs with her "filmy, flimsy dresses."[45] In the Los Angeles scene of celebrity scandal, political corruption, and economic degradation, McPherson seemed to fit right in, wanting to save the worst of what Los Angeles had to offer.

What Pentecostals did not count on, and no doubt would vigorously oppose, is the idea that Pentecostalism itself promoted an unhealthy and spiritually suspect physicality. Grant Wacker's notable work includes this amusing but telling story of how Pentecostals were opposed by other evangelicals because "men and women fell together, swooning and moaning in the most indelicate positions."[46] These events demonstrate that firstly, the idea that men and women worshiped that closely, experienced what amounted to a euphoric climatic experience, caused consternation and probably more than a little embarrassment. That men and women fell on the floor together, and laid hands on each other was also another cause of concern. That McPherson's appearance would cause such an uproar, may be simply because of her Pentecostal theatrics, but undoubtedly also included the fact that she was a woman.

McPherson's life and her mixing with the Los Angeles political machine, her performances, her divorcee status, and yes, her self-consciously flowing filmy dresses, all make for a rather non-Pentecostal view of the founder of the Foursquare church. Los Angeles was not and is not ultimately all about celebrity, despite the denizens who have tried to make it live up to its publicity. The Los Angeles that McPherson moved to, founded her denomination in, and relished being a part of, was also a place wracked by political graft, stifling poverty for many of its people stuck with no way out of the pre- or post-Depression era. Los Angeles was (and still is) a Mexican city, perpetually on the verge of having any memory of that past erased by boosteristic progress. What did Sister Aimee do in this Los Angeles? And how did those actions make her a Pentecostal innovator? Aimee fused Hollywood and Pentecostalism. When most of the Pentecostalism that the West Coast had known up until then was marked by its southern and midwestern roots: conservative, white, pietistic, and severe, Aimee flashed flamboyance.

Historian Matthew Sutton's biography of McPherson does an exceptional job of placing McPherson in 1920s and 1930s Los Angeles, when battles between newspaper editors, celebrities, and local politicians made for wonderful copy. McPherson's flair for the dramatic and for publicity made her a favorite of Los Angeles' civic booster crowd. Angelus Temple became a "must see" on the typical tourist agenda for Los Angeles.[47]

A theatrically oriented preacher, a politically savvy player in city politics, and a tireless advocate for her Foursquare denomination, McPherson made her ministry life a spectacle. It is no wonder that she had a brief stint in the theater—although her reenactment of her life apparently did not grab audiences and her show closed down shortly after it started.

But in her ministry, McPherson was masterful in directing, set design, and lighting, all intended for dramatic sermons. Some of her best known theatrics included driving up on stage with a motorcycle in full police uniform and bringing a sheep on stage to illustrate the story of the Prodigal Son. McPherson stressed healing and would have wheelchairs, crutches, glasses, and other personal items that people healed in her services no longer needed, displayed. Those items are still on display at Angelus Temple. McPherson also used parts of her life to illustrate her religious messages. Indeed, a *Vanity Fair* article placed her in the company of P. T. Barnum, Harry Houdini, and Greta Garbo.[48]

Aimee's legacy as a pioneering Pentecostal evangelist is secure. There would be a lot at stake historically if Aimee turned out to be little more than what the popular media of the time often painted her as—a fraud. Frank Capra's movie *The Miracle Woman* (1931), starring Barbara Stanwyck as a thinly veiled Aimee, is more generous to the evangelist than Jean Simmons's take on the evangelist in *Elmer Gantry* (1960). What is clear is that Aimee is a media creation and a Hollywood creation, and for that, the Foursquare church owes her all the respect and accolades she is due.

A. A. Allen

In 1970, Asa Alonzo Allen, tent revivalist extraordinaire, died at the Jack Tar Hotel in San Francisco. Reports differ regarding the circumstances of his death. While newspapers reported that empty liquor bottles as well as several bottles of pills were strewn around the hotel room, sources from the Miracle Valley Ministerial Association (Allen's organization, still in existence in Arizona) disputed those reports. According to them, Allen died of cardiac arrest (though controversy and conspiracy would also cloud the role played by the coroner, more on that later), and they deny that there were any signs of alcohol or drug abuse. Other accounts had Don Stewart, a self-proclaimed successor to Allen and active evangelist, finding his mentor in the hotel room and removing the bottles of alcohol and pills before authorities arrived. Whatever the actual narrative, in such a high tension faith[49] as Pentecostalism, divine healing is possible, an encounter with the Holy Spirit can break the stranglehold of alcoholism, disease, or depression. For more than a century,

Pentecostals have been loath to question that basic premise and have had surprising tolerance for the leaders who have transgressed. Thus, A. A. Allen's biography reads like hundreds of narratives that Pentecostals have told and retold about hard living on the margins of poverty, violence, and hopelessness. Why it is important for contemporary Pentecostals to retell such stories has much to do with the idea that those who represent the faith to a hostile and unbelieving world need to "collectively" represent Pentecostalism.[50]

Asa Alonzo Allen was born on March 27, 1911, in Sulphur Rock, Arkansas, into an abusive family. Allen's father was an alcoholic wandering musician who gave Allen alcohol and tobacco very early in his life. Allen's mother left his father when he was four, but ended up marrying another man who was also an alcoholic.[51] According to evangelist Melvin Harter, who took over the abandoned Miracle Valley property in the early 1990s with the desire to revitalize Allen's ministry, Allen's early years were very difficult. On the Miracle Valley website (on a page now archived), Harter wrote details from Allen's life that he seemingly accumulated through time spent listening to Allen's sermons and mostly from Allen's books. From these sources, that Harter does not cite completely, he notes that Allen stopped attending school in the eighth grade because he was ashamed of his clothes. His stepfather, whom Allen characterized as a "big old milado [*sic*: mulatto]," was violent—so much so that Allen said that he would have "murdered all of us if he could have." To keep her six children safe, Allen's mother, a half-Cherokee woman, allegedly did not leave the house unless she was armed and carried things like icepicks and knives with her. Allen concluded his life story by relating a story of how he and his family picked off chunks of coal thrown off passing trains, which was, as he notes, much better than stealing the coal.[52] There are allusions to Allen's stepfather's racial identity in his official biography, but he is not referred to as a "milado." Neither is Allen's mother referred to specifically as a Cherokee, though the allusion is to her Native American heritage. Given that a large part of Allen's image was as an integrationist and a pioneer of multiracial, multi-ethnic revivals (who had an African American, Gene Martin, as one of his first worship leaders), it would be beneficial for the official biography to clean up the racialized language and the linking of Allen's mother's race with her propensity to violence and arming herself with knives. Allen's audience—a unique mixture of African Americans, whites, Latinas/os, and Native Americans—could have found Harter's depictions insensitive. In any case, both Allen's wife and one of his most prominent supporters, John L. Carver, who keeps an online archive of Allen's work operating today, maintain Allen's legacy as a pioneer of racial tolerance.

In 1936, after several years in the Methodist church, Allen was ordained in the Assemblies of God, began his work in Colorado, and eventually landed in Corpus Christi, Texas, in 1947. Disappointed that the Assemblies refused to sponsor his radio program and would not construct a new church building for him, he formed A. A. Allen Revivals and became an independent evangelist. Around 1950, Allen drove to Dallas to attend an Oral Roberts tent meeting and came away convinced that Roberts's tent ministry was the future of Pentecostal outreach. Allen began holding tent revival meetings shortly thereafter under a used tent he bought from fellow traveler Jack Coe.[53] Allen's issues with drinking grew worse, and in 1955 he was arrested in Knoxville, Tennessee, for driving under the influence of alcohol, and he jumped bail. Allen returned his ministerial credentials to the AG; he said because he was insulted that the AG asked him to step down from his ministry, pending an investigation into the incident.[54] Allen then founded his own ministry, a traveling healing and evangelistic ministry under the auspices of the "Miracle Revival Fellowship." Allen also pioneered prosperity teachings on television. Kate Bowler adds that the uniformity of the prosperity gospel message was in some respects due to the influence of televangelism. Prosperity preachers appeared on more stations as technology advanced production of shows and distribution of a strikingly similar idea of reciprocity based on tithing to a minister's coffers.[55]

In 1958 Allen founded Miracle Valley ministries in Arizona.[56] The idea to make church property multi-use and all in one may have originated with Allen, and was later adopted by other prosperity pioneers such as Roberts and Kenneth E. Hagin. Allen's entrepreneurial talents were on display when his ministry began selling such items as "miracle" water, dirt from his compound, real estate from the same acreage, and even shreds of his used tents, which he packaged as "power-packed prayer rugs."[57] Throughout the 1960s Allen's revivals constantly referred to the "spirit of poverty," suggesting that poverty was one of the ailments God healed.

One can see Allen's presence and style today courtesy of YouTube, where many of his sermons receive regular viewings. While mocking people with too much education, he preaches heartfelt sermons about the miraculous nature of God and exhorts his audience to have faith. Allen represents the cultural populism of mid-century American Pentecostalism, which veered away from theological education and denominational authority. Convinced that he should take his case directly to the people, Allen coupled a suspicion of religious and educational elites with a democratizing feel for the Holy Spirit. Faith would unleash the power of living a Spirit-filled life. Holy Spirit living would cause people to lose weight, to be healed of cancer, to be freed from poverty.

Allen's coupling of healing to include financial health was not new. Oral Roberts had done much the same without the outreach to the ordinary folks. What was new was his channeling of a populist impulse and making the prosperity gospel become part of American Pentecostalism. God cared about paying bills, filling bank accounts, and making sure that ordinary folks were as prosperous as those educated elites whom Allen loathed. Faith in the prosperity gospel produced an avenue of power that uneducated ordinary folks did not have. Faith equaled the economic playing field, or at least, that was and is its enduring claim to fame, to bring the wealth of secular elites to the people. To accomplish this, Allen had to convince his audiences that he knew their pain, that he was one of them; if he could heal the sick and overcome his family circumstances, then so could anyone in the audience. In one of his more audacious stunts, Allen brought a church member's Cadillac up to the altar so she could testify that after she prayed for a Cadillac and additional monies in the pages of Allen's *Miracle* magazine, she received them. Allen shouted to the audience that the Cadillac was a way of showing God's promised blessings of prosperity to the devout. Allen concluded this segment of his television show by having one of his staff drive the Cadillac out of the tent and adding, "Beat-up old cars don't glorify the Lord."[58]

Folklorist Ronald L. Baker, who examined over ten years' worth of Allen's *Miracle* magazine, notes that Allen's ministry claimed to be saving Christianity from the "cold dead hand" of denominations, which were lost to "liberalism, intellectuals, and sin."[59] Allen's brand of folksy populist preaching, coupled with his racial tolerance marked him as different from white Pentecostals of the time, especially those who belonged to denominations that essentially operated as nearly all-white organizations. In a video that may date to the mid-1960s, Allen chastises his former denomination for deflecting their racist views and supporting missions in Africa while doing little to reach African Americans in the United States. Allen also recounts a time when he was preaching in an Assemblies church and the pastor had a "colored" woman removed from the church. Allen responded: "Don't you dare run that colored woman out of this church!" In fact, the whole thirty-minute television show is Allen preaching about his interracial ministry and criticizing others who are not integrated. Before moving on to criticizing ongoing police brutality against African Americans, Allen calls on his worship leader, Gene Martin, to join him on stage. When Martin approaches, Allen rubs his cheek on Martin's startled face. Allen notes that nothing has rubbed off. The audience seems surprised by the display, and Allen, sensing he may have gone too far, tells the crowd: "I know some of you don't like this, but Jesus likes it."[60] Allen's patronizing racial tolerance was made more palatable to white audiences probably because he was not a religious elite. His desire for racial harmony was not based on intellectual argument or an overtly political civil rights agenda. Allen's constant referral to the Bible as his source of inspiration for his interracial ministry was all the authority many of his followers needed.

Allen's outreach to racial minorities coupled with his open embrace of the prosperity gospel made him exceptionally popular. Poverty, a condition Allen knew well, was not sanctioned by virtuous Christian living; it was demonic. Therefore, seeking to get out of that state and seeking wealth were God-ordained goals for the faithful. All one had to do was ask for that favor, wait for it, the heavens would open.

For Allen, becoming wealthy was not dependent on any terrestrial variable; God determines your wealth. He also equates being "rich" in God with material possessions. Allen's remark that women would no longer have to rely on their husbands for money if they trusted God to provide all the wealth that they needed may say a great deal about his mostly female audience. It also helped that Allen blamed being poor on demonic activity. No respectable Pentecostal would want to give the devil that victory.[61]

Allen also began dispensing prosperity cloths, prayed over by him and his staff for the expressed purpose of breaking that spirit of poverty and that they could be had for donations between $100 and $1,000.

According to Allen's ministry association, at the height of his popularity, Allen broadcasted on over fifty radio stations and over forty television stations. While his demise in San Francisco is still shrouded in mystery, supporters claim on various websites that the coroner was bribed with $10,000 to doctor Allen's autopsy report and then, in a fit of guilt, sent the money back to the Miracle Valley Association before taking his own life.[62] For Allen's detractors and supporters, it does not matter what newspapers print, what the autopsy report says, or whether Allen's successor admitted to cleaning up the hotel room after finding him dead.[63]

Allen and other notable Pentecostal figures, past and present, are allowed to be transgressive "artists" as it were because ultimately they are not viewed as detrimental to the overall goals of the movement.[64] On the contrary, Allen's revivals, according to the Miracle Valley Association, were responsible for thousands of people converting to Christianity. For many Pentecostals, the behavior of secular transgressive artists is subject to correction, repentance, and forgiveness. In this schema, only sin explains people's consistent inability to overcome their self-destructive tendencies. Allen's life and his work as an evangelist and healer are legendary among Pentecostals. For many Pentecostals, trying to examine Allen's successes and failures is impossible because they feel obligated to rescue his reputation. Any negative assessment of Allen's life is itself subjected to doubt. Allen's influence, the narrative he created for himself and one that his followers continue to support as an alleviator of illness and poverty, as an integrationist, as someone unafraid to touch an African American—that, for the devout, is the only legacy they care to maintain.

CHAPTER THREE

Gender, Sexualities, and Pentecostalism

Saying that the 1906 Azusa Street Revival was mostly, if not all, mythology may seem to be getting old by now. One cannot stress how strenuous an effort was and is made by adherents and scholars alike to make Azusa Street mean something that historically it simply cannot bear the weight of. One of the more fanciful claims was that after Azusa Street, and even during the height of its revival, women received an unprecedented entryway into the halls of pastoral power. But in fact, it is not that women were not prominent, but they have not become equals in Pentecostalism.[1] Gender in general is a tricky issue in Pentecostalism. In order to do justice to its complexity, we need to go beyond traditional heterosexual identities and relationships and consider homosexuality, the subordination of women, and the construction of a form of genteel evangelical masculinity that privileges their supremacy—soft power, if you will.

Insofar as women are concerned, Pentecostalism does have female ministers, missionaries, teachers, and congregants, but very few, if any, denominations have ever given women central places of power in the hierarchy. However, it would be shortsighted for this chapter to take the traditional path and discuss the role of "important" women in American Pentecostalism, select a few historic figures, discuss their accomplishments and how gender played a role in their successes or failures, and leave it at that. That would not do justice to the complex relationship that Pentecostalism has always had with sexuality and its insistence that gender and sexuality be subsumed to its high-tension piety.

Focusing on a few major figures that fell short of that piety and became embroiled in scandal and controversy (such as Parham and McPherson)[2] is also not adequate to flesh out the complexities of the issues. This is especially true with sexuality, or as the title of the chapter indicates, a multiplicity of sexualities that exist in both the public and private lives of Pentecostals. The literature here is vast and beyond the scope of this chapter.[3] This chapter then assumes that sexualities exist in the Pentecostal movement and that whereas for some their own sexual identity is a non-issue, for others it is something to be suppressed. Either way, there are many who believe that any hint of their "aberrant" sexual identity requires healing as a part of their living out their lives as Pentecostals.

Part of this chapter discusses how gender roles and sexual identities are inscribed in approved behavioral and moral codes for young adults, at a time in their lives when they are most vulnerable to leaving the fold and most ready to become monogamous married couples. First, however, it will examine how theological institutions of higher education help shape and reinforce ideas of gender and sexuality in ways that are acceptable to the church.

Bible Colleges and Universities

Pentecostal bible colleges and universities are known by insiders as institutions that young men and women attend with the idea of finding suitable spouses.[4] They also serve as sites where young people, who are perhaps for the first time outside of the purview of their youth-oriented ministries and parents, can choose either to partake of the sexual purity narrative created for them by their churches and their parents or not to partake. Since there are few regulators outside of their church life and home life, bible colleges and universities fill the role of maintaining sexual purity and traditional gender roles.

Pentecostal bible institutes are staples in the educational landscape of a movement that maintains a tepid relationship with higher education. Given the fact that there are more bible institutes that are Pentecostal than there are colleges or universities says much about the movement's attitudes. Their handbooks are themselves revealing; for the sake of geographic and denominational diversity, I chose to examine those of Emmanuel College, founded in 1919 in Franklin Springs, Georgia; Elim Bible Institute, founded in 1924 in Lima, New York; NorthPoint Bible College (formerly Zion Bible College), founded in 1924 in Haverhill, Massachusetts; Life Pacific College (formerly Life Bible College), founded in 1924 in Los Angeles, California; and Evangel University, founded in 1955 in Springfield, Missouri.

Many of these Pentecostal college students are already familiar with the regulations imposed on their behavior because they come from a purity culture that emphasizes modest dress and a restricted sex life, especially for young women.[5] Perhaps because Pentecostalism has not developed a rite of passage from the high school years to the college years, bible institutes take on added significance. Not only are they places where people prepare for ministry, but they also instill ideas about gender, proper sexual behavior, and the sanctity of marriage among eighteen- to twenty-four-year-olds, beyond the years when parents exert some control over their children's lives.

Emmanuel College, located in rural Georgia, is one of the oldest Pentecostal bible institutes and is part of the International Pentecostal Holiness denomination. Emmanuel's behavior codes and dress codes are fairly typical of most Pentecostal bible colleges. Also typical is that it is difficult to disentangle the behavior codes from the dress codes or to separate either or both from the way that this and other bible institutes take on the role of preparing their students for marriage. Emmanuel College students' lives are strictly regulated in accordance with what the college believes is biblical teaching. Thus, premarital, extramarital, and homosexual relationships, acts, and practices are forbidden. So, too, is abortion. While Emmanuel frowns upon conception outside the confines of marriage, it will not support a female student's choice to have an abortion in keeping with the belief that it will "violate the sanctity of life."[6]

Emmanuel's dress code, like that of many of the organizations I examined, explicitly aims to de-sexualize women by emphasizing modesty in everything from skirt length to how low a blouse is cut. Men's dress on the other hand is meant to make them more professional, to erase the boyish appearance of youthful immaturity with the more "grown-up" look of shirts and slacks.

Behavior codes are equally restrictive. Students can listen only to so-called Christian genres of music. They cannot watch R-rated movies on campus and must exercise good judgment off campus. A perennial favorite for restriction since the late nineteenth-century Holiness movement is the prohibition on dancing in "dance clubs, bars, taverns, and gentleman's clubs." For Emmanuel, the key words here are "provocative and suggestive." Likewise, students are forbidden to engage in overt demonstrations of affection, as well as "excessive kissing, inappropriate touching or laying down on couches" in private.[7]

Punishments for breaking the rules vary. Most interesting here is the fact that Emmanuel seeks to regulate private and public behavior on and off campus without much of a strategy for doing so. But then if one has truly received the optimum benefit of the teachings of the church and is living a Spirit-filled life, the theory is that one regulates one's own behavior in public and will not be seen in places such as bars or be caught listening to forbidden music. At the same time, their piety is what keeps them in high tension with their environs. The punishments and expulsions work to continually keep students in check and maintain that high tension as a standard as well as to weed out those students who are not capable or willing to subject themselves to the regulations.

Elim Bible Institute in upstate New York is one of the first Pentecostal denominations to have been founded in the early twentieth century. Elim's dress codes, like those of other schools, focus on professionalizing the students, minimizing their casual appearance, and deemphasizing women's sexuality much more than that of men. For men, there are no muscle shirts, shorts, hats, or earrings. For women, there are no low-cut blouses or sleeveless tops. Modesty seems to be the modus operandi. While the rules governing behavior reflect the moral codes of the school, Elim regulates students' social lives more than Emmanuel.

At Elim, freshmen cannot date. This prohibition probably mirrors what many of these young people experience in their home life where dating is questioned and oftentimes discouraged.[8] Older students need written permission from college officials to have relationships; there is a dating approval worksheet that asks questions about student's peers, parents, and what their plan is to guard their "sexual purity."[9] Such rules, according to the student handbook, are not aimed at deterring mature relationships.[10] Rather, they are meant to keep students from interrupting their studies by getting married. If the idea that a school official will deter an engaged couple from holding hands seems quaint to an outsider, it makes perfect sense in a Pentecostal context where bible institutes serve as a traditional bridge from adolescence to adulthood.

Students found in violation of these policies are subject to counseling and disciplinary action. There is also a rewards system wherein good behavior receives "honor" points. Even with a small school like Elim (it has only 150 students), located in upstate New York and dedicated to educating students in their denomination, the geographic and demographic isolation (it is an overwhelmingly white denomination) creates a space for Elim to enforce its strict moral code. Since its founding in 1924, Elim has not grown much beyond its northeastern U.S. base, where only a dozen or so Elim churches exist.[11] As the teaching arm of the denomination, Elim seeks to make sure that its core values are maintained and to attract students to their brand of Pentecostalism.

NorthPoint Bible College and Graduate School in Massachusetts, another college founded in 1924, supports my contention that geographic and demographic isolation have at least a part to play in the level of strictness that Pentecostal bible colleges deploy to ensure appropriate levels of conduct and distinctiveness. While NorthPoint is an Assemblies of God school, it has the same kinds of rules governing dress and behavior as Elim. Formerly Zion Bible College, NorthPoint was refashioned on the grounds of the recently closed Bradford College. Hobby Lobby heir Mart Green bought Bradford and donated it to Zion. In keeping with its AG heritage, NorthPoint's focus is similar to the other schools. Abortion and homosexuality are chief concerns, as are modest dress and regulating sexual behavior.

Though NorthPoint is not as geographically isolated as Elim, its spiritual and demographic isolation in secular New England[12] is striking. Catering to an older immigrant population (Italian and Eastern European Pentecostal immigrants), NorthPoint has 302 students—and does not attract nearly as many as competing conservative evangelical school Gordon-Conwell Seminary, which regularly attracts over two thousand students from nearly fifteen different denominational backgrounds.[13] Also, when one examines bible colleges on the West Coast compared to those on the East Coast, there is a marked difference—not so much in the behavioral codes, but in the dress codes.

The location of Life Bible Institute (now known as Life Pacific College) in Southern California has shaped its policies. For example, Life has virtually no dress code, and compared to the other schools discussed in this chapter, it has the least specific punishments for infractions. It does, however, have a fairly typical code of conduct. The college "rejects all inappropriate behavior," which means not only no (sexual) relations outside of marriage, but also no sleepovers. Under the circumstances, it would appear that these rules, which seem obvious, required codification after infractions. Life Pacific's other behavioral codes fit right into the standards of most Pentecostal colleges: no drinking, smoking, gambling, and social dancing, although perhaps it is harsher than most in requiring students who divorce or are separated during their time at school to withdraw from school.[14]

Compared to Life Pacific and the other schools discussed above, the Assemblies of God's Evangel University in Springfield, Missouri, is unique in several ways. In terms of behavioral codes, it is fairly similar. There is to be no consumption of alcohol or tobacco. There is to be no co-ed campus dancing (and presumably no same-sex dancing either). Evangel notes that everything that is not in keeping with "biblical principles" is forbidden and leaves it at that. In contrast, their system of punishments for varying levels of infractions is almost dizzying in its detail.

One reason for this may be that Evangel is a relatively new school, founded in the 1950s, and thus has a strong desire to be professional and has an obvious infatuation with the gospel of efficiency. Also, Evangel is a university, so it is subject to different standards of accreditation than bible colleges and must also have some measure of quality control for its moral codes so that they are not perceived as unfair or unequal. In any case, the elaborate system of punishments and fines demonstrate how Evangel approaches inculcating a specific view of morality and gender among their students.

First offenses for improper displays of affection have no punishment. Social dancing is an "Alert Level 1," as are dress code infractions and "displays of affection." Second offenses are punishable by up to eight weeks probation and another fine. When it comes to sexual infractions, there are levels of punishment for having sex outside of marriage, which is a "Probation Level 1" infraction, with a $100 fine. If the offenders are involved in extracurricular activities such as sports, they are banned from those activities.[15] What all the dress and behavioral codes reinforce is that the ideal relationship for young men and women is marriage, and that any deviation from that is prohibited. For Pentecostal higher education, these rules are not arbitrary or capricious; they are biblically mandated as part of the continued demonstration of a transformed life. Moreover, the institutionalizing of dress and behavior codes serves to cement the purity narrative onto young adulthood, just as the varied options available to these young people becomes much more complex. This is especially important given that, by and large, the general population sees the ages of eighteen through twenty-four as years that no longer automatically include marriage.[16] It is this demographic shift that often serves as the strongest argument for the "secularization" of society since this idealized moment when people married young, had children, and women stayed home to raise those children remains a strong trope in Pentecostalism. To suggest that it no longer is the dominant trope, not only among the general population, but among the emergent millennial population of the Pentecostal church,[17] causes great consternation among many in church leadership and one reason why augural discussions of "war against marriage" are more than rhetorical flourishes. Countervailing realities such as sexual promiscuity, divorce, and same-sex marriage are perceived as real threats to what I would like to call "marriage imaginaries."[18] Before delving briefly into the public marriages and divorces of some well-known Pentecostal figures, another story from my ethnographic work among Pentecostals that may help place marriage in some context.

Marriage: Ideal and Real

Terry was a friend of the pastor. He was an occasional visitor to the Saturday night service, and people knew that his marriage was in trouble, so, in an attempt not to make him feel uncomfortable, they invited him to the after service dinner, always held at the same Chicago institution. Terry sat down with Andy, a married man older than Terry and someone who generally did not make the rounds to the after dinner service. This night, though, he was in for quite a story. Andy was a straight-laced Presbyterian, fairly liberal, and not at all Pentecostal; he was sharing this table with these Pentecostal folks courtesy of his wife, who was out of town. After some small talk and food, Terry confided in Andy that he was going to be getting a divorce.

Terry said that his wife and he had not been getting along for a while; he suspected she was having an affair, but never asked her. He noticed that the first couple of years, their marriage was fine; they were inseparable and began attending church together. Then, to hear Terry tell it, she changed, for no apparent reason. She became distant, they argued, she stopped going to church. After months of trying to reconcile, Terry and his wife agreed that it was not going to work. Terry became quiet and less expressive. "I know what the problem was and I got rid of it." Andy paused to wait for the rest of the answer. "I got rid of them, they were the problem, those rabbits were possessed." Terry blamed his wife's pet rabbits for their pending divorce, believing that their presence had introduced a demonic presence into their lives a year ago (about when the marriage began to go sour), and he let them go, releasing them out into a particularly cold Chicago winter.[19]

Unable to make sense of his wife's estrangement, Terry blamed her pets. Their demonic activity had to be a part of his deteriorating marriage. There are many places to take this true story. One surely is that Pentecostals take marriage seriously because for them it is not a civil procedure, but sacred, and they take the Devil's attempts to crush marriage serious, even if it means unlatching bunny cages in the dead of winter. Pentecostals, like their evangelical cousins, have literally thousands of ministries dedicated to marriage counseling, therapy, and anti-divorce interventions. There is a veritable and very determined marriage industry in Pentecostalism that views this institution as spiritual and its failure is viewed as a severe blow to another institution—the nuclear family.

All Pentecostal denominations believe marriage to be a sacred, God-instituted relationship that is male/female and, as Elim Fellowship's statement on marriage and divorce note, "terminates in death."[21]

The statement of marriage of the Assemblies of God, the largest white Pentecostal denomination in the United States, mirrors most of the statements I found. It is longer but the sentiment is similar.[22] The Assemblies, like many conservative Christian organizations, believes that traditional marriage and the family are "under attack," which presumes many things, among them that what exists now in terms of marriages and families are radically different than from what existed in the past, and that this desire to restore traditional marriage and family means restoring it to male/female heterosexual families with children. One singular idea undergirds all this: biblical literalism. As the statement notes, the Assemblies of God support the idea of an Adam and Eve according to the account in Genesis. As such, ideas such as women being subjected to men, as men are to Jesus; women being helpmates as noted in Genesis; and marriage being a religious institution are all valuable assets in the religious economy of the Assemblies of God, if not the whole of most Pentecostals. What is unclear is that divorce—viewed uniformly as bad, to be avoided, and unbiblical—is largely accepted as the influential 2006 Pew study of Pentecostals/charismatics found.[23] It is beyond the scope of this chapter to uncover all the reasons why divorce has become de-stigmatized in Pentecostalism, but we can try.

Injunctions against transgressive behavior are staples of high-tension religious groups. For those who transgress, there are warnings not to, punishments should that happen, and in all cases, paths to redemption. The question is then why, with the reality of something like divorce a given, does Pentecostalism still insist on biblical literalist interpretations of things like marriage, divorce, homosexuality, and a host of other prohibited behaviors? If the statistics are clear—that Pentecostals divorce at similar or higher rates than the general population, a population believed by many Pentecostals to be unbelievers—why the continued idealization of marriage as a "life-long relationship . . . terminated in death"?[24] Such cognitive dissonance does not have easy answers. Suffice to say, it may be that the Assemblies of God and the other denominations featured in this chapter simply have failed to acknowledge that their religious standards do not conform to the cultural destigmatization of issues of marriage and divorce.

Admitting that something as sacred as marriage and divorce are viewed by the general population in nearly legal terms—and largely based on whether the individual receives the maximum amount of benefits and personal growth—lies at the crux of what Pentecostal denominations mean when they talk about traditional ideas of marriage. It is essentially the same argument made by most high tension groups who see prized non-negotiables such as drinking, gambling, or divorce over a span of a generation or two become negotiable plausible activities to engage in. Since, like most things, the certainty of one's piety is often defined outside the realm of one's faith, it is usually defined and stretched by cultural and social factors that do not bow to religious dictates.

Marriage then is the glue to much of this exercise in high tension piety. What some Pentecostals are just coming to terms with, if they are at all, are the numbers of young people who simply do not see marriage as a religious or tradition-bound step to adulthood, but a legal contract through which the individualized desires of both partners for personal growth and comfort can be secured.[25] In keeping with this idea, in the following section, the issue of marriage and divorce, the ceremony, the pomp, and circumstances of the ritual will be viewed through three very different lenses: the choice of ministry over marriage of Maria Atkinson, the broadcasted wedding of Sister Rosetta Tharpe, the televised wedding of Juanita Bynum, and the complicated married life of Ted Haggard.

Some Married Lives of Pentecostals

Maria Atkinson was born into a Catholic upper-middle class family in Sonora, Mexico, in 1879. Atkinson seems to have experienced ecstatic experiences early on in her life, as the semi-hagiographic biography of her and her denomination note.[26] At the age of fourteen, Atkinson experienced a vision of Jesus at Mass and remained in a state of ecstasy for several hours. Church of God author Charles Conn notes that at that point Atkinson exchanged the "mariolatry of Romanism for the simple faith of evangelical Protestants."[27]

Atkinson came from a privileged background. Her family owned land and had various mining interests. After her parents died, Atkinson was tutored privately, and her first job was working as a teacher. Her first husband, Dionisio Chomina, died in 1905 shortly after transferring to Douglas, Arizona, where he worked for the railroads. Atkinson made her way to Los Angeles in 1916 and, like many Mexicana and Mexican American women, made her living making dresses. A friend of a client introduced her to her second husband, Mark Atkinson, and they were married in 1920.

Maria's story of how she became Pentecostal is typical of hundreds, if not thousands of people who have come to the faith by a healing experience, or as religious studies scholar Hector Avalos aptly characterizes it, utilizing Pentecostalism as an alternative health care system.[28]

Diagnosed with cancer in 1924, it was Maria's washwoman who suggested the possibility of faith healing. Subsequently, Atkinson sought treatment and healing throughout the Southwest, reportedly being healed at an Assemblies of God church, and joined the denomination. Healing evangelist Peggy Scarborough, in a laudatory biographical sketch, notes that Atkinson received a vision from God that she was supposed to go into missions. After this vision she left her husband. That would be important to readers whose denominations have very strict rules about marriage and divorce. An edict from God in the guise of a vision would give Atkinson license to leave her husband and go into ministry as a single woman, whereas just about any other rationale to leave her husband would be unacceptable. In 1926, she returned to Mexico as a missionary. She established Pentecostal communities in Nogales, Santa Ana, Hermosillo, and Ciudad, Obregon.

Atkinson tended to focus on preparing other missionaries and on training her charges on the proper way to conduct themselves. Her wealthy upbringing instilled in her a sense of propriety she apparently felt was missing among her followers. Anthropologist Mary I. O'Conner suggests that Atkinson trained her people to be respectable.[29] In addition to this socialization, Atkinson, who had been trained as a teacher, taught people to read. Avalos notes that Atkinson's power as a single woman in Mexico came from her socioeconomic status and her personality. Surviving church members told Avalos that Atkinson was a strong-willed disciplinarian whose signature white dresses and light skin demonstrated to them that she was an "upper-class lady."[30] Atkinson was a woman who could afford to live her life as a single woman who'd left her husband because of her economic status and her "chromatic privilege." Coupled with her desire to serve as a maternalistic white savior to her "indios," Atkinson served as transmitter of assimilation to American Protestant cultural values and norms.[31] Atkinson represented the apex of American Protestant culture that privileged assimilation: melding Christianization with Americanization by "transmitting Appalachia to Mexico" through worship music and style.[32] Atkinson, like so many early Pentecostal missionaries, viewed her job as twofold: to Christianize and to civilize. Since this colonial project has never quite left its European/American Christian roots, Atkinson's worth, as it were, was not in demonstrating the sanctity of marriage, but the urgency of conversion. Pentecostal women, and it will be mostly women, may or may not serve as weather vanes for the marriage pedestal. If they can serve the cause of holiness in another capacity, their less-than-stellar marriages will be ignored or excused as part of their sacrifice for ministry. As concerned as she appeared to be about social propriety, she eventually asked for and received a divorce from her second husband in 1930. For some women in ministry, marriage and divorce and re-marriage were often the ways they made themselves acceptable to Pentecostal audiences who needed assurance of women's place in the movement and of their piety. For other women, like COGIC musician Sister Rosetta Tharpe, maintaining the appearance of a woman whose singleness was more about bad timing and bad choices of men, meant not having to face questions about her sexuality, at a time when staying closeted was the only choice for church folk.

Sister Rosetta Tharpe was a gospel singer and guitarist extraordinaire, whose influence broadened out beyond her gospel circuit to include early rock 'n' roll and country performers such as Elvis Presley (more on him in chapter 4), Jerry Lee Lewis, and Johnny Cash. She was also part of COGIC and of its musical legacy. Tharpe was born to Mother Katie Bell Nubin in 1915 in Cotton Plant, Arkansas. Nubin was an established musician and traveling evangelist for COGIC, who ministered along with her husband, a healing evangelist. In the 1920s the family relocated to Chicago, where the family could make a living as church musicians and, for Rosetta, a place where her virtuosity as a guitarist would gain her more attention. Black Pentecostals, as historian Lerone Martin perceptively notes, were not ascetics. They engaged in consumer culture, buying records, attending concerts, and selling ministry related products in order to support preachers and church musicians.[33]

Throughout the early 1920s, the family toured various Holiness churches and campgrounds. By six years old, Rosetta had achieved enough mastery of the guitar to accompany her mother, who played the mandolin. By the time she was in her early teens, however, Rosetta moved to New York, fueled by musical ambition and a desire to move beyond the cloistered gospel circuit.

In New York, Rosetta married a pastor, Thomas J. Thorpe, who was affiliated with a non-COGIC church. Thorpe did not accept Rosetta's performing and expected her to adhere to traditional notions of what a Pentecostal wife should be, going so far as to chastise her in public for not wearing a hat at the Cotton Club.[34] Her marriage to Thorpe would not last, not only because of the way he treated her, but Rosetta could not accept Thomas's adultery, since that would have certainly been at odds with her strict COGIC upbringing. She did keep a version of his last name, changing the "o" for an "a," hence the unconventional spelling of her last name.[35]

Tharpe played the New York club circuit, including the Cotton Club, with Cab Calloway, and eventually earned a spot with her own back-up band, which included famed boogie-woogie jazz pianist Albert Ammons.[36] Tharpe became a successful crossover artist, playing other clubs, theaters, and adding the electric guitar to her repertoire. Tharpe dressed like an entertainer, wearing wigs and feathered boas while performing. For her, adopting a transgressive dress code had to do with moving beyond the gospel circuit to gain acceptance from mainstream audiences, whereas for Aimee Semple McPherson, it meant using popular culture accouterments to expand her ministry. For both, dressing in a very un-churchlike manner signaled to a church audience they did not see the boundary between sacred and secular as intractable as some church members probably wished it was.

In the 1940s, Tharpe married again, this time to Forrest Allen, a gospel booking agent. It is unknown why, but that marriage ended as well in 1950. Tharpe decided to go live with her mother until her third and most well-known marriage. Biographer Gayle F. Wald, who has done work on Tharpe's musical legacy, notes that the gendered relations that existed during Tharpe's career in gospel music have not received enough attention, even as race has. As Wald writes of female African American artists: "Their gender extracted additional dues from these women gospel musicians who like all such women performers had to negotiate their publicity as professional entertainers in the context of ongoing and sometimes ruthless sexualization and constant pressure to deploy their mature femininity."[37] Tharpe's mainstream success and influence perhaps insulated her from the more extreme exploitation. But as her career began to wane in the late 1940s and early 1950s, Tharpe planned a publicity event that would bolster her career and perhaps help her out with a certain sector of her audience who might have accepted her musical ambitions if she had a husband.

Gospel promoters Irvin and Israel (Izzy) Feld met Tharpe in 1949 and they devised ways to get Tharpe out in front of a large audience, perhaps a concert at Griffith Stadium in Washington, D.C. A problem—at least according to one source, Izzy's wife Shirley—was that Rosetta needed to find a husband, otherwise Irvin did not want to promote the concert. Rosetta, a thirty-five-year-old, twice-divorced woman, signed a contract with the Feld brothers promising to produce a groom by the New Year. By spring 1951, she found Russell Morrison, who worked for the Ink Spots and was two years her junior. The wedding was broadcast on July 3, 1951.

There were 22,000 people that day at Griffith Stadium. This was a spectacle on a scale that few had seen from a gospel singer. Programs memorialized the event; the Feld brothers sold key chains, holy handkerchiefs, and small bibles. Samuel Kelsey, a COGIC minister, performed the ceremony, and given some of his comments, seemed ambivalent about the spectacle. Kelsey mentioned divorce as a negative; that in marriage, one was to forsake all others; and one was to obey and serve. Kelsey also seemed to be aware of Morrison's "semi-ornamental" role, asking Morrison in a quizzical tone, if he indeed had a ring?

Once the ceremony ended, Rosetta played guitar in her wedding dress, playing some of her classics like "So High" and the anti-alcohol gospel song "God Don't Like It." The wedding ended with fireworks and a life-size reproduction of Tharpe and her guitar paraded throughout the stadium. Wald notes that the "wedding concert thumbed its nose at middle-class convention of piety." From Tharpe's perspective, the event was a success—it displayed her ambitions, her entrepreneurial, spiritual, and artistic desires to a national audience.[38]

There are so many places to take this one event, let alone Tharpe's remarkable career. For now, the purpose of including this vignette about Tharpe is to lead in to the larger discussion of how gender and sexuality inevitably fall into binary categories for Pentecostals. Gender and sexuality are not easily managed, but the idea of marriage is, since that is the consummation of all successful relationships. The marriage/divorce binary is something that Pentecostals have only recently begun to deal with. What the Tharpe narrative says is that among her many complexities, among her "transgressions" if you will, the secularization of her music and her choice to play "in and for the world" were only part of the problem. It was an open secret that Tharpe had both male and female sexual partners.[39] For the promoters to sell Tharpe as a gospel singer, to be able to sell religious paraphernalia, she had to rectify the previous two marriage/divorces, she had to find a husband, even though this latest marriage was one of convenience and ended in divorce. Marriage then for Tharpe was a means to an end: a way to resurrect a career, a way to legitimate her already tenuous grasp on her gospel audience. As we will see next, with the stories of Juanita Bynum and Ted Haggard, problems with marriage and divorce are not new, not rare, and says much about what may lie at the heart of the marriage imaginary many contemporary Pentecostals believe has been lost to the secularization of a sacred vow.

In a very perceptive article, historian Monique Moultrie examined the recent difficulties of popular televangelist Prophetess Juanita Bynum from her marriage to Bishop Thomas Weeks in 2002 to their divorce in 2008, which ended ignominiously with a very public battering of Bynum by Weeks in the parking lot of an Atlanta hotel. Moultrie's article mentions several prominent Pentecostal women, including Lucy Smith and Mother Rosa Horn, leaders and broadcasters both "married to men whose presence was inconsequential to their religious lives."[40] Husbands, to many public female leaders, it seems, cannot be seen as taking a higher place in the religious hierarchy of their lives. As Moultrie says, these women wanted to be known for "choosing Spirit over Flesh."[41] Bynum's story fits this notion well. Born in Chicago in 1959, Bynum was involved in church life from an early age and sang in her local COGIC congregation. According to her best-selling book *No More Sheets*, Bynum married a man for the wrong reasons in 1981; that is, she married "for sex and for what the man looked like."[42] Miserable and depressed, Bynum reportedly attempted suicide and was committed to a mental hospital. After overcoming her depression, Bynum embarked on a very successful career as an evangelist, first appearing on popular shows with T. D. Jakes and becoming a fixture on the Trinity Broadcasting Network (TBN). With Jakes's backing, she embarked on a tour for her book. Her *No More Sheets* tour ends dramatically with her removing sheets from her body, symbolizing a tearing away at the misdirected sexual desire that she felt tugging at her as a single woman. Historian Amy DeRogatis believes Bynum's appeal is a combination of conservative theology and contextual language that connects with her audience. Unlike many white evangelical/Pentecostal women who preach sexual purity, Bynum does not presume the purity of her audience, whereas white evangelical/Pentecostal women's contextual language would assume sexual purity.[43]

In 2002, before an estimated broadcast audience of millions (TBN and later YouTube viewings combined), Bynum married Bishop Thomas Weeks, a prominent Pentecostal minister in the Atlanta area. The wedding was elaborate to say the least. It was attended by eighty family members and friends and one thousand guests and featured a twelve-piece orchestra and a 7.76-carat diamond ring. The black-tie wedding cost "more than a million," the bride said, and included flowers flown in from around the world. "My dress," she says, "took nine months to make. All the crystals on the gown were hand-sewn. The headpiece was sterling silver, hand-designed."[44]

Why did she spend so much time and effort on the wedding? "This," she said, "was my once-in-a-lifetime wedding, and I did it this way because I plan to stay married."[45] One might speculate that in her case, as in Tharpe's, the wedding was supposed to help her career. (Bynum sold DVDs of the event for years afterward.)

By 2008, though the marriage was in trouble. Bynum and Weeks met at the Renaissance Hotel in Atlanta to attempt reconciliation. Unsuccessful, Bynum left and Weeks followed her to the parking lot. Witnesses said he beat her, pushing her down on the pavement and stomping on her until a bystander intervened. Weeks ran off and for a time was considered a fugitive, but then surrendered to charges of battery. This cast Bynum in a new role—battered wife, which she ultimately turned into another cause, becoming a vocal advocate against domestic violence and ministering to her followers from her Atlanta headquarters. Weeks re-married in 2010, but his church, a victim of the ongoing recession that had hit churches hard, went into foreclosure in 2011. Bynum's story—from depressed single woman to elated married woman, to troubled married woman, and now to something akin to a liberated divorced woman—is instructive in supporting traditional ideas about marriage and sexuality.

Moultrie's analysis of Bynum's life is very instructive here since she sees Bynum's marriage as a byproduct of a desire for Pentecostal ministers not to see the end of one's sexuality in a chaste singleness but in marriage. She writes: "The sexual pairing of these women and God is a reiteration of heteronormativity and reflects what theorist Adrienne Rich deems as compulsory heterosexuality in which heterosexuality is 'imposed, managed, organized, propagandized' . . . Those engaged in heterosexual relationships are considered normal and in good relationship with God, which demonized those of differing orientations and even those active heterosexual singles."[46] Part of the marriage imaginary insists that marriage precludes any problems that might be found in the temptations living as a chaste single person, and it also supports the idea that sexual identity is fixed at heterosexuality. Tharpe managed to keep her sexual life private because the media apparatus of the 1940s and 1950s was primitive compared to today. Other prominent Pentecostals, like one-time megachurch pastor and head of the National Association of Evangelicals (NAE) Ted Haggard, could not escape such scrutiny.

In 2006, a Denver-area man claimed he had an affair with Haggard, and during those times, they also consumed methamphetamines. Haggard initially denied the allegations, but the male escort kept the phone messages where Haggard purportedly asked him to buy more drugs. Haggard soon resigned from his church. Three years after the scandal, Haggard chose to make his return to public life in a 2009 HBO documentary, *The Trials of Ted Haggard*. The former pastor of New Life Church in Colorado is seen traveling hundreds of miles throughout the southwestern United States to sell health insurance. After another unsuccessful sale, Haggard is driving back to his hotel where he and his family live as he undergoes months of exile, and in a mixture of self-reflection and self-pity, Haggard says that he is a loser. Unable to support his family, unable to get a job, Haggard is at a loss to explain his dramatic downfall, except to say that he is a loser.

When asked by the off-camera producer, if he is now "completely heterosexual," Haggard notes that he did not answer that question in front of the church-related board charged with his rehabilitation counseling, and he was never going to address the question again. Haggard's previous twenty years of public ministry are reduced to shouted questions as he drives around selling insurance in front of HBO's prying cameras. This scene and others may draw sympathy for him from even his most vociferous critics. A former head of the NAE, megachurch pastor, and a gay man for at least part of his life, Haggard's rehabilitation in Pentecostal circles is as fascinating as was his very public humiliation. Not only did his 2006 ousting as head pastor of New Life bring his sexuality to the fore, his later rehabilitation also brought accusations that Haggard had continued a long-term relationship with a younger male church member when he was pastor of New Life. This revelation caused his brief stay at Tommy Barnett's megachurch in Phoenix, Arizona, to end; it also precipitated his public campaigns on the Oprah Winfrey Show to demonstrate his heterosexual rehabilitation. In October 2009, Haggard moved back to Colorado Springs, Colorado, and has a house church that meets in his barn. One might ask, how is it that Haggard was able to move back to his exiled Colorado and continue ministry in the face of much public and private speculation that he was and is and will remain a gay man?

Part of the answers lies in the ways in which Pentecostals relate to what they would call sin and temptation, and what psychologists would term transgressive behavior. For Pentecostals, the reality of this behavior is not in question; they know that people sin, that they "fall" into temptation. When prominent people, especially those with a track record in public ministry, engage in transgressive behavior, the remedy is always for them to repent and seek to not engage in that behavior again. Haggard's public confession, and especially his wife's continual support and acceptance as well as his three weeks of rehabilitative work with fellow pastors, supports the idea that Haggard was willing to yield to their authority and by extension to obey biblical injunctions that most Pentecostals view as squarely against homosexuality. Haggard may not have the megachurch that he once had, but he was able, in the aftermath of his scandal, to ask for and received thousands of dollars in donations so that he and his wife could go back to school.

The business of rehabilitation for Ted Haggard has not been easy, but it became easier by one significant fact: Haggard has never changed his theological position that homosexuality is sinful and that his engagement in the behavior was wrong. Therefore, Haggard maintains his theological credibility and his viability as a minister. Similarly, pastors who do not appear to be able to stop engaging in transgressive behavior—pastors like A. A. Allen, who was a lifelong alcoholic—become theologically safe because they are in a state of perpetual repentance proclaiming their cure one day and descending back into the behavior the next, until it no longer becomes an issue for their followers.

Similarly, Tharpe's marriages and divorces are not issues with most contemporary Pentecostals, because even if they know about them, or the personal issues of other public Pentecostals for that matter, the end result is that they find a way to make the problems a way of reinforcing established theological certainties: women should be married; they should only divorce for very good reasons; if they do not marry, they should live chaste single lives. That they do not seems irrelevant: it is the ideal that matters—not the reality.

There is little to no evidence that Tharpe faced censure for the seemingly cavalier way she married and divorced her husbands. Bynum rebounded from her ostentatious and controversial wedding and her very public break with her abusive husband by becoming an advocate for battered wives and supporting traditional views of gender, sexuality, marriage, and divorce in her ministry. Haggard is making the most of his public disgrace by using media attention to draw people to his church. Of utmost importance to Haggard's redemption story is his wife Gayle, who wrote a book about why she did not leave Ted even after his gay affairs.[47] Gayle's actions solidified again the idealized marriage views of many who would have never forgiven Haggard had he not received the endorsement of his wife. What Haggard probably could not accomplish because of his complicated sexuality, his wife did, by providing him with enough pious reverence for marriage. Thus, any who wish to view Haggard in a positive light probably do so because of his wife and not because he admitted to his sexual orientation.

It is the binary with which most Pentecostals view gender and sexuality then that makes these stories so interesting and for some so contradictory, what psychologists view as cognitive dissonance writ large. To conclude this chapter, and to try and make some sense of these often confusing views, we turn to philosopher Martha Nussbaum, whose work examining marriage in the light of same-sex marriage debates proves very instructive in this case.

Pentecostals evoke a sense of urgency and danger about the "crisis" of marriage, and according to Nussbaum, this has more to do with the "primitive idea of stigma and taint."[48] Nussbaum uses the language of anthropologists here to describe what I have described as stigmatized and de-stigmatized behavior. The binaries of marriage/divorce, gay/straight, moral/immoral for Nussbaum have much more to do with a meta-binary of clean/unclean, and until those deeply held notions of unclean are diminished, gender and sexuality in most Pentecostal communities will mean one thing, but it will never be lived out that way. To see how far Pentecostals have sought to engage the world, while desperately trying to convince their unbelieving neighbors that they are not bound to this ground—the next chapter will examine Pentecostalism and popular culture, specifically how a hallmark of Pentecostalism, healing, has become a public performance and part of the therapeutic culture of contemporary American life.

CHAPTER FOUR

Pentecostalism and Popular Culture

Rock music has been a part of my life since my dad bought the Beatles' *White Album* for me in 1969, when I was three years old. Some of my academic peers grew up in households in which they were forbidden to listen to or purchase such music. As much as I have tried to understand the animus Pentecostals have towards secular music, particularly rock music, it bewilders me. No more bewildering than when a colleague of mine looked perplexed when I took one of my cherished album covers down from my office wall. It was the Clash's *London Calling*. To my shock, she had never heard of the Clash. Never heard of the Clash? My desire to be snarky and dismissive turned to curiosity because I knew she grew up in a midwestern Pentecostal household where the immutable laws about what is sacred and profane were clear.

I wonder if my friend knew that her denomination had been in the forefront of the record-burning rage of the 1960s? I doubt that she was surprised that her behavior as a good Pentecostal youth was exactly the kind of inculcated piety that Rev. Bob Larson was looking for when he established his traveling evangelistic mission against rock music in the 1960s. Bob Larson, a pioneer in what is now commonly called "deliverance" ministry (exorcism of evil spirits), traveled all over the United States, especially to Assemblies of God (AG) churches rallying them to keep their children away from the demonic call of rock music. To exorcise those demons, in effect, Larson encouraged youth to bring their records to church and burn them.

This chapter explores Pentecostalism, popular culture, and healing, all of which broadly construed expands our vista on how diverse Pentecostalism is and how pervasive Pentecostalism is in popular culture, especially as a signifier of one of its most prominent characteristics, healing. Healing is a holistic endeavor that includes body, mind, emotions, psyche, careers, sexuality, and finances. This chapter examines aspects of the lives of four charismatics/Pentecostals. There will be two famous ministers, Joel Osteen and Agnes Sanford, and two famous musicians. Elvis Presley and Marvin Gaye warrant inclusion because their Pentecostalism informed their artistic and literary contributions and they in turn used their Pentecostal upbringing to bear on their need for healing from the rigors of celebrity.

Elvis Presley's Prodigal Pentecostalism

Visiting Graceland, for me, was a pilgrimage. Beneath the ostentatiousness of Graceland is a home, a place of refuge, and a gravesite. I took my requisite pictures of the big Vegas-era suits, the wall full of gold records, but I spent more time outside at the gravesite, which seemed the proper place for me to think about the irony of Elvis's life: white working class, Assemblies of God member, lover of African American music, someone who did not run away from the blackness he absorbed through the radio or the black church living in the segregated South. Elvis took the most dynamic parts of Pentecostalism's embodied performance, added blues, country, and gospel to it, and created what I call a religious miscegenation of sound and culture that 1950s Pentecostalism was simply unable to comprehend and actively rejected. The South where Elvis was born and where he spent most of his formative years was infused with what historian Paul Harvey calls the "racial interchange" at the margins of southern religious culture. As Harvey notes, this culture shaped Pentecostalism and, I would add, shaped Elvis Presley.

By most accounts, Elvis had a typical church upbringing in the AG. For most of his youth, he took an active role in church. He went to Sunday school and learned guitar from an AG minister named Frank Smith.[1] Around the same time that Elvis worked with Sam Philips at Sun Studios, his church in Memphis received a new pastor, James Hamill. Hamill was a well-educated, fiery preacher who denounced movies and dancing from the pulpit and encouraged speaking in tongues in church. Under his leadership, the church grew to over two thousand members.[2] Elvis, who sang in church, was also a member of the AG's youth ministry, Christ's Ambassadors, which is where he met his first serious girlfriend, Dixie Locke.[3] They attended church, bible studies, and even snuck out together to attend the African American church, the Church of God in Christ, to listen to the music Elvis preferred.[4] Elvis's well-known gospel influences included the Blackwood Brothers, Sister Rosetta Tharpe, and the Clara Ward Singers.

Elvis was a Depression-era baby, born to a father, Vernon, who seemed to lack ambition for the better part of his life, and to a mother, Gladys, who doted on her sensitive, shy son. The family moved to the housing projects of Memphis, Tennessee, where they lived on welfare. Elvis, according to Peter Guralinick's definitive biography, was a loner. He did whatever he could to earn some money, including selling his blood, ushering in movie theaters, and eventually driving a truck as a teenager.[5]

The aesthetics that shaped Elvis—southern evangelically tinged country music, working-class humility, and the music of the black church—are all covered at length by music scholars and historians. For our purposes, it will be enough to summarize the life and times of Elvis, examine his religious life in some depth, and see how that life created this most unique blend of religious miscegenation. For many youths in the 1950s, Elvis was as close as they ever got to a Pentecostal preacher. Elvis did not promote a specific theology; instead, he was the kind of preacher who embodied the ecstatic shout, the holy dance, and the clandestine sexuality that institutional Pentecostalism suppressed.

Historian Bill C. Malone, in his perceptive work on country music and the southern working class, points to the immense influence evangelical Christianity has on country music, stating that the entirety of the genre is permeated with religion. He notes that all manner of guilt and self-pity are unconsciously expressed in country music.[6] This may be why Elvis internalized feelings of inferiority, because, as cultural critic Gail Sweeney noted about many poor southern whites, they were considered "trash." She adds that "much of the disdain held for white trash by the dominant society may be bound up in the foggy racial histories of such peripheral people and in a fear of miscegenation and contamination from mixing with them."[7] These anxious racial feelings are key to understanding Elvis's conflicted faith. Elvis feared contamination by the unsavory elements of the music business but became subservient to its grueling schedule, its glamorization of excess, and its banal acceptance of self-destruction. Similarly, Elvis's denomination feared contamination on many fronts: from rock 'n' roll music, from immorality, and from racial integration.

It is a given that Elvis owed nearly everything to listening to and mimicking African American artists, as he himself admitted. Historian Michael Bertrand writes that while it was unusual for southern whites to credit African Americans for anything positive, Elvis seemed intent on acknowledging his black roots: "I got my singing style listening to colored spiritual quartets down South," he said. "The colored folks been singing it and playing it just like I'm doin' now, man, for more years than I know."[8] In fact, as Bertrand notes, it was often the poor white underclass that Elvis belonged to that was subjected to derision and the contempt of being called "trash," as they were called in the antebellum South even by slaves.[9]

Paul Harvey explains that post–World War II southerners were "raised as cultural products of this racial interchange as the religious expression entered the public world of broadcasting and performing in the mid-twentieth century." Harvey adds that Elvis "intuitively grasped its kinship to his own AG background. He listened avidly to black religious orator W. Herbert Brewster on the radio, went to a COGIC church."[10] Elvis appropriated African American musical styles in much the way early Pentecostals appropriated this African American religious form,[11] the difference being that Elvis gave credit to his musical influences. It is my contention that the AG rejection of their son on the surface was a rejection of Elvis's moral compromise with the secular world of rock music, but hidden deeper beneath that was Elvis's religious and musical miscegenation. Elvis's open embrace of a music tainted with immorality and racial impurity horrified listeners as much as his first appearance on the *Steve Allen Show* and the infamous hip shake. As Bertrand notes, "After reading how Presley professed to have learned from its black counterpart, the pastor of a white AG congregation in Memphis exploded: 'The inference that the white Assembly of God congregation borrowed heavily from negro sects is not only a slur, but it is too stupid for words.' "[12]

Elvis internalized Pentecostal social norms to some extent. According to his friends, he did not allow smoking or drinking in his house. He did not want to be around people when they were drinking, and he himself resisted imbibing.[13] Particularly during the first few years of his career, Elvis stayed close to his faith. A family friend quoted in Guralnick's biography said that she and Elvis read the Bible every night and that he seemed very serious and sincere about his faith.[14] Elvis also learned from AG pastors' frenetic styles and integrated that into his on-stage dancing. He noted: "When preachers were not animated, no one paid attention, but when they cut up all over the place, jumped on the piano . . . I guess I learned from them singers."[15] He could be protective and defensive about his AG background. Once he became irate at the suggestion made by a reporter that his gyrations were part of his "Holy Roller" upbringing: "I have never used that expression," Elvis exploded angrily. "That's another deal. See, I belong to an Assembly of God church, which is a Holiness church. I was raised up in a little Assembly of God church, and some character called them Holy Rollers." Elvis continued: "I always attended church where people sang, stood up and sang in the choir and worshiped God, you know. I never used the expression 'Holy Roller.'" The reporter continued pressing the point, and Elvis retorted that his religious upbringing had nothing to do with his music today. He concluded angrily: "My religion has nothing to do with what I do now. Because this type of stuff I do now is not religious music, and my religious background has nothing to do with the way I sing."[16] Elvis was stung by the moniker "Holy Roller," used for decades to dismiss Pentecostals as little more than an overly excited and potentially unstable religious group that offered little more than an ecstatic worship service bereft of theological depth. Future critics examining Elvis's influence should rightly note his social location as well as his Pentecostal upbringing as being two sides to the same musical coin.

According to music critic Greil Marcus, musically and religiously, Elvis symbolized the triumph of "white trash" over Southern gentility. "No white man has so deeply absorbed black music, and transformed it," writes Marcus. "Elvis didn't have to exile himself from his own community to justify and make real his use of an outsider's culture. . . . As a Southerner and white trash to boot, Elvis was already outside."[17]

Marcus's limited reading of Elvis's Pentecostalism is not totally off the mark. In typical Marcus style, he places Pentecostal worship in the context of "Saturday night, the impulse to dream, the need to escape, the romance and the contradictions of the land, this was a source of energy, tension, and power."[18] This sentiment, coupled with my idea about religious miscegenation, may be a fitful way to conclude this section.

Borrowing Marcus's riff on Pentecostalism, Elvis's Pentecostalism could fit the descriptor "Saturday Night." Elvis appropriated Pentecostalism, yet rejected its whiteness and its high-tension piety to create his own Pentecostal aesthetic. This aesthetic brought forth the emotional energy of the black church, heard in such songs as "Where Could I Go But to the Lord" (a gospel song complete with backbeat), "Heartbreak Hotel" (with lonely cries that echo the blues), and the sexually playful "Little Sister" (whose leering at young girls reminds one of the dangerous sexuality Elvis embodied).

Elvis embodied the physical, emotional, and sexual aesthetic that his Pentecostalism contained and unloosed it on a worldwide audience. Elvis sold Pentecostalism's true sexual aesthetic, not the confused jumble that at once delights in sex and condemns it. Instead Elvis sold the idea of being taken over by the Holy Spirit, the common schema that people describe as a spiritual act that is ecstatic, freeing, electric, and physically exhilarating.

Elvis meanwhile knew that his success meant the end of his days pursuing the normal life of a potential husband to his girlfriend Dixie. According to Guralnick, Dixie realized that rock 'n' roll was not fit for either of them. She described Elvis as quiet and pensive when discussing the potential end of his Christian upbringing. Later in life, Elvis went beyond his Pentecostal faith. He read books by Kahlil Gibran, met Sri Daya Mata (leader of the Self-Realization Fellowship), and asked for and received prayer from AG pastors Rex Humbard and his home pastor Peter Hamill on the eve on leaving for Germany to begin his stint in the army.[19] Eventually, when Elvis tried to make sense of how his life had unraveled as he descended in to drug use and serious health problems in the 1970s, he still clung to the deeply held Pentecostal belief that God had ordered his steps even if he did not understand why.[20]

Agnes Sanford's Healing Ministry

Agnes Sanford was born in China in 1897 to Southern Presbyterian missionaries. Sanford, first as the daughter of missionaries, then as a pastor's wife, had her life planned out for her. But Sanford found being a pastor's wife stifling and depressing. Adding to her depression was seeing her pacifist son go to war in Europe in the 1940s. Sanford began writing to cope with her depression and became one of the first mainline Protestants to write about healing experiences. These narratives were rooted in a mid-twentieth-century religious amalgam of Orthodoxy, Episcopalianism, and Catholicism. Sanford's irenic spirit allowed her to appropriate ideas about healing from these traditions, but also, from outside the boundaries of orthodox Christianity.

Rather than take the road many women did, which was to leave the "dead formalism" of mainline Protestantism, Sanford stayed in the Episcopal Church and became a sought-after speaker and writer. In one of the few avenues available to women who did not dissolve their marriages, even though they were unhappy, Sanford found writing and speaking to be acceptable outlets.

As a pastor's wife, Sanford felt trapped in what pioneering feminist writer Betty Friedan called the "problem with no name." During the 1940s and especially the 1950s, when women lived isolated private lives as wives and mothers without any outlet to display any self-created identities, they suffered from a "bored, diffuse feeling of purposelessness, non-existence, non-involvement with the world."[21] Sanford never accepted the feminist mantle as her own. However, her writing about dissatisfaction, isolation, and depression rooted in diminished expectations of a pastoral life make it easier for people to place her in context of a whole generation of women who felt left out.

Sanford wrote about her expectations of becoming esteemed in her role as pastor's wife, welcomed by parishioners with "flowers and cakes," neither of which happened.[22] Instead, she punished herself for being a housewife, scolded by her husband for inadequate housekeeping and her inability to be content with her children: "There was always the feeling that the real me was dead."[23] Rather than criticizing her husband, Sanford blamed herself, because she was not living for her original purpose.[24] She was overcome by guilt and depression, which she struggled to hide from her family. "I was a good actress and had been brought up to contain and control myself."[25] Inculcated into her religious identity was the idea that her depression was rooted in a satanic attack, and she wondered whether God permitted Satan to afflict her with depression as a kind of a test in order to prepare her to help others.[26]

After prayer and intercession by friends, Sanford began writing to counteract her severe bouts with depression. Her friend Glenn Clark picked up her once-dismissed manuscript. In 1947 Clark helped publish *The Healing Light,* which became a classic of contemporary devotional literature. Soon thereafter, she began holding regular talks at Clark's "Camps Farthest Out" organization in New Hampshire, and eventually became a popular speaker on the charismatic Episcopal circuit.

Early in her search for healing methods, she traveled to Philadelphia and attended a New Thought church called the Chapel of Truth, where, according to theologian Pavel Hezjlar, she learned some of her healing techniques.[27] Sanford found parts of Catholic and Orthodox healing traditions useful, praying the Jesus prayer she had learned from an Orthodox priest friend, and she also incorporated the work of New Thought writer Emmet Fox into her work. Regarding Fox's *Sermon on the Mount*, she said that "the language of this book was not that to which I was accustomed," but, she added, it "fulfilled my soul because it made dear to me the reality of the spiritual body that interpenetrates the physical body."[28] Sanford uses similar vocabulary to describe healing; particularly important to her were the New Thought ideas of everything being comprised of vibrations.

Throughout the 1950s and 1960s Sanford was one of the most popular conference speakers working the network of charismatic mainline churches, mostly Episcopalian, whose members wanted to be taught how to pray for healing. It is also during this time that she moved with her husband to Massachusetts and opened a School of Pastoral Care on their church property in 1958 to teach ministers "that area of Christian faith that is not taught at seminaries—healing of the soul, mind, and body through faith and prayer."[29] The school chose not to emphasize the Pentecostal baptism of the Holy Spirit, though Sanford had received that in 1953 in a private meeting with charismatic Episcopal ministers. For Sanford, teaching about tongues was "imposing" a gift on her students that might distract their attention from them seeking the power of God to heal.[30] In fact, Sanford earlier had disavowed any connection to Pentecostals, calling them "weird and off base." This anti-Pentecostal bias was very much in keeping with the charismatic movement's de-emphasis of tongues as a prerequisite gift.

Sanford created a series of healing scripts, the goal of which was to prepare oneself to be an effective channel for the healing power that she believed flowed through her to her "patients." In praying for another, Sanford writes, "the essence of all healing is to become so immersed in the being of God that one forgets himself [sic] entirely."[31] Sanford even advocated praying for nonbelievers to be healed, going so far as to say that faith was not a requisite to bring "God's healing energy into the afflicted portion of [a person's] mind."[32] She also said that when thinking of the person needing prayer, we "create in our minds the picture of that person well. Thus we set in motion our powers of creating."[33] Visualization could have been one of the healing scripts she learned from Fox. Throughout her writing and in her talks, she mentions the mind's creative power. Since the mind was capable of creative action, she exhorted her followers not to dwell on the negative, and to banish doubt from their minds. "Just believing a set of facts about God does not necessarily turn on the power in a single one of our prayer objectives. To do that we must believe that we are receiving the thing we desire."[34] She also seemed to suggest that one could somehow starve out doubt—that "gradually the voice of doubt will speak no more within us, as we will be re-made in His image and likeness."[35]

Sanford believed that the subconscious needed to be re-educated, and "every thought of fear replaced with a thought of health, every thought of death with a thought of life."[36] Her advocacy of healing of memories and inner healing spawned an entire movement of Christian psychotherapy, while her larger idea, learned from her New Thought training and familiar biblical verse, that the "Kingdom of God was within" was especially potent. Sanford called this Kingdom, the "Indwelling Light, the secret place of consciousness of the Most High that is the Kingdom of Heaven in its present manifestation on earth. Learning to live in the Kingdom of Heaven is learning to turn on the Light of God within."[37]

In her later years Sanford prayed not only for healing, but also that the "light-energy of God be built up in homes, schools, and businesses."[38] By the end of her life in the early 1980s, Sanford became fully immersed in the metaphysical language of her New Thought teachers.

Because she did not belong to a particularly conservative denomination, she did not have gatekeepers asking her to retract her words. It also helps that she was not ordained, nor did she want to be, perhaps because being part of a nondenominational ministry provided Sanford with the freedom to be the kind of eclectic minister she was.

As an older woman, freed from the objectifying lens that tends to befall many evangelical women in ministry, Sanford became an advocate for unconventional modes of healing. With her interest in the unconscious mind, Sanford uncovered new territory for charismatics. It is not a stretch to say that Sanford's ministry opened new avenues where mainline Protestants peered into the Pentecostal world they often belittled and feared, only to find a kindly grandma speaking softly about God's power to heal anything and everything.

Marvin Gaye's Pentecostal Healing Aesthetic

There was a pall cast over my high school one April morning. The large urban campus, normally bustling, crowded, and loud, was silent. The previous evening, Marvin Gaye had been killed by his father. For us at school, this was senseless and crazy. But according to most journalistic accounts and biographies of Gaye after his death, the father and son in this Oedipal drama fed off each other's jealousy and hatred for years until it destroyed them both.

Despite the tortured relationship he had with his abusive father, Gaye took the theology of the Pentecostal church, its aesthetics of healing and the freedom of worship, and repackaged it as sexual liberation. As an artist, Gaye did what his high-tension Pentecostal church could not do—harness the innate sensuality of Pentecostal experience onto a black musical aesthetic and wed them both together.

Part of what this section explains is this uneasy tension Pentecostalism has with its own innate sensuality and its attempts to rein in the sexual desires of its adherents. This tension led Gaye to claim his liberation boldly, not in the holiness tradition of his youth, but as the sexual healing of his troubled adulthood. Gaye found solace from depression and drug addiction in a never-ending spiritual quest.

Marvin Gaye grew up in the housing projects of Washington, D.C. His father, Marvin Gay Sr., and mother, Alberta, married in the 1930s and raised four children in an African American Pentecostal denomination called the

House of God, which mixed together Holiness Pentecostalism and Jewish rituals.[39] When Gaye began singing in this church at the age of two, he became subject to what would be years of physical violence and psychological abuse at the hands of his father. According to biographer David Ritz, Alberta and the other children were terrorized by the brutality of their father, leading Ritz to conclude: "Certain he could never win his father's approval, Gaye sought his attention through antagonism. For the rest of his life, Marvin would express his need for affection through provocations of violence, the perverse pattern of behavior which would literally kill him."[40]

Gaye played music by ear and sang, which he enjoyed because it made the "church mothers" like him.[41] By the time he was a teenager, Gaye was still singing in church, but also found time to sing in a local doo-wop group. Along with doo-wop, Gaye was also proficient at singing popular standards. His father and the House of God in general were displeased with Gaye's singing secular music.[42] Gay Sr., in an interview with Ritz, told him that the "House of God would never approve of any music that did not praise God."[43] Nonetheless, Gaye continued to sing and to receive regular beatings from his father until he escaped to enlist in the air force after dropping out of high school at age seventeen.

The violence of his home life did not sour Gaye on church. He particularly enjoyed the Pentecostal practice called "tarrying," as he explained to Ritz: "The idea of tarrying thrilled and fascinated me. That's where you wait for the Holy Ghost, where you repeat over and over again, thank you Jesus, thank you Jesus . . . until the Spirit arrives."[44] Gaye was active in church life, going on mission trips, where he was exposed to the realities of life on the road for gospel singers. Gaye said that his fellow performers gave into temptations, but despite that, "devotion to Jesus was real. The spirit was there, in the room, in the songs. The Spirit enraptured me."[45]

According to African American religion scholar Michael E. Dyson, Gaye was also sexually assaulted as a young teen by an uncle. There is little indication that Gaye ever received counseling or other kinds of treatment in the aftermath of this trauma. Gaye explained his views to Ritz:

> If we stop long enough to listen to the rhythm of our heartbeat, that's the rhythm of God's voice. After leaving Washington, I've never regularly attended church, but neither did I leave the church. . . . I had religion, so why did I need head doctors? No, I didn't need to go to cocktail parties and talk about my psychoanalysis. . . . I didn't need no shrink.[46]

With little but his music and spirituality to comfort him, once the heyday of Motown was over by the early 1970s, Gaye began to explore more serious themes and continue to expand his Pentecostal notions of healing to include sexuality to grow closer to God. Like Elvis, Gaye was torn between the sacred and the secular in becoming a musician. Sensitive to the strict piety the House of God espoused, he judged himself harshly for his transgressions, even though, according to Ritz, he vacillated between believing he was a good person and believing he was "Satan's pawn."[47] Ritz concluded from these discussions with Gaye that these two forces, loving Jesus and playing the "backslidden" devil, would never make peace.[48]

Like Billie Holiday and other great tortured artists, Gaye "felt the hurt of humanity," though he also recognized that no one had perfected suffering for humanity like Jesus.[49] Dyson believes Gaye's gift was to transmit "sacred power" that this was his true calling, and that the two reactions generated from Gaye's music were sexual and spiritual. Only one of these was acceptable to his Pentecostal beliefs, and as his church commented, Marvin's defiance of God would come with a terrible price to pay.[50]

For Gaye, the years encompassing the 1970s until his death in 1984 were productive. Music seemed to be a way for him to dig out of the depression that paralyzed him for years, as well as escape the violence of his childhood. His ruminations about dislocation, death, sex, desire, all emanated from the depths of his chaotic life—a life that never removed the heartfelt desire that one day Jesus would heal him.

Attempts to salvage Gaye's reputation and explain the tragic circumstances that lead to his death and life-long battles with depression and drug addiction are largely left to his biographer David Ritz and religion scholar Michael E. Dyson. Both want to rescue Gaye from that unforgiving dustbin of dead celebrities whose excesses are all that people remember of their careers. Both Ritz and Dyson do admirable jobs at explaining the nexus between Gaye's music and his faith life. Ritz's copious quotations of Gaye discussing faith leave little to say except that Gaye clearly believed in Jesus and in healing: "My own beliefs come down to two simple points. One, believe in Jesus, and two, expand love. Both points, you see, are really the same."[51] Ritz notes that as he and Gaye became close friends, Gaye tried to convert him and prayed for the healing of Ritz's stutter."[52]

Dyson vigorously defends Gaye against critics who believe he abandoned his faith because he incorporated some beliefs culled from a vague understanding of Eastern religions such as reincarnation.[53] While conceding that Gaye's views were contradictory and conflicted, Dyson contends that they nevertheless deserve consideration. Seeing Gaye as a transgressive artist, Dyson describes him as someone who "inspired irreverence as he was exercising prophetic prerogatives."[54] Specifically, for the purposes of this chapter, Gaye's work subverted notions of sanctification and healing, two religious ideas that Pentecostalism has closely guarded as part of its own claims to being part of the final outpouring of God's Spirit.

To sever himself from his troubled childhood, Gaye went against nearly all of what his father taught him about holiness, sanctification, and healing. As Ritz succinctly put it, in the Gay/Gaye household, sex was trouble. Ritz says that Gaye always felt sexually inadequate. Losing his virginity to a prostitute while he was in the air force "freaked him out." Compounding matters was Gay Sr.'s sexual ambivalence. "Both men saw sex as a dangerous force that threatened and finally destroyed their peace of mind and their virtuous life they aspired to lead."[55] Ritz says that Gaye's self-reflection, painful as it may have been, was a way for Gaye to grow closer to God.[56] One might ask at this point, if Gaye was honest with his brokenness, if he was so "drug-addicted and God-intoxicated," as Dyson put it, why didn't his denomination try to rehabilitate him? Why, as in the case of Elvis, did the church largely view him as a tragic example of backslidden faith?

For Pentecostalism, confession requires authenticity and most importantly, repentance. To be "laid bare before God" means accepting contrition and ceasing the questionable behavior or repenting of the unorthodox beliefs. Gaye's heartfelt cries for prayer, for Jesus, were judged inadequate because Gaye never abandoned his sexual promiscuity or sought healing or help for his drug addiction.

Gaye's refashioning of the work of the Holy Spirit as a sexual/spiritual healing agent placed him outside the church's theological norms. Perhaps Gaye's refashioning of sexuality/spirituality as having a sanctifying and healing properties is seen most clearly in his classic song "Let's Get It On." This song is only one of at least a dozen examples of Gaye's working out his notions of sanctification as having erotic possibilities. This well-known song has Gaye trying to seduce a woman, pleading with her, trying to convince her that there is nothing wrong with their desire for each other, since the agent of this desire is the Holy Spirit.[57]

Repurposing sanctification, for Gaye, meant fulfilling sexual desire. In an outtake from an undated concert during the early 1980s, Gaye closes his concert with what amounts to a benediction and an altar call. Gaye says goodbye to the audience, telling his audience that this may be his last time on stage, because he might "just start serving the Lord." He tells his fans that they should not take him too seriously, but that he has "lots of spirituality" in him. He alternately tells the audience to "go out and make babies" and asks them to pray for his mom, who was sick at the time. Finally he offers a prayer for anyone in the audience who had a sick family member.[58] Not knowing if Gaye concluded any other concerts like this, it does strike a familiar chord—this narrative of wanting to leave the sinful life behind to serve the Lord and exhorting the audience to pray for healing is familiar. Sex mystified Gaye, from the confusion in his home to the abject cruelty of his sexually promiscuous father, a cruel, hypocritical, and hateful man. Gay Sr. offered the rules and precepts of a pietistic Pentecostalism in such a chaotic swirl of spiritual dissociation, it probably made perfect sense for his son to seek to redeem that one thing he could salvage from his life. Gaye re-sacralized sex and in doing so wrested it away from his denomination's rigid pronouncements, using it to free himself from his own personal demons.

By removing the taint of demonization placed on illicit sexual acts, Gaye tried to live very close to his own adage, that "beyond sex—is God." Gaye understood the problem with his valorization of sex. However, the devaluing of the violence, especially in the African American neighborhoods he wrote about in the masterful work "What's Going On," bothered him more and he was angry. This is the message of his song "The World Is X-Rated," where Gaye asks: What about crime, killing, fighting, and stealing? Why is sexual immorality seemingly more important than those things? He concludes his song by noting the irony that children are subjected to seeing life's most violent endings, which does not seem to bother pious church folks, but children are shielded from seeing people procreate.[59]

Gaye's anger at hypocrisy has no satisfactory answers. This tension between this hierarchy of spiritual disapprobation can be seen even more clearly in the next chapter on race, ethnicity, and American Pentecostalism. Before that however, one more take on re-purposing Pentecostalism from one of the most polarizing figures in contemporary Christianity, who has made a living by trying to be as non-threatening as possible.

Joel Osteen's Repurposing of American Pentecostalism

When I spent my sabbatical teaching in Texas a few years ago, I visited Joel Osteen's Lakewood church in Houston. Before that, I saw Joel on television several times and found him to be—soothing. He was pleasant, he seemed younger than his fifty years, and his blue eyes really did seem to sparkle. Listening to him over the course of several months, I'll admit, Joel grew on me. I shared my stories of listening to Joel with my class, most of whom disliked and even detested his "puffy" theology. Underneath that showy handsome exterior, they assured me, was a pillowy message of comfort without commitment, of prosperity without responsibility. Be that as it may, Joel has repurposed Pentecostalism, expanded the nature of healing, enhanced the use of media and popular culture, and reanimated Christian publishing like no other figure has in recent memory.

As an innovator, Osteen has employed market researchers to craft his message, and for him, Satan does not sell. He has neutralized that old devil, a standard of most Pentecostal preachers for over a century. In Osteen's Lakewood church, material blessings are providential markers of God's working in your favor. Physical, emotional, and psychological healing are possible without too much struggle. Gone is the expectation of suffering, of sin, of hell. Nor is there a spiritual gifts hierarchy through which one secures the outpouring of the Holy Spirit. All you need now is to believe that material blessings are there for you, because God is always on your side. In effect, Osteen has disarmed Pentecostalism.

To see how he accomplished this, we should begin with where Joel's message originated, with his father, John Osteen. After he experienced Spirit baptism in 1958, he became an advocate of charismatic experiences, healing, and the prosperity gospel. When John and his wife's first child, Lisa, was born with health problems, John prayed constantly. Believing that this helped heal his daughter, he became a confirmed advocate of divine healing. Like many evangelicals who came of age in the 1960s and 1970s, John had little interest in belonging to a denomination. On the contrary, while preaching as an itinerant evangelist for healing and Spirit baptism, he was also trying to de-couple Pentecostal practice from Pentecostal denominations, according to historian Phil Sinitiere.[60] As a member of the Full Gospel Businessmen's Association, John fully embraced its agenda of professionalizing and "quest for respectability." He also looked around at the post-1960s United States and became a culture warrior, unlike his son. Warning that "legions of demons were unleashed on humanity" he engaged in fiery rhetoric that was also the opposite of the style his son would come to adopt.

When John Osteen died of a heart attack in 1999, Joel, who studied broadcasting and business at Oral Roberts University for one year, took over his father's church and transformed it. Already a megachurch with 6,000 members in 1990, its numbers mushroomed to 45,000 by of 2012. Joel Osteen's rise to fame is equally staggering. His first book, *Your Best Life Now*, sold five million copies and was translated into twenty-five different languages. His second book, *Become a Better You*, spent twenty-nine weeks on the *New York Times* bestseller list when it was released in 2007. His latest book, *I Declare*, has met with similar success, and, according to the *New York Times*, netted him $13 million advance.[61]

One reason for this popularity, I believe, is that Osteen offers a new Pentecostal aesthetic that burnishes away the rough edges of his father's generation. His soft prosperity gospel is attractive to many who would otherwise not find Pentecostalism palatable. But his impact also has a great deal to do with how he has crafted his spiritual life story. It is this Joel Osteen, this simulacrum, whom people see; it is the Joel they want him to be and the one they can emulate; and it is this image of Joel that he himself seeks to maintain.

At the service that I attended, Joel's opening prayer was very emotional. Focused on loss, it certainly was not the sunny optimistic picture that Joel usually paints about life, and it was about as close to Pentecostal as I have ever seen Joel let himself get. When I watched that service later in the week on television, I noticed that his crying at the service was edited out of the broadcast. Keenly aware that religious broadcasting is dominated by Pentecostals and charismatics, Osteen understands that his people have a publicity problem. Hence, he edits vestiges of those practices, particularly the emotionally draining aspects of prayer, out of his shows. As he puts it, he does not want to give people any reason to turn off the television.[62]

To see how this aspect of marketing works, it may help to look at what Charles Brown calls "proactive and passive" tactics to make their product more attractive. Among the former is refraining from using evangelical language. Thus, Osteen's mode of preaching is not exegetical. Rather, he is a storyteller, interweaving biblical stories with those of ordinary people in a plain language, stripped of religious fervor. A related proactive tactic is to stick to universal themes. Those Osteen refers to over and over include the abundance of God, trust, overcoming obstacles, thinking positively, trusting in people's ability to see the best in themselves, tuning out the negative messages in their lives, and focusing on the inevitable triumph of believers because that is what God wants for them. Then there is also the way that Joel sells himself outside the Sunday service,[63] and here product diversification is key, as Osteen's Lakewood bookstore demonstrates amply. It sells bibles that cater to every taste—the Marine's Bible, bibles for women, kids, African Americans. There is an entire section of Spanish-language books. Visitors can also buy dozens of items as mementos of their trip to Lakewood—pillows, water bottles, key chains, fleece blankets, clothing, and miniatures evoking the warmth of home, motherhood, and childhood. Beyond the bookstore, product diversification is evident in the variety of classes that visitors and potential members can take before every Sunday service.

A young African American woman taught the beginner's class the day I visited. She countered nearly every signal that Joel sends to his weekly audience of over seven million viewers. The women began the class with a prayer, invoking Jesus and the Holy Spirit; her script taken from passages in Ephesians about arming oneself for spiritual protection against the attacks of the "enemy." She also spoke of how she prepared herself for her day by using her "spiritual language," which is code for speaking in tongues. She recommended that everyone do so and proceeded to demonstrate how easy it was, mimicking tongues speech and saying that all you had to do was start it yourself and allow the Spirit to continue the process. The effect of all this is not to depart from or contradict Osteen's teaching, but rather to compartmentalize Pentecostal experience for a segment of his audience, the ones who know he is charismatic, that he believes in healing, and that it is a pretty safe bet that he speaks in tongues, but would never allow that to become a focus of his broadcast ministry. But for those visitors who are deciding whether to visit again or become members, this kind of class will either validate their own desire to be charismatic or solidify their aversion to such practices. The key here is that people have a choice.

In a study of Osteen's ministry, pastoral psychologists Christine Miller and Nathan Carlin identify several qualities that make it appealing. One is that Lakewood is set up in such a way that going there resembles going to a "leisure activity."[64] People "flock to Osteen not for [the] theological content of his sermons or his books," they add, "but for the way in which Osteen binds with his audience," which in itself "brings healing."[65] Analyzing how he works his audience, Miller and Carlin note that he never criticizes them; rather, he seeks to help them break destructive patterns of thinking and behavior, and as a result the audience is uplifted by his presence and they have their sense of self-worth restored. The encounter with Osteen is "therapeutic," and given his television ministry, the therapy does not depend on going to Lakewood.[66]

What Miller and Carlin also call attention to is how ordinary Osteen is. Son of a previously divorced father, with a half-brother from that relationship, Osteen is also a college dropout, and until he found his niche as a broadcaster, he seemed like an underachieving son of a minor charismatic minister. Now famous and wealthy, Osteen is idolized and idealized by many because "they see themselves reflected in his lifestyle and they too want to overcome any obstacle."⁶⁷ Moreover, the message of Providence always being on your side extends to racial minorities and economically disadvantaged persons who come to believe that despite their reality, they have a chance to achieve their dreams. Not only does Osteen put members of these communities front and center in worship settings, but as volunteers and teachers, they themselves become the transmitters of the narratives of success that are ongoing at every service. Still, the question remains, if they are not experiencing success, how do people become convinced to go along?

Osteen makes people comfortable with their desire for abundance by telling them that that is what God wants for them. The Pentecostalism offered at Lakewood and throughout Osteen's media empire, free of the cultural warrior rhetoric his father deployed and from nearly all mention of sin or evil, makes Pentecostalism a private reserve and is used almost exclusively as means of self-improvement and self-realization. Osteen represents refinement without appearing elite. He transcends Pentecostalism precisely because he does not appear or sound like one. He is southern without relying on the cultural norms of the South. He is evangelical without engaging in propositional debates over doctrine. He is an exceptionally ordinary middle-aged Texan with a wife and two kids and knack for marketing an image that draws a devoted audience longing to be just like him. Re-purposing and re-packaging the strictness of the theology and the harshness of the unyielding piety is one thing. However, where Pentecostalism faces its most daunting challenges to re-shape narratives to bend their stories into tales of victorious living, is demonstrated most clearly in the following chapter on race, ethnicity, and the construction of an American Pentecostal identity.

CHAPTER FIVE

Race, Ethnicity, and the Construction of an American Pentecostal Identity

Some believe that Agnes Ozman, a member of Charles Parham's church in Topeka, Kansas, spoke Chinese on New Year's Day in 1900, but there are plenty who dismissed the event and mocked the Chinese allegedly spoken as being simply the argot of a local laundry business.[1] In turn-of-the century Kansas, Chinese immigrants dominated this industry.

Such racializing of language in Kansas is not surprising, given that fifteen years earlier, in 1886, Wichita passed laws to forcibly remove any Chinese residents.[2] The Chinese Ozman allegedly spoke would not have meant much to anti-Chinese Kansans. Speaking in tongues was not about breaking down racial barriers in Kansas; rather Parham always promoted that it was meant for missions to China. For him, it was not about building churches in the United States, but about furthering the cause of Pentecostalism abroad. The Chinese in Kansas, and indeed until 1965, the Chinese in the United States, were rarely a part of the community that white Pentecostals created.

White American Pentecostal identity was, for nearly a century, marked by racial and ethnic separation and by an assimilationist drive. Nevertheless, people of color have engaged Pentecostalism in various ways over time. African Americans and Native Americans have used the faith to strengthen their racial identities.

For example, historian Angela Tarango's study of Native Americans in the Assemblies of God describes how Native peoples used the AG's own missions idea, called the "indigenous principle" (the idea that to be an effective missionary meant supporting the indigenous culture rather than trying to change it), to create a space for themselves and their brethren.³ Through her case studies of Native AG leaders Charlie Lee, Jimmie Dann, and Andrew Maracle—all converts who experienced healing, whether from alcoholism or racism—Tarango shows that when these Native leaders remade the white Pentecostalism of the AG into Native Pentecostalism. Jesus changed from a "white man's God" to a "Great Healer."⁴

Pentecostalism demonstrated integrationist tendencies since its Azusa Street days, and it also demonstrated a hyper-spiritualized neutrality that often completely ignored racism. But this story is obviously more complicated than the well-known narratives of race relations in the United States. An African American, William J. Seymour's founding of the movement, accomplished by his leadership at the Azusa Street Revival, went unacknowledged for decades.⁵ American Pentecostalism is, then, an African American religious movement. Some of its earliest leaders—including Seymour, Charles H. Mason, and Garfield T. Haywood—were raised in the denominations of the historic black church before they developed their faith through various iterations of African American Pentecostalism. It is beyond the scope of this book to explore the incredible variety and diversity of African American Pentecostalism, which includes Trinitarian, Oneness, Afro-Centric, Hebraic, and esoteric forms.⁶

As ethicist Leonard Lovett writes, "the twentieth-century Pentecostal movement in America originated from the womb of the Black religious experience."⁷ However, the disagreements that beset Pentecostals were evident in the African American church as well. These included disagreements over the nature and importance of sanctification, Oneness vs. Trinitarian formulations of baptism, the nature of God, views of women in ministry, and piety codes. Historian Anthea Butler notes that women made a home for themselves in the COGIC denomination. In her case studies of church mothers like Mother Lizzie Robinson, Butler finds that they had a distinctive view of how to promote a sanctified life: "Rather than pursuing cleanliness and abstinence for social reasons, many African American women were inspired to right living by scriptural admonitions . . . [they were] special and set apart despite what any white southerner could say."⁸ In effect, moral uplift and racial uplift were intertwined. Native Americans and African Americans found the seeds of their own healing and liberation within Pentecostalism. Nevertheless, resistance to change at the institutional levels still meant certain corridors of power remained closed to people on the periphery, and that included women.

According to historian Estrelda Alexander, the divisiveness over women in ministry, evident under Seymour's leadership at the Azusa Street Mission, meant all-male ordination; while women were allowed to be ministers, they could not baptize or ordain.[9] Even today, the only women on many church boards are pastors' wives. Nonetheless, women did make their mark on the movement, and one African American woman, Rosa A. Horn, who pioneered Pentecostal radio broadcasting in the 1930s was especially influential.

Rosa was born in Sumter, South Carolina in 1880, the granddaughter of former slaves who had purchased their freedom before Emancipation. She married musician William Artimus, who developed terminal tuberculosis and became "crazed" enough to try to kill her, according to Rosa. But as Artimus shot her, "[the Lord] lifted her bodily from one chair to another" to safety.[10] Several years after William died, Rosa found out that she and her daughter Jessie were also sick with tuberculosis. Heading south to Georgia with Jessie, Rosa attended a Fire Baptized Holiness church and then reported being healed. She and her daughter then went to Indiana, where another pioneering Pentecostal woman, Maria Woodworth Etter, ordained her in 1913. Moving to establish her own ministry in Evanston, Illinois, Rosa married a man named William Horn.[11]

In Evanston, a white follower, the father of Gladys Brandhagen, asked Horn to pray for his daughter's healing from a chronic stomach ailment stemming from an untreated appendectomy. Gladys was healed and joined Horn's ministry.[12]

Horn's ministry in New York attracted thousands, and her soup kitchen fed over 48,000. Her competition feared her popularity. According to her attorney, famed Scottsboro Boys lawyer Sam Leibowitz, Horn's ministry fought being run out of town by its key rival, Father Divine. In 1934, she also started a radio broadcast called *Church of the Air*, heard throughout much of the East Coast until the 1960s.[13]

Aside from helping with wartime support of troops during the 1940s, the church operated several prayer ministries. Horn acknowledged that a significant number of her followers drafted into service during World War II chose to be conscientious objectors. Horn's pacifist work was well in keeping with the black Pentecostal tradition, especially Charles Harrison Mason's Church of God in Christ during World War I and Willliam S. Cowdry's Church of God and Saints of Christ. Both churches found themselves subjected to government surveillance because of their refusals to submit their members to the draft.[14] Mother Horn's ministry is also a story of the historic "Great Migration" of African Americans from the South to the urban centers of the Midwest and Northeast. A later migration, from that same Midwest to the Sunbelt in the mid- to late twentieth century helps situate our last group of stories. The first migratory stream is from south to north, bringing Mexicano workers to the borderlands and in contact with earnest AG missionaries. The next migration is a continuation of the Great Migration chain of African Americans, from the urban Midwest to the Sunbelt. Finally, the last migration is a flow from the cities to the suburbs, where suburban white Pentecostalism found a home in the mid-twentieth century and where it still finds itself most comfortable.

A Convenient Apocalypse: The Assemblies of God and the Problem of Mexico

AG minister and missionary to Mexico Henry Ball, whose career began in Texas in 1914, extended his work across the border as well. "This is a great field for work among the Americans, as well as the Mexicans, as there have [sic] never been any Pentecostal work," he wrote. "Much of the population from the Mexican side is over here now, many of them unable to find shelter and sleeping on the ground along the railroad tracks."[15] Ball, along with fellow missionary F. C. Hale, interpreted the Mexican Revolution in terms of a prophetic imperative. It became their duty to "save" Mexicans and eventually to save Mexico. Hale writes: "Those who know of the superstition of the Mexican race will appreciate what a wonderful victory has been won. These poor people had been brought up to worship images and know nothing of a living God. . . . God is sending them across the border to us in multitudes. . . . We must gospelize these hundreds of thousands of heathens whom God is thrusting into our midst."[16] A few months later, Hale wrote:

> Five of these Mexicans are now studying to fit themselves as ministers of the gospel to their own race. . . . All of this country was once part of Mexico and a large proportion of the inhabitants are now Mexicans. Besides these many thousands of refugees have come to this country from Mexico during the last 4 years. Many of these are now preparing to return to their country, and if we are to reach them with the Gospel, we will have to act quick."[17]

AG missions efforts were working. Mexican ministers were trained to reach their own "race," and the presumption at the end of the article was that Mexican Pentecostals were going back to Mexico. The idea of a temporary Mexican migration, especially on the Borderlands, alleviated the anxiety of the average *Pentecostal Evangel* reader who worried about Mexicans settling permanently. The anxiety arose from a discomfort not only of having to assimilate immigrants, but having to assimilate potentially unconverted Catholic immigrants.

Ball's intense anti-Catholicism fueled the urgency of his missionary efforts. Catholics, he said, were "wolves," and Pentecostals had to "rescue" Mexicans lost to the "darkness of Romanism." Mexicans lived under the "curse of Catholicism," which blighted everywhere it touched.[18] He considered Mexicans themselves to be thrifty, hard-working, and patient who lived on practically nothing and never complained. For Ball, this made them exceptional candidates for ministry.[19] Writing back to AG headquarters in 1916, he praised the Mexican work ethic and the fact that they ate very little, which Ball interpreted as fasting. Ball mentioned that his workers ate only cactus, not realizing that cactus (*nopales*) was a staple of the Mexican diet for millennia.

Ball blamed Catholicism for the dire situation of many Mexican refugees from the Mexican Revolution. Meanwhile, women missionaries like Alice E. Luce and Florence Murcutt spent time writing in the *Pentecostal Evangel* about the plight of their Mexican charges; both expressed anti-Catholic views as well. In their view "Romanism" led not only to degradation, but also to vice.[20] Narratives of salvations, Spirit baptisms, and healings in turn helped to make the case for the need for more money for more missionaries. Throughout the 1920s, missionaries like Ball, Luce, and others continued to paint Mexico and the rest of Latin America as living in the spiritual dark ages. The only missionary to go against this portrayal was healing evangelist Francisco Olazábal.

Writing in the *Latter Rain Evangel*, Olazábal (whose name was misspelled Olazabel), a former Methodist turned Pentecostal, wrote: "We want those who do not criticize the way Mexicans act, and the way the Mexicans live, but who come to suffer with the Mexicans and die for them if necessary."[21] Olazábal mentioned Ball and was effusive with praise of Ball's work with Mexicans. He repeated many of the same critiques of Mexicans that Ball and others shared with the readers of these magazines.[22] One cannot know why Olazábal chose not to critique Ball, though later he would critique the AG as a whole and be demoted from his position as the de facto leader of the Mexican AG in South Texas. Olazábal blamed his demotion on the racism of the AG.[23]

As a pastor who fought a nearly decade-long battle against the leadership of the AG for autonomy to run his own district, Olazábal had enough credibility to critique AG leaders. However, was not until after he left the AG and formed his denomination (*Concilio Latino Americano de Iglesias Cristianas*) two years later in 1923, that he felt able to criticize his former denomination.

Ball, Luce, and Murcutt wrote articles in Pentecostal magazines that critiqued Mexicans as spiritually and morally inferior, exactly what Olazábal pleaded with them not to do. These racialized criticisms did not cross the theological threshold of "false" teaching or aberrant theology. Pentecostalism's threshold for racism as an unacceptable and aberrant theology historically is very high. With the specter of Mexico being "lost" to Catholicism, Olazábal defaulted to a position that sought to preserve his tenuous status within the AG, while at the same time vaguely criticizing the anti-Mexican rhetoric of the leaders of Borderlands missions.

One should not forget that for all the criticism aimed at Mexicans, it was primarily their Catholicism, not their ethnicity, that was the main issue. Ball himself noted that as these relationships continued into the 1920s and 30s he displayed some sympathy for the plight of Mexicanos. In the 1930s, when Mexicanos and Mexican Americans were repatriated back to Mexico, Ball wrote that 200,000 have "left the states and returned to Mexico, not that Mexico is better off than we, but being able to get work here and having homes or land in Mexico, they return home in hope of getting by in some way." He appeared aware of the plight of Mexican workers, "[who] have been laid off to give their work to American citizens. Even American born Mexicans have been discriminated against most unjustly, as they are as much American as we."[24] However sympathetic Ball was, the overriding goal for his work was ridding his Mexican charges of their "superstitious" beliefs and making sure that the dark forces of communism not gain a hold on the laboring classes.

For Ball, the anti-clerical policies of the Cárdenas administration lay the groundwork for moving Mexico from the urgent mission field category to that of the harbinger of the Last Days. Ball wrote:

> The activities of the representatives of communism are very manifest in many Latin American countries, and now that the door of Mexico has been closed to further foreign missionary effort it seems that there is a challenge before us to ensure these doors that are still open and sow gospel seed while we yet have the opportunity.[25]

Sometime during the 1930s, the *Pentecostal Evangel* began running a column that focused on biblical prophecy entitled "The Passing and the Permanent: A Review of Current Life and Thought in the Light of Scripture." In it, Mexico came to figure in the ongoing effort to examine current events for clues about the *eschaton*. Concerned with the anti-religious activities of the Mexican government, one writer bemoaned the destruction of "religious images"—though without noting that they were Catholic images—saying that "the object is obvious—to put the stamp of atheism upon the Mexican children." This, the article concluded, was surely a sign of the Antichrist.[26] The fear that Mexico was becoming a communist atheistic country consumed AG's borderlands missions and missions to Mexico, so much so that Mexico as a harbinger of the Second Coming was also featured prominently in the AG's *Christ's Ambassadors Herald*, the magazine of AG youth ministry.

Author Otto Klink, in his column "Otto-Graphs" wrote of "blood-drenched altars" and how Mexicans were being killed for following Jesus.[27] That most were Catholic was secondary to the AG's claim that religious persecution was part of an end-time schema. According to this logic, Mexico needed more missionaries as its salvation became more urgent. Mexicans, in effect, became weather vanes of the *eschaton*.

One of the articles from that same year (1935) in the *Pentecostal Evangel* headlined "Bolshevistic Mexico" alleged that the "Mexican government is as communistic as the Russians, and considering the nearness of Mexico to us, the fact should become a matter of grave concern and much prayer. A few years ago Mexican Christians little dreamed that Christianity would be practically outlawed, many churches closed and in some states the number of ministers restricted."[28] Again, like the youth ministry magazine, this article does not mention that the main targets of the closures and anti-clerical laws were Catholics.

Another proof that Mexico fit into bible prophecy was the supposed growth of anti-Semitism. One month later, the *Pentecostal Evangel* reported on a boycott of Jewish businesses in Sonora, attributing this to yet another sign of the end times. Quoting Deuteronomy 28:65, "Among these nations shalt thou find no ease," the correlation the *Pentecostal Evangel* drew was that this business boycott might hasten Jesus's return.[29] On the other hand, where communism was represented as "the 20th century scourge of God on a Christless Christianity,"[30] Mexican Catholicism could be to blame, because it did not resist the Cárdenas regime and because it did not offer the power of Pentecostal spirituality. Mexican Catholicism had displeased God so much that God allowed communism to take over Mexico, and thus threatened the evangelism Pentecostals began to sow in that country in the 1910s.[31] The AG then used anti-Catholic and anti-communist rhetoric as a two-way strategy to promote more financial backing for missions. However, it was the underlying fear of Mexicans overstaying their training in the United States and not going back home that served as another source of anxiety for Ball, who wrote for decades in the pages of the *Pentecostal Evangel* that he was training workers to go back home to save their Mexican homeland. For Mexicans to be useful, they had to be compliant, pious, and ready to go back to where they came from. Fear then—of migration, of different people moving from place to place and building new communities, of new migration patterns upsetting the prevailing legal and political order—forms the backstory of our next case study as we revisit A. A. Allen's Miracle Valley compound.

Shoot-Out in Miracle Valley: Racial Violence and the Fear of the City

A. A. Allen's belief in racial integration allowed him to hire gospel singer Gene Martin, integrate services, and finally move to Miracle Valley, Arizona, where Allen hoped to build his healing and deliverance ministry. This section focuses on Allen's ideas on racial integration and the Gene Martin years as a context for what happened at Miracle Valley twelve years after Allen's death in 1970.

In 1982, Cochise County sheriffs confronted Mother Frances Thomas, leader of the Christ Miracle Healing Center and Church (CMHCC), who claimed that Allen had ordained her and that she moved her church from Chicago to Arizona accordingly. Almost immediately, the CMHCC registered complaints of harassment to the local sheriffs only to have their complaints largely ignored by the authorities. This situation ended badly, with the deaths of two church members in a flurry of police activity that effectively ended the church's stay in Arizona and symbolically ended Allen's racial integration efforts begun decades before. This tragic event might have been an isolated event, but the bias against an "urban" church "from somewhere else" was not new. Also not new was the use of police against a group of African Americans perceived to be dangerous—that is a story as old as the United States itself.

But it was specifically the racial tensions of the 1960s that formed the backdrop to Allen's integrating his audiences and hiring Gene Martin as a worship leader. He also promoted racial integration in a sermon that for its time was quite striking. Though undated, it appears to have been preached sometime between 1964 and 1968. Like the man, the sermon is raw and unpolished, angry and impassioned, especially in its condemnation of those who used race to exclude people from church. Allen begins with an anecdote about overhearing a conversation at a coffee shop in which a man said that he was glad that Kennedy was dead because "he was a nigger-lover" and that he hated Johnson because he was a "nigger-lover too." Allen told the crowd that he did not agree with the sentiments of that man and exclaimed that "my Jesus was a nigger-lover too!" Claiming that there are no racial, social, or sexual barriers in the Bible, Allen asserted that blacks, whites, men, and women are called to preach. He also claimed that the Bible depicted integrated baptismal services and that the Apostle Paul was ordained by a black man in the church at Antioch.[32] Thus, he was critical of "colored men" who were content to preach to "colored folks," and, in a similar vein, he also chastised his audience: "Don't bother bleaching your hair, skin, straightening your hair, it's a waste of money. We've all got the same heart." And when faced with the notion that blacks needed to "stay in their place," Allen assured his audience that "their place is in the Kingdom of God."[33] Despite Allen's vehemence, he did not integrate his personal beliefs about race into a broader vision for countering the oppressive racial climate of the 1960s. In an ethnographic article published in 1965, sociologist Howard Elinson took on the question of why Allen's Pentecostalism was theologically inert and did not offer any effective answers to racism. This article also demonstrates how some academics viewed Allen and his "lower class" church. Miracle Valley's members are depicted as little more than sheep led by a theological lightweight. Elinson described church members as "lower class, poorly educated Negroes, white trash, [and] Puerto Rican."[34] He characterized Allen as an "ascetic" who combined moralism with apocalyptic thinking in forbidding tobacco, liquor, baseball, bingo, table tennis, and movies.[35] Elinson concluded that Allen's racial integration ideas were "purely religious," and that he had no interest in the secular struggle for civil rights or indeed any worldly issues.[36] He also made the perceptive observation that there may be something to the intensity of Pentecostal religious fellowship that "may be capable of eradicating, at least in the religious context, concern with race."[37] I do not have much evidence to support this reasoning, but in some ways, the neutralizing of race is what I have found in nearly twenty years of studying the faith lives of American Pentecostals. Some nexus is missing between the intensity of their spirituality and a desire to work for social justice.

For Allen, and for those who followed his path even after his death, Miracle Valley was infused with prophetic significance. Rancher Urbane Leiendecker had a vision and his account was reprinted in the Miracle Valley website several years later: "My son, from the place the Gospel shall go out to all the world . . . with signs and wonders and miracles. Lo from faraway places, they shall come to this valley to be instructed and taught my ways and from here they shall go to take the world My deliverance."[38] Nevertheless, the property lay dormant for a number of years after Allen's death in 1970 until Mother Thomas moved her church to the property in 1979. After the shoot-out, the land was dormant again from 1983 to 1999, where it lay in disarray as a garbage-strewn, graffitied outpost in the desert. The prophetic significance of Miracle Valley continued again when Rev. Mel Harter bought the property in 1999 and tried to resurrect Allen's ministry and reputation. He too gave up, selling the property to a Canadian couple, Gilles and Diane Langevin, who started their own ministry on the property in 2009. As of last year, the Canadians had sold the property back to a local Arizona ministry. Significantly, none of the above ministries exhibited any desire to continue Allen's work on racial integration and reconciliation. This legacy makes the events of 1980–1982 all the more poignant.

A few things should be noted about the historical context out of which the shoot-out at Miracle Valley transpired. Taking place a few years removed from the tragedy of Jonestown, it may be viewed as a tragic confrontation between religious "extremists" and the government. The CMHCC experienced difficulties almost immediately upon moving from Chicago to Cochise County, and it escalated in the fall of 1981, when church member Dorothy Collins was arrested for carrying nunchucks that September. Church members devised a plot to free her from jail by blowing it up. When the bomb blew up prematurely, it killed church member Steven Lindsey.[39] The CMHCC reported threats and rocks thrown at their property on a consistent basis. According to them, they began arming themselves when the local authorities continued to ignore their complaints.

Helpful to piecing together this scattered history is a piece of historical ephemera, an unfinished student film from 2008 that provides some clues to the bombing incident and to the shoot-out. The film, by Thomas Javier Castillo, describes the church as being founded in 1962 (actually 1963) by "poor" blacks. Castillo describes Frances Thomas as a "self-described prophet," adding that she was a smart and intelligent woman. He claims that Thomas distrusted whites and that the church bought lots of weapons in response to harassment. Castillo corroborates the story that church members were on their way to free church members from jail when the dynamite bomb exploded. According to the church, they stockpiled dynamite for their mine, and they blamed white townspeople for the van explosion.[40] What was not at issue in the many accounts of the contentious relationship between the church and the town was that the church members armed themselves. What varies greatly is why they armed themselves, and whether there was sufficient distrust between townspeople and church members to warrant the violence that befell Miracle Valley.

According to John J. Lyon, quoting church bishop Julius Gillespie's 1987 interview with the *Arizona Republic*, Mother Thomas put into place a practice that restricted church members from associating with whites because it was against "God's ordinances."[41] According to one researcher, she may have gone further, turning her church in the direction of "Black Power attitudes and confrontation."[42]

Church members armed themselves, they said, for self-defense but reactions to their actions were overwhelmingly negative. Before the October 1982 confrontation that marked the beginning of the end of the CMHCC in Arizona, tensions between the church members and the town were already high.

Thomas's son, William Jr., compared living in Cochise County to living under the Third Reich, saying that "Hitler's way is very much alive and kicking."[43] Relations deteriorated to the point that a few weeks before the shootout, some residents of Miracle Valley held a closed meeting of a community action group, Citizens for Equal Justice, co-chaired by Eli Duran, president of the Southern Arizona Bible College (an AG school). Frustrated by the inaction of the Cochise law and civic officials to quell the armed patrols of the CMHCC, Duran and the group called for staging public protests, demanded action, and if that did not work, they supported creating their own security patrols to counter the church's patrols.[44]

On a Saturday morning in October 1982, Cochise County sheriffs arrived at the church to serve outstanding traffic warrants to two church members. This began what would be a day-long siege of the property and ended with two church members dead. The deputies who fired on them claimed that the church members first threw all manner of objects at them and then started shooting. The dead included William Jr. and Aruguster Tate. In all, there were thirty-seven deputies and 150 church members said to be involved in the melee.

In examining media reporting of the raid and the following weeks of investigations and legal proceedings, clearly the racial composition of the church members and the surrounding areas played a part in creating the tensions that ignited the violence in October.

The shoot-out made national news, with all major broadcasters characterizing the CMHCC as a "black fundamentalist sect," a "black religious sect," or an "all-Black sect [that] believes in faith healing," and reporting that it was "armed" in addition to being a "cult." Subsequently, media accounts continued playing up the race angle of the participants and supporting the allegation that CMHCC was a cult. One article, by Ben Bradlee Jr., pulled no punches: "What had unfolded in Miracle Valley, they say is a mini-Jonestown, where a sect of urban outsiders grew increasingly paranoid about those outside the group and became responsive only to their charismatic leader."[45] The use of the words "urban" and "ghetto" become intermingled with ideas of what is law abiding (white citizens of Miracle Valley) with law breakers (CMHCC). Eyewitness and reporter Paul Brinkley-Rogers took a different angle, saying that "white sheriff's deputies of rural Cochise County were ill-prepared by background, training, and temperament to deal with the problems of having '300 urban blacks in their midst.'"[46] Among locals, "urban" easily became "ghetto." "They came from a city ghetto to a real rural area and they couldn't adjust," said a gas station owner, quoted in Bradlee's article. "Maybe on the South Side of Chicago no one noticed what they did. But out here, everyone did."[47] A white couple who worshipped at the CMHCC church believed that the problem was that "the church got the idea it didn't have to obey white man's laws."[48]

Subsequent accounts of the shoot-out have not been the only reinterpretations of events that have been spun to focus on the alleged inability of church members to adjust to their rural surroundings. Rev. Mel Harter wrote another version of the story that diminished the impact of the shoot-out story on his ministry. Harter told a matter-of-fact story of "black people who moved from Chicago," then the ensuing events were recalled, and concluded with two blacks shot and killed. Harter minimized the violence of the shoot-out and claimed that the media "sensationalized" the events to make money. Seeming sympathetic to Mother Thomas, Harter supported Thomas's claim that Allen ordained her. But he reverts to the racialized script created by law enforcement and the media, claiming that "[f]rom the start there was mistrust and dislike between tough urban Chicago transplants and set in their ways rural Cochise County residents."[49] Harter did support the church's claims that it was subjected to racial slurs, burglaries, and vandalism and that only after those incidents did the church start the security patrols. Harter located the beginning of the troubles with law enforcement a year earlier, when four of the church members' children were said to have died due to medical neglect. (There is a discrepancy in the number of children who were said to have died, other reports only mention two.) Harter noted that the church was a "fundamentalist" church advocated against administering medication, and thus authorities tried unsuccessfully to place other children under state supervision, and church members resisted.[50]

From the beginning, this story was shaped by reaction to the ingress of African Americans into a white, mostly Latter-Day Saints population, who did not understand the church's beliefs nor the authoritarian nature of their founder. Painting the CMHCC as a violent apocalyptic cult became an especially powerful tool for evading or discounting African Americans' allegations of racism. Cochise locals did not understand why the CMHCC chose to move to a nearly all-white rural area and by most accounts, the church either chose not to fit in or was prevented from fitting in. Either way, historically, the African American presence in many quarters of the United States has been an ingress of necessity rather than of choice, and more often than not, the onus on "fitting in" has fallen on them.

Jesse Jackson arrived in Miracle Valley in early 1983 to help reconcile the parties involved in the incidents and quell the unrest. He held a series of community meetings and the residents of Cochise County held nothing back. Elaine Duran, wife of college president and co-founder of Citizens for Justice Eli Duran, told the audience that her son prayed before bed: "Dear God, please don't let the blacks kill us." Another person at the meeting blamed the violence on the "belligerence" of the church, while an elderly white man added, "What we had here was a cult, a controlled dictatorship, just the same as Hitler or Mussolini did to their groups or like that Jim Jones did when 900 died."[51] Jackson, according to the media, simply sat and listened. Miracle Valley, like Azusa Street, has taken on a mythic character all its own. It may be that the segregated nature of nearly all American institutions tends to be something Pentecostals understand, and though they may say they abhor it, historically there is very little they, or any other institutions, have been able to do about it.

Building Suburban Pentecostalism

Growing up a Latina Catholic in East Los Angeles skewed my sense of what diversity was. It was simple: everyone around us in our neighborhood and at church looked and sounded like us. Years later, when I was well into my research, I was convinced that most churches I visited were segregated on purpose. People really did not want to go to church with people who were different from them. When it came to Pentecostals, they rationalized their segregation the same way. Then, upon visiting a Foursquare church, I was surprised when the pastor, a Latino, took great pains to affirm his ethnicity while at the same time diminishing its importance as a formative factor in his life. What was the rationale for that?

On the surface, this church was multicultural, but as sociologist Michael Emerson observes, there is a great deal of difference between an assemblage of different people of color and a cultural ethos that accepts multicultural realities. That is what I found in Foursquare—that it was essentially a culturally white church with lots of different people attending.[52] What I also saw there was an unease with ethnicity, projected by the pastor. Ethnicity became acceptable only when neutralized and its ability to influence people to act in their vested interests as people of color diminished. For example, the Foursquare pastor, Pastor Ken, on several occasions uttered things so disturbing, I wondered if I mentioned these things to him, would he ever realize his own self-loathing? How had his Pentecostal identity neutralized his ethnic identity? It was difficult for him to even see past things like the genocide of Native Americans, saying in one sermon that the genocide of Native Americans was "okay, because those savages needed to hear the gospel."[53] Later that year, after attending a local missions meeting at a Foursquare bible school, I saw that same pastor wearing a t-shirt with a picture of him on it in full Native American headdress. He mentioned that they were selling the t-shirts along with nachos to raise funds for a missions trip. When asked if he was insulted by his portrayal on the shirt or the connection to nachos, he retorted, "I'm not insulted because I AM Indian." Again, I sat there, unsure why racializing did not bother him, why a smart, well-read pastor would make such statements about genocide and at the same time tout his ethnicity as something he was proud of, at least when it suited him.

What I have learned over time, though, is that this seeming contradiction is embedded in Pentecostalism. For Pastor Ken genocide is acceptable when considering the Christianization of the Americas. Of first order of importance for Pentecostals is a person's soul. Genocide, according to this logic, was an unfortunate by product of Spanish and Portuguese colonialism. By identifying later as "Indian," Pastor Ken further complicated his ethnic profile, since the conflating of Mexican American and Native American identities has a long history in the Southwest U.S., as is the conflating of Americanized culinary creations (nachos) with authentic Mexican food (no nachos). That Pastor Ken had no qualms about accepting his "Indian-ness" coupled with an accidental Americanized creation of mass-produced yellow corn chips covered with cheese product sprinkled with jalapeño peppers may be quite the apt metaphor.

White Pentecostalism deploys a host of controls to ensure that ethnic identity is both subservient to religious identity and supportive of theological stances and conservative political views. Often these communities are marginalized politically, culturally, and socially by the dominant white culture. For Pastor Ken, a Mexican American from Northern California who marched with Cesar Chavez, who married a white woman and who experienced racial taunting because of his choice of spouse, to embrace his ethnic identity as "Indian" and Mexican is acceptable. Thus, race and ethnicity in Pentecostalism can be prized commodities as much as they are troublesome identities. Moreover, insofar as these identities are neutralized, this neutralization is accomplished, in the Foursquare denomination in particular, by the reverse operation—that is, by a drive for diversity.

For many Pentecostals, evangelism transcends the human calculus of numbers and political motives. Defining what is diversity, and claiming success at becoming multicultural are all spiritual concerns. As such, diversity is effectively neutralized of any substantial power for what educator Paolo Friere called conscientization. Examining the attempt of the Foursquare denomination to claim their multicultural mantle through where it opens its churches paints a very different picture of what the church believes about its diversity and how it views its multicultural vision.

This reality came to light about ten years ago, when faced with dwindling attendance at its flagship church, Angelus Temple, in the Echo Park section of Los Angeles, one of the most demographically diverse areas in the city. The Foursquare denomination recruited Ed and Ivy Stanton from Oregon to revitalize the church. When they arrived in 1999, they saw their task as revising the architecture of Angelus Temple, which, according to Ed, made the acoustics of the place inferior. The Stantons set out to modernize the historical landmark, perhaps unaware of the resistance they received from long-standing Foursquare members displeased with the renovations the Stantons planned and who began a campaign to stop the process. A subtext to this story that did not go reported was that, according to anti-renovation activist Ana Crist, the "Stantons seemed preoccupied with looking for new worshippers from affluent white areas, while ignoring the poorer black and Latino parts of the city."[54] Indeed the unofficial slogan for the Stantons' recruitment strategy was "A Suburban Church in an Urban Oasis." The goal was to have suburban churchgoers drive into Los Angeles on Sundays to go to church and then go home to their suburbs. For his part, Ed Stanton rejected the criticism that race played a role in the strategy, telling British newspaper *The Guardian* that the Angelus Temple staff was very "multicultural" and that he was sensitive to that.[55] Whether it was the renovations strategy that failed to get support from church members, or the resistance from the city's heritage agencies, or the recruitment strategy that went awry, by 2001 the Stantons were gone, replaced by Matt Barnett, who merged his Dream Center church with Angelus Temple and did not renovate the facilities.[56]

The contemporary drive for "diversity" as part of the mission of many Pentecostal denominations deserves some discussion. Most classical denominations have been historically reluctant or resistant to actively trying to diversify their populations. If it came naturally, it was something God did. If it was part of a secular political agenda, it was dismissed as such, because the overarching idea was that such artificial building of God's kingdom would fail. The Foursquare denomination both illustrates and complicates these attitudes toward diversification.

Foursquare is a denomination that is strongest in the West Coast and Mountain West, with scant representation in the Deep South and the Northeast. The reasons for this are historical and have to do with the way the church developed after the death of Aimee Semple McPherson in 1946. Foursquare became a denomination run by the McPherson family, and as such focused heavily on churches in California (528), Washington (161), and Oregon (106). After that, growth followed networks of pastors to places like Montana. Foursquare churches thus continued to multiply in the Northwest and Mountain West, but did not extend beyond until the late twentieth century.[57]

This "organic" model of growth may have been partially effective, but it did not align with demographic shifts in the United States. After successive tries at re-organizing itself, and focusing on "diversity" as part of its mission, Foursquare tried again. Its focus on diversity though did not result in any measurable change in terms of leadership, and actually, the denomination ended its experiment with "Hispanic" supervisors, folding that district into a larger one controlled by a white supervisor.

Between 2000 and 2010, Latinos/as were responsible for most, if not all the country's population growth, and in certain Rust Belt and Plains states, they were the only reason there was not a population loss. Latinos/as have also been a stable and sizeable minority in Foursquare since its founding. Thus, it would have been sensible to build on that base and take advantage of the recent demographic shift. However, in the twelve states that saw growth in Latino/a population, Foursquare opened churches in only three states—two in North Carolina and Georgia, respectively, and two in Maryland. Moreover, even in states where the Foursquare Latino/a population has traditionally been strongest, the church has not made much of a push towards growing its presence in the community. The closest seems to be Colorado, where Latino/a churches make up twenty-three of the sixty-nine Foursquare churches, while in Fourquare's home state of California Latino/a churches account for one-fifth of the denomination. But in some states with sizable Latino/a populations, the number of churches are few. In Florida, New Mexico, and Texas numbers vary, but none of these states has more than fifteen; of Illinois's forty-seven churches only two are Latino/a and only one of those is in the Chicago area; and in New Jersey and New York, which have twenty churches total, there are no Latino/a churches.

So, what does this picture tell us? For one, it is a stubborn reality among Foursquare pastors that many default to the "organic" model of growth and throw in a dose of spirituality when trying to explain why there has not been more growth, particularly among Latinos/as, outside the denomination's main geographical base.

And, in fact, hyper-spiritualizing an answer tends to be the default for most Pentecostals when I ask about what such numbers mean and whether overt or subtle racism is at play. Mostly, they individualize the problem and proclaim that they are not racist, that God must "open the doors" for more "urban" churches, and that they are just waiting for God's timing. Talking about racial or ethnic tensions with Pentecostals often means hearing how their movement was founded as a multiracial endeavor (Azusa Street or PAW), and how the ultimate concern for those pioneering women and men was preaching the gospel—they did not see color. But by focusing on a seemingly endless string of spiritual genealogies tracing who ordained whom, and whether any of those people were black, scholars of Pentecostalism, confessional or not, are missing the point. It is not numbers that create racial and ethnic hush harbors; it is unequal power sharing—something very few, if any Pentecostal denominations believe is subject to human intervention. Pentecostalism, for adherents, is supernatural and outside the boundaries of human design, but since it is these very ordinary, very flawed humans who populate their churches, it is fitting to conclude with some very human stories about outliers.

In our final chapter, we examine some Pentecostal "outliers" some who began as beloved figures and ended as heretics, some who are still polarizing figures, and some who may be creating a future profile of what American Pentecostalism might become as it shifts theologically and demographically into the twenty-first century. Pentecostalism resists specific definition. Most global Pentecostals do not speak in tongues, many adhere to the prosperity gospel, and we can say fairly accurately that what one sees today in the United States and abroad are really variations of charismatic Christianity positioned to appeal to various audiences. Pentecostalism spins endless sequels, the most prominent being the charismatic movement. As such, examining this movement through lives and ministries of Kathryn Kuhlman, Joyce Meyer, Carleton Pearson, and Jay Bakker seems like a good way to end this part of the story.

CHAPTER SIX

Outliers in American Pentecostalism

"Outlier" is a sociological term that entered the pop-culture lexicon with Malcolm Gladwell's 2008 bestselling book *Outliers* (2008). Like Gladwell, I am using the term "outliers" loosely and in doing so I may come under the same criticism he did. Sociologists did not appreciate Gladwell's elasticity with the term. For our purposes, the "outliers" examined in this chapter are either "heretics" who rehabilitated themselves or individuals who have chosen to live on the periphery of Pentecostalism. These individuals include Kathryn Kuhlman and Joyce Meyer, the former seen by some as little more than a charlatan and the latter considered to be a prosperity gospel promoter with little else to show for it but her lavish lifestyle. In some circles, though, they are idealized as faithful anointed women of God. The two male outliers, Carlton Pearson and Jay Bakker, are the heretics. For a religious tradition that privileges male leadership and has a historically significant African American male presence, both Pearson and Bakker are outliers because both failed as it were to pick up the prefabricated mantle of leadership and run with it. Making the decision to shift theologically and become outliers is not something that most public Pentecostal figures do because they know that doing so would separate them from their audience, and they thus would have to repurpose themselves and sell their new personas to different audiences. That is what Pearson and Bakker have done.

Riding out there on the outskirts of orthodoxy are persons who are either today's heretics or tomorrow's saints. Consistent with the history of Christianity, creating, maintaining, and reorganizing the boundaries of orthodoxy are dependent on certain factors. For this select group, some of the factors that determine whether they fit the definition of orthodoxy or if they indeed have driven their Pentecostalism off the cliff are theological; others are not. What bothers detractors about Meyer, for example, is the way she looks; her demeanor and her gender are wrapped up in an incongruous package that marks her as a false teacher.

Kuhlman became popular for her televised ministry. Like many women who preceded her, she was a divorced older woman whose ministry reached beyond Pentecostal circles. Like most televangelists, she was often mired in scandal, and like some of the more well-known healers, she suffered from a variety of ailments. Kuhlman was a crossover artist of sorts, watched by people who would never set foot in a Pentecostal church, but who admired her style. She made Pentecostalism palatable to millions of viewers and as a life-long Baptist, proved that the charismatic movement was a potent force for disseminating Pentecostalism's most popular spiritual gift, healing.

While Jay Bakker belongs to a millennial generation descended from Pentecostal royalty—he is the son of televangelists Jim and Tammy Faye Bakker—he recently became a heretic first by airing the hardball tactics that fellow Christian Right leaders used to oust his father from his ministry, and then by saying that he was pro-same-sex marriage, and of late, by writing fairly openly about doubting faith. Pearson's heresy was quite different. It came in the form of a vision in 1996, which went against the teachings of Pentecostalism's exclusive view that only believers in Jesus's Divinity will be saved.

Pentecostalism usually has filters to mitigate against revelations, prophecies, and visions that counter its tightly drawn boundaries of orthodoxy. When that filter does not work, for whatever reason, the result is heresy. What causes these filters to fail? And given that they do fail more times than not, what is the glue that keeps Pentecostal orthodoxy together? Traditionalists maintain that it depends on being firmly rooted in the Bible. Accordingly, false teachers are those who do not know their Bible, while those who do know their Bible are not prone to heretical beliefs. This, of course, is too simplistic. Some outliers attract followers *specifically* because they are considered great Bible teachers. One of these was Kathryn Kuhlman, a Baptist divorcee from Missouri, a renowned healer who was never healed.

Kathryn Kuhlman: Close-Up

Kathryn Kuhlman was born in Missouri in 1907 into a Baptist/Methodist family and began ministry in 1924, when she went on an evangelistic tour with her sister and brother-in-law, which lasted until 1928. Historian Amy Artman notes Kuhlman refused to acknowledge that she had any kind of formal education, and that she was probably influenced by noted healing evangelists Charles Price, Aimee Semple McPherson, and A. B. Simpson. Kuhlman also attended Simpson College in 1924. Nevertheless, Kuhlman did not credit them for her spiritual development. Like most Pentecostals and charismatics, all credit was due to the Holy Spirit.[1]

In the early 1930s, Kuhlman began associating with another evangelist, Burroughs A. Waltrip Sr., a former Baptist turned Pentecostal evangelist who began a church in Iowa called the Radio Chapel. The suspicions of their congregation that they were romantically involved proved true, and in 1937, Waltrip sent his wife a letter asking for a divorce, leaving her and their two children to fend for themselves and marrying Kuhlman. In 1938, the Radio Chapel became financially insolvent. Waltrip and the church board wrangled legally to determine control of the church. Ultimately, Waltrip left town, leaving Radio Chapel $40,000 in debt. Kuhlman went with him, but she was unhappy in her marriage, and like Aimee Semple McPherson and Maria Atkinson before her, turned divorce into an opportunity to establish her own ministry.[2]

Working in the Youngstown and Pittsburgh areas of Pennsylvania, particularly with men who lived hard lives and were alcoholics, Kuhlman built her reputation as a healer. Soon after, though, in 1948, financial supporters of her ministry claimed that she had shortchanged them $20,000 in back pay for using rental facilities to hold her services at the Gospel Tabernacle in Franklin, Pennsylvania. Eventually, the matter was settled out of court, and by 1950, Kuhlman ventured into television ministry, a medium that helped bring about what Artman calls the "gentrification" of charismatic Christianity.[3]

In the 1960s, Kuhlman began making an impact with the show entitled *I Believe in Miracles*. With total creative control over the program, Kuhlman demonstrated to a nationwide audience that as a healing evangelist, she was like everyone's grandma. Acknowledging that she never had kids, she said she felt as if she had dozens of spiritual children. Her interest in what she called the "youth movement" is apparent from a segment in which she sits with young people on the stage floor, listening to Lonnie Frisbee, one of the most famous and controversial evangelists of the 1960s Jesus movement in California, who enthusiastically answers her questions about what Jesus has done in his life. Frisbee, wearing his most California hippie look, explains how Jesus changed his life completely and how the new birth he experienced was real. When Kuhlman queries the audience about whether they received the new birth experience, most of them raise their hands in affirmation. While Kuhlman's typical audience wore their Sunday best, played traditional hymns, and usually did not include young people, a segment like this exposed Kuhlman to wider audiences, and the endorsement of wildly popular evangelists like Frisbee gave her further legitimacy.[4]

Kuhlman had the ability to secure for herself a national pastorate when most evangelical/charismatic or Pentecostal women in ministry were not in such positions. She, like Agnes Sanford (see chapter 4), disavowed any link to the growing feminist movement. On the contrary, she spoke out in support of a traditional domestic model for women and said that she wished she were a good cook and had twelve kids. "I would just love to have a man boss me,"[5] she added. In spite of her anti-feminism, Kuhlman was able to pursue her work as a result of the social forces of feminism that created space for women to occupy more roles than in previous eras.

Kuhlman continued her television ministries, with a foray into the talk-show circuit in the early 1970s. This endeavor did not come without further controversy. One of the more famous musicians Kuhlman recruited to play for her television show was classically trained Dino Kartsonakis. As they traveled together to support her television ministry, they became good friends. But their relationship soon soured. Kuhlman did not support Dino's choice of girlfriend and did not give him a raise.[6] The bitterness over their fallout resulted in more rumors alleging Kuhlman's lavish spending and lifestyle. But in any case, financial troubles plagued her relationships with people close to her ministries, including her personal manager, Paul Bartholomew, who sued her for breaking a contract, with the result that yet again her finances were in disarray.

Kuhlman suffered for years with heart problems, which eventually led to her death in 1976. A healer herself, she apparently did not seek healing for her condition. Nor did she let anyone know how sick she was aside from a few close associates. Kuhlman, like Aimee Semple McPherson, seemed to lead a solitary life, but whether that was by choice, we do not know. Very much in keeping with her growing celebrity, Kuhlman was not buried in working-class Youngstown or Pittsburgh, but in Los Angeles, in the same cemetery as McPherson.

Kuhlman created a new media image as a holy healing grandmother, dressed in white and high heels. She led a choir of hardened men in the working-class city of Pittsburgh. As a media star, she helped pioneer the tactic of "calling out" healing to audiences waiting to hear their affliction called out. She did the same thing to her television audiences, who did not care that these shows were taped days in advance, edited for maximum effect, and mediated through the larger-than-life persona Kuhlman created for herself. Kuhlman survived moral and financial scandals; she survived a deadly heart condition for many years, and would offer her own version of a charismatic/Pentecostal "dharma transmission" to devoted fans like Benny Hinn and Joyce Meyer.

Joyce Meyer in the Confessional

Joyce Meyer, like most outliers, can be a polarizing figure. I have met plenty of people who love Meyer because she is fearless, a survivor and a straight talker in a sea of evangelical therapeutic fluff. Others hate her, her lavish lifestyle, and her prosperity teachings. Regardless of what Pentecostals think, she is probably the most prominent female preacher in global Pentecostalism today.

She herself has quite a testimony. As a young girl, her father sexually, psychologically, and verbally abused her, destroying her self-esteem and as she grew older, sending her looking for approval from men with some awful results. Her conversion and healing of her traumas are a source of her popularity. Meyer also succeeds because, despite her circumstances, she has not defied the authorities that privilege stratified gender hierarchies and believe women's submission to men is the way to a peaceful married life. Rather than blame the religious culture for her problems, she supports every aspect of that culture, and in doing so supports the idea that she is only in ministry because her husband "allows" it. Moreover, Meyer flies in the face of the idea that Pentecostal female ministers are sexually tempting to the point that people inevitably blame them for their moral failings à la McPherson. Meyer may be many things, but there is little in the literature, in social media, and in her own created profile that views her as sexy. Rather, like Agnes Sanford and Kathryn Kuhlman, Meyer is a grandmotherly figure; but, unlike Sanford's kindly diminutive grandma, Meyer is the a tough-talking grandma who tells it like it is. Perhaps it is the luck of their chronology that Sanford and Meyer escaped the public eye in their younger years, avoiding being judged chiefly by how they looked, what they wore, and how they comported themselves. Both Sanford and Meyer entered ministry later, with their sexuality neutralized by their ages.

Meyer's media presence is extensive. Her website advertises her books, CDs, upcoming conferences, newsletters, and just about anything else her followers need to keep up with her ministry. She also has a Facebook and Twitter presence with over four million followers. The material on these sites reinforce both her no-nonsense persona and traditional gender roles and stereotypes. As a straight-talking, pioneering woman in the ministry, she casts herself as different but the same, a threat but not a threat.

Meyer's "Confessions" demonstrate these tendencies,[7] along with her Word of Faith leanings and how those affirmations lead right into traditional gender roles for her and for her followers.

Out of the twenty or so confessions, four stand out as affirming Meyer's promotion of gender ideals. One states, "All my children have Christian friends and God has set aside a Christian wife or husband for each of them." This is not a statement about what is but is an affirmation of something that will be. In another confession, when Meyer says, "I am an obedient wife and no rebellion operates in me," she asks that her followers say the same. But is her ministry a rebellion? Fundamentalists might say yes, simply because she is a woman preaching the Bible. For Meyer, though, another confession serves as a cover: "My husband is wise. He is the King and priest of our home. He makes godly decisions." Ministry thus falls to second place in this hierarchy.

Meyer's statements of faith and affirmations of health and prosperity in her "Confessions" ultimately fall in with these traditional notions of gender and female submission, while also including a healthy dose of transpersonal self-esteem psychology. Thus, Meyer is wise; she never gets tired; she weighs the correct weight; she answers all her speaking requests; she does not allow any measure of negativity to enter her life. These are admirable if unrealistic goals for many, but the magic here is Meyer's confidence that making these confessions on a regular basis will make them manifest in reality. In spite of the traumas she has suffered, Meyer comes out of those experiences not as embittered or as agnostic. On the contrary, she is quite positive—especially in reaffirming what traditional evangelical or Pentecostal women need or want to hear. Whatever problem they had or are having, staying within the framework of traditional marriage is of utmost importance. In her reading of the Bible, she emphasizes those passages that assert the privilege of men to head the household and the responsibility of women not to be rebellious. That is what makes Meyer so popular. She is a survivor who does not locate her misery in a church culture that often silences women's abuse and pain; instead she continues submitting to male hierarchy.

Joyce is a winner and a survivor. Her advice hovers around the practical and uncomplicated as often as possible, and she proves capable of overcoming the controversies surrounding her excessive wealth. As a minister, she is not required to file public records about her finances, but various media report her evangelism organization is worth $57 million.[8] A more serious accusation occurred a few years ago when her head of security became the focus of a criminal murder investigation.[9] Scandals like these, which normally doom most public personalities, do not stick to Meyer. Indeed, she is as popular as ever. For Pentecostals, who have a powerful ability to create narratives of healing, redemption, and the miraculous, creating narratives of invincibility around figures who demonstrate their convictions comes naturally. Meyer succeeds, then, despite being a woman with a hard life and a plainspoken person in a culture that does not accept that trait in women, because she and her audience create a Christian domestic fiction, with Meyer as the heroine passing along her hard-earned pearls of wisdom.

Part of Meyer's appeal is also how her testimony reads like a martyrology, which is an eternal source of inspiration and passion. Historian Jennifer Heller argues that Meyer skillfully tells women they need to submit for their own sacrificial good.[10] Meyer's emphasis on women's submission is something of an effort to return to Eden, a call for a return to a divine order that is comforting for her followers. Meyer succeeds because she sticks to the script. Yet there are other outliers who push the boundaries of that script so far out that they find themselves completely outside the boundaries of what Pentecostalism is willing to accept, even from its famous celebrity preachers.

Carlton Pearson: From Favorite Son to Heretic

What Pentecostals do not get over is betrayal. Especially irksome is the kind of betrayal that noted evangelist, singer, and pastor Carlton Pearson supposedly committed more than ten years ago, when his formerly solid grasp of the certainties of the faith, taught to him by his parents and grandparents, began to unravel in a vision. Pearson betrayed decades of tightly stitched-together biblical inerrancy that offered non-Christians no effective way out of spending eternity in hell. Pearson's vision upended all he believed about non-Christians' condemnation to hell. Pearson felt compelled to preach this new message to his Tulsa, Oklahoma, church, and it did not go well. Before getting into the story, some background.

Carlton D. Pearson was born in San Diego in 1953, a fourth-generation Pentecostal from the Church of God in Christ. Growing up as an African American in California, he encountered racism and prejudice, but said "as I grew older and got more involved in the broader religious world, I discovered that the seductive vices of religious prejudice far outstripped those of racial hatred."[11]

Pearson's grandfather, a pioneer in the COGIC movement in San Diego, built and pastored the St. Luke Church. His grandmother, on the other hand, "backslid" into a life of drinking, smoking, and gambling on race dogs in Tijuana, Mexico. But then, as Pearson acknowledged, his grandfather was a womanizer. Why then were he and his family so sure that only his grandmother was in hell? Reflecting on this period in his youth, Pearson later wrote that this was the first time he wondered why certain people were going to hell and others, like his grandfather, were not.

After moving to Oklahoma, Pearson attended Oral Roberts University, the Pentecostal college, where he was groomed for stardom. His Azusa Conferences, annual ministry showcases, were standouts in the Pentecostal world, and he soon planted a church called Higher Dimensions Ministries in 1977. At its peak, Higher Dimensions had five thousand members. By all accounts, Pearson was at the height of the Pentecostal ministry world throughout the 1980s and most of the 1990s, until he experienced a vision while watching television news.

The story of the vision is simple, with broad implications. While Pearson was watching news reports about the horrible killings in Rwanda, he felt God speak to him about the erroneous nature of his belief that those who did not have a personal relationship with Jesus would spend eternity in hell.[12] Pearson told his congregation about his vision and began preaching universal salvation. Subsequently, his once-thriving megachurch lost so many members that after a few weeks only about six hundred were left. Pearson tried to restart his church, but it went into foreclosure, and he lost it a couple of years later.

Since Pearson has been on a quest to find a denomination that welcomed his new "gospel of inclusivity." He has worshipped in a United Church of Christ, a Unitarian Universalist church, and a Unity church. Currently, he leads his own New Thought–inspired church, Higher Dimensions Center, in Tulsa with a branch in Chicago. Pearson settled on New Thought after leading Christ Universal Temple in Chicago in 2009, founded by legendary African American New Thought pioneer Johnnie Coleman. It was an unhappy union. The experiment lasted two years, and by 2011, Pearson resigned,[13] although he retained the basics of New Thought theology.

In the span of fifteen years, Pearson lost his church, his home, and was branded a heretic by a liturgical body called the Joint College of African American Pentecostal Bishops. Pearson reimagined himself as a "metacostal," a metaphysically-inclined Pentecostal who accepts New Thought teachings of Jesus as a symbolic figure promoting Christ consciousness but allows for Pentecostal-style worship.

This hybridizing of New Thought and Pentecostalism is not in itself unusual, particularly for African Americans and former COGIC members. As Darnise Martin explains, in the 1920s and 1930s, New Thought was overwhelmingly white and not concerned with race issues. By adapting their variations of Protestantism with New Thought ideas, people like Father Hurley, Father Divine, Reverend Ike, and Daddy Grace taught African American congregations an amalgam of self-determination, self-worth, prosperity teaching, often wrapped in Pentecostal-style worship.[14] Pearson, in his latest book, offers a sample of this theological style: "If you exist in Christ consciousness, where thought becomes reality and you give thanks to God for what you have in your life. . . . All poverty is artificial. Lack and want are delusions. They are produced out of spiritual amnesia. In a more severe sense, poverty is a form of insanity."[15]

In the case of Martin's pastor, "Rev. E," her COGIC background helps her maintain a thread of Pentecostalism within a New Thought context. "Rev. E" left COGIC because there was no room for women in terms of ordination. However, she does not accept that she left all Pentecostal theology behind since "everybody is teaching the same thing."[16] Despite "Rev E's" seeming ease at blending religious traditions, it is risky for those with a large public profile and large churches, and most do not attempt it. Martin maintains that New Thought teachings are expanding through the growth of independent Black New Thought churches and the continued growth of megachurches that teach the prosperity gospel. Though Pentecostal prosperity gospel churches denounce inclusion in this group, that is precisely the space Pearson inhabits. Listening to his YouTube channel and following the company he keeps, like prominent New Thought pastor Michael Beckwith and author Neale Donald Walsch, Pearson believes that they occupy a religious space ripe for a spiritual revolution.[17]

Pearson's vast social media output and his writings help to show how his religious inclusivism is now the lens that he uses to examine his past experiences. For example, looking back on growing up and going to school with mostly Catholic Mexican Americans, Pearson says that he never "really believed that God would reject these dear friends. . . . It seemed unnecessary that all these people were going to end up in hell."[18] As his memoir demonstrates, Pearson's theological transformation colors the entirety of who he is now, though in earlier decades of public ministry, Pearson never seemed to have given a second thought to his Catholic classmates being subject to endless torment. Race is another subject that Pearson did not really begin to reflect on publicly until after his theological shift. Now, however, he claims that his race played a part in the "campaign to destroy Carlton Pearson." In a chapter of his memoir entitled, "Exile: A Price Worth Paying," Pearson says that he knew the response to his message of inclusion would be "explosive," but that he was unprepared for the level of "hatred" that came from his own church. "What hurt most was that my own church members, people I had served faithfully and lovingly for over two decades, along with some members of my family, left by the thousands."[19] While Pearson's bitterness is aimed at those who condemned him for believing in universalism, I believe that the reason Pearson became a pariah was that he disappointed his white benefactors, who groomed him for years to be a major public figure, only to be betrayed by Pearson's soul searching.

One of the most illuminating interviews during his last ten years in "exile" occurred in 2011 with noted African American pastor, author, and businessperson Bishop George Bloomer,[20] who tried to coax out of Pearson an answer to the question: Does Pearson still believe? Does he believe enough to have the mantle of Pentecostal be a part of his life? Pearson tells Bloomer that he not only prays every day, but that he prays in tongues, explaining that it is all he has ever known. He also says that he is still Pentecostal because that is who he is, who he has been for generations, and that that he responds to the sense of transcendence in the faith. When Bloomer asks if he is "saved," Pearson responds, "Yes, he is, and Carlton Pearson is safe." He explains that for the first time he feels completely safe with God, because God will not punish him for his views; in fact, God will not punish anyone, because all God has is unconditional love for everyone. At the end of the interview, though, when Bloomer asks him repeatedly if he's "coming back" to traditional Pentecostal faith, Pearson says no: "You'll join me before I join you again." As an outcast, Pearson's position is especially difficult. It is one thing to do something wrong: in that case, Pentecostals can make a space to accept repentant believers back into the fold. Change in belief, though, is harder to come back from, since that is pretty much what holds all manner of conservative forms of Protestant Christianity together—correct belief. Pearson believed wrongly, acted on those beliefs, and dared to expand accepted Pentecostal theology. Not only did he preach his gospel of inclusion, first in Pentecostal churches, then outside them, Pearson broke with established norms vis-à-vis nonbelievers, and instead of trying to convert them, Pearson accepted them as saved.

It is a testament to the tightly scripted theological worlds that Pentecostals inhabit that Pearson remains exiled from the church. He is also in the paradoxical situation of considering himself part of a movement that has no use for him. Pearson became an outlier because he offered his congregation an unthinkable theological conclusion to their countless triumphant narratives about how God saves. In the view of his congregation, Pentecostal leaders, and others, Pearson opened the gates of heaven without permission. As a man in a decidedly male Pentecostal world, Pearson threw away his birthright; that and his new theological outlook make his potential repentance narrative unlikely. Equally unlikely is the repentance narrative of another favorite son, who did not throw away his birthright so much as mess with the firmament of Pentecostal belief—certainty.

Jay Bakker: Son of a Preacher Man

Jay Bakker is nearly always described as the "prodigal son" of his famous parents, Jim and Tammy Faye. He is the legacy child gone wrong, the son who refused to take up his father's damaged mantle. When his parents' ministry notoriously imploded, he did not attempt to pick up where his father left off. Instead, he lost himself for a time in alcohol and drugs.

Pentecostalism and, more broadly, evangelicalism operate on a basis of "spiritual primogeniture." Sons are crucial to the movement; they easily become pastors, often to continue the family line. There are no better suited legacy builders in American Pentecostalism than straight white males; they are the most revered, the most theologically vested in the tradition and in maintaining it. Sons who leave, sons who change their theology, sons who indulge in a diet of hedonism and substance abuse—as Jay Bakker did—those are not sons that Pentecostalism desires. Like Pearson, Bakker holds views that make him an outlier. His support for LGBT rights put him on the farthest reaches of Pentecostalism. Indeed, some would say that Bakker is no longer Pentecostal. But then it is my contention that American Pentecostalism may be more like Jay Bakker than it might like to imagine. One cannot tell the story of Jay Bakker without some reference to his famous parents. Both came from modest means and met at North Central College, an Assemblies of God school in Minnesota. They got married in 1961. North Central then kicked the Bakkers out, because the school forbade students from getting married. Jim and

Tammy began a children's ministry in North Carolina, but Jim's ambition was to be in the televangelism business. Jim and Tammy's ministry became very popular on Pat Robertson's Christian Broadcasting Network (CBN) around 1965. Soon thereafter, Jim began co-hosting the network's flagship show, *The 700 Club*. This became a springboard to Jim Bakker's own Praise the Lord (PTL) network, which he started in 1973. Throughout the 1970s, Bakker built his televangelism empire to unprecedented heights, with the worth of his broadcasting network valued at $172 million by 1987.

Maintaining Bakker's dream of PTL and an adjoining Christian amusement park, Heritage USA, soon became an all-consuming search for money.[21] Problems with money paled in comparison to Bakker's dalliance with Jessica Hahn in 1990. Proving once again, the cover-up is usually worse than the crime, Bakker drew on the depleted funds of a debt-ridden PTL and paid her hush money to keep the affair quiet. This, coupled with the discovery that PTL had debts of nearly $70 million and that Bakker was still drawing a yearly salary of $1.6 million, resulted in Bakker's eventual conviction for fraud in 1989. He served five years in prison.

According to Jay, his father was the victim of a conspiracy where Bakker's competitors were tipped off that the rumors of an affair were indeed true. Then the frenzy to ruin Bakker's reputation became the logical next step. The conspirators included Jerry Falwell and Jimmy Swaggart.

Jay's writing about his father is emotionally raw, where the men who Jay trusted seem to take great pleasure in denouncing his father's behavior. Jay recounts that Swaggart said, "Jim Bakker is a cancer on the body of Christ."[22] The Assemblies of God soon defrocked Bakker. Why Bakker did not survive his sex scandal and Swaggart weathered out his own may have much to do with the money that Bakker supposedly diverted from contributions to his Heritage USA park to pay Hahn.

Jay does not mention why other televangelists thought it was their purview to involve themselves in the Bakker scandal. But they did. Swaggart denounced him. Falwell decided to ask Bakker to tape an apology for the PTL partners group, and Bakker acquiesced. According to Jay, Falwell edited out the portion where Bakker admitted that the affair lasted only fifteen minutes. The partners group never saw the whole tape.[23] Jay seems to suggest that the root of Falwell's ferocity at Bakker was their theological disagreements, which Jay says was "at the center of the scandal."[24]

Bakker accused Falwell of staging a "corporate takeover" and launching TV attacks accusing Bakker of being "gay and a thief."[25] Jay adamantly denies that these accusations were true and in his book seems incredulous at the level of vituperation Falwell had for his father. Falwell's takeover of PTL also included the Bakker family home and personal items that Falwell claimed Bakker purchased with partner funds.

Probably no event is more excruciating for Jay than the prison time his father served after his fraud conviction. It was the prison term that precipitated the Bakkers' divorce and Jay's descent into substance abuse. For Jay, "the theological pettiness of others, along with their lust for power, and plain old greed, destroyed my father's ministry, just as it's destroying the church today."[26] Jay spent most of the 1990s trying to recover from the aftermath of the scandal.

Jay is still a pastor and still interested in promoting Christianity. Despite his deep feelings of betrayal against Falwell, his narrative vis-à-vis Falwell reads very much like a good old-fashioned Pentecostal testimonial. Jay seethes with hatred at Falwell for what he's done to his father and family. At one of his prison visits, his father tells him that he is going to meet with Falwell and they are going to reconcile. This sets Jay off and he cannot believe his father is going to meet with his nemesis. Falwell and Bakker meet. Bakker forgives him and tells Jay that he should do the same because forgiveness is more about Jay moving on, not so much about Falwell accepting responsibility for his actions. Jay in fact did meet with Falwell—he was angry, he wanted answers, and as he reports, Falwell did not admit to anything, hinting that Jay did not know the whole story. After not receiving answers from Falwell, Jay tells him that he forgives him anyway, regardless of Falwell's inability to accept that he did anything wrong. Lesson learned. For Jay, forgiving Falwell became unconditional; it is the essence of grace, and that is the essence of the Christian faith. Added to the reconciliation meeting he has with Falwell, after many fruitless phone calls, Jay gets Swaggart to write a letter on behalf of his father to try to earn early release from prison.

Jay Bakker's tone in his next two books is very different. *Son of a Preacher Man* is deeply personal, raw storytelling that veers often into clichés about a naive young man being disappointed by the hypocrisy of religious leaders, lamenting why all these televangelists are being so mean to his father. Two of Jay's books, *Fall to Grace* and *Faith, Doubt and Other Lines I've Crossed*, show his transformation into a Pentecostal outlier on his own terms. Jay is a preacher; he is interested in teaching theology, using the Bible as a centerpiece of religious authority. He wants to reclaim Christianity lost to ego, money, greed, and right-wing politics. In *Fall to Grace* Jay grows in awareness of the peculiarity of growing up Pentecostal, that it often seems far removed from Christianity. This small volume focuses on grace and forgiveness—on how Jay overcame his own issues and how that has informed his understanding of how to relate to other outliers. For Jay taking up the LGBT cause is a way to make his case that grace is foundational to his Christian message. His most amusing and touching chapter is entitled "St. Peter and RuPaul."

After an invitation to a RuPaul drag show, Jay faces having to be more vocal and open about his LGBT-affirming stance, and he knows that this revelation makes him a pariah in Pentecostal circles. Jay, having a cigarette outside the show during intermission, is approached by a drag queen who tells him that he was a preacher's kid too, and that he loved Jay's mother Tammy Faye and that he is worried about her because her health had begun to deteriorate.[27] Jay does not go into detail about his mother and her role as a gay icon, except to note that he is aware of it, but it is fair to speculate that one reason Jay found a point of contact with the community was his mother's open embrace of LGBT people. It may be that Jay is an outlier because he was simply following his mother's footsteps and is continuing her path. Back at RuPaul's show, the host notices that Jay is in the audience, and mentions that he's there, he then says that "You know, this is where Jesus would be if He were alive today. Jesus hung out with the tax collectors and the prostitutes and the sinners."[28] The host wished Jay well on his new church venture.

Jay's latest book ventures even farther away from traditional notions of Pentecostal orthodoxy. In it, he largely dispenses with biblical quotations, and, rather than preaching, he focuses more introspectively on the cost of being an outlier. If there is one thing that outliers understand about their choices, it is that they will no longer be part of the larger Pentecostal community, whether they still identify as Pentecostals as Pearson does or they are more circumspect about their faith allegiances as Jay Bakker is.

Jay hints at the idea that he might be a universalist, or at least that he believes as some do that hell is not a place in the afterlife, but it is a place or state of being that exists right now. In that, his trajectory is less dramatic than Pearson, but as important in that it may be that for some outliers raised in the spotlight of popular Pentecostalism, the move out toward a theological broadening marks the edges of a new orthodoxy.

Like Pearson, Jay lost his church. He reflects on the loss, and concludes that it was worth it:

> I realized that none of that mattered. I said the Bible has been abused, has been used to justify discrimination, and that it was wrong to do so. I

said that they [LGBT] are loved and accepted, that that from now on I would be preaching grace that includes them, not excludes then. And I lost everything I thought I'd lose. But it did not matter, because I freed myself from the burden of indifference.[29]

In Pentecostalism, a revelation, a calling, a prophetic word, a dream, or vision usually characterizes choosing a successor. This has the effect of legitimizing the technique. Since Pentecostals are socialized to accept religious instruction by those means, this in effect legitimizes the successor. The other characteristic of a successor is the imprint of designation. Designating a successor is legitimate by the very act itself according to sociologist Max Weber, creating a "hereditary charisma."[30] For Pentecostals, creating this "hereditary charisma" would mean not only the theological beliefs of the faith, but the exercise of spiritual gifts and, I would add, extending the theological beliefs to include political stances that reflect the conservative politics expected of most white evangelicals. Maintaining this position as a charismatic leader then includes a theological, experiential, and political component. It may be the case that in the era of televangelism scandals that befell the Bakkers and Swaggart, and that have become commonplace, one of the ways to maintain some semblance of religious authority is to have a son who takes over after the scandal. Donny Swaggart managed to stay in ministry after his father's fall and defrocking by the Assemblies of God. The Bakkers then had a chance to recoup their losses, and in a sense, they have. Jim Bakker has a ministry in Branson, Missouri, and his theology and politics now veer toward the hard right survivalist fringe. Jay Bakker has become a successor of a different kind. Rather than accepting the succession available to him if he had followed his father to Missouri, Jay's traumatic teen years, his drug and alcohol abuse, and his own theological wanderings have pushed him out onto the ledge of what is acceptable in Pentecostalism. It is for that reason that I believe Jay Bakker not only is an outlier, but he very well may be what remains of white American Pentecostalism once the larger millennial drift moves away from organized forms of the faith.

EPILOGUE

A Whole New Thing—The Future of Pentecostalism in America

Pentecostals tell great stories. How they tell their stories, why they tell their stories, and how their stories affect others help craft their success globally. There is little doubt that Pentecostalism is a growth industry. Globally, Pentecostalism is often synonymous with the prosperity gospel/Word of Faith movement. Globally there are approximately 280 million Pentecostals and 305 million charismatics according to Pew Study data,[1] who together make up about 27 percent of all Christians. Currently, the region with the largest percentage of Pentecostals is sub-Saharan Africa (15 percent), followed by the Americas (11 percent). It is the reverse for charismatics, more of whom live in the Americas (16 percent) than in sub-Saharan Africa (7 percent). Eight out of ten Pentecostals are African or from the Americas, and half of the world's charismatics are from the Americas.[2]

Moreover, in the United States Pentecostalism has not experienced the kind of decline that other religions have. On the contrary, while Protestantism has lost about 5 percent of its followers, going from 51 percent of the population to around 46, the percentage of Pentecostals among U.S. Protestants has grown from about 8 percent to 13 percent; in other words, out of approximately 152 million Protestants, roughly 20 million are Pentecostals.[3] Healing is one engine that drives Pentecostal growth.[4] The prosperity gospel is another. Looking at the geographic locations where the Pentecostal presence is largest, it makes perfect sense that healing is the draw that it is, and that the desire to turn one's reciprocal arrangement with God into tangible material benefits is as strong as it is.

In terms of U.S. Pentecostalism, growth comes overwhelmingly from communities of color. The three largest Pentecostal denominations in the United States are the Assemblies of God, the Church of God in Christ, and the Church of God, Cleveland, Tennessee, and people of color have recently played a significant role in their growth. While the largest white denomination, the Assemblies of God, lost 14 percent of its white members between 2001 and 2015, the proportion of Latinos/as has grown from 16 to 23 percent during that same time. The numbers of African Americans, Native Americans, and other people of color have also increased. Whites comprise roughly 1.8 million members, while combined, people of color comprise 1.2 million. The second largest denomination, the Church of God in Christ, a historically African American church, has a membership of roughly 5 million, 84 percent of whom are African American and 8 percent of whom are Latinas/os, who form the second largest demographic in the denomination. The third largest denomination, the Church of God, Cleveland, Tennessee, has seen similar trends. It, too, has grown by over 1 million members. At the same time, the proportion of white members has decreased dramatically, from 91 percent in 2007 to 65 percent in 2014, and the denomination's proportion of Latinos/as has grown from 10 percent in 2007 to 28 percent in 2014.[5] This latter figure is notable, considering that the church is geographically strongest in the Southeast. It may be that this is a reflection of the general drift of Christianity from the West to the Global South.

Migration characterizes how Pentecostalism in the United States, like its global counterpart, moves around the globe. Place plays a central part in the movement's story. After examining place, the epilogue will move on to the question of power—cultural and political, as well as spiritual—and focus finally on its paradoxical qualities.

Place

Brazilian Pentecostal churches in Cape Cod, Mexican Pentecostal churches in Anchorage, West Indian Pentecostal churches in New York, Scandinavian Pentecostal churches on the Great Plains—American Pentecostalism travels through the lives of immigrant populations, who either bring their particular brand of Pentecostalism from their home countries or convert to it here in the United States. Moreover, for more than a century, Pentecostals have moved around this country in search of places to ply their trade, with the Great

Migration of African Americans to the West Coast from the 1920s through the 1950s being particularly significant.

The founding of McGlothen Temple Church of God in Christ in the San Francisco Bay Area in 1925 by black migrants from Oklahoma and Texas began the process, which continued for decades, with southerners bringing with them staples of their culture and religious tradition from places like Arkansas, Mississippi, Texas, and Oklahoma.[6] Their new churches tended to exhibit a degree of sectarianism and competitiveness, at least according to mainline Protestants. They improvised their places of worship. COGIC folks regularly met in tents, and some took their talents outside to the fields, and when they did open brick-and-mortar churches, these were often in unadorned store fronts in run-down parts of town. Black and white preachers both made inroads among the workers in the burgeoning defense and military industries in the Bay Area. Unlike their mainline Protestant co-religionists, black Pentecostal preachers were more likely to open up storefront churches, an affront to the propriety of mainline Protestant organizations like the Oakland Federal Council of Churches (OFCC). The OFCC noted in one report that these churches sprang up like "weeds in uncultivated areas."[7] The local ministry arm of the OFCC, United Ministry, also noted that Pentecostal churches were sectarian and did not cooperate with local efforts at ministering to the community. Religious competition became one of the ramifications of how Southern Pentecostals re-imagined place in moving to the West.

One of those families who made the move to the Bay Area was the Stewart family from Denton, Texas. F. L. Haynes founded the first COGIC church in Denton, Texas, the historic St. Andrews COGIC. There were other black churches in segregated Denton, but St. Andrews gained the distinction of being loud. St. Andrews was different than the established black Protestant churches. The founding families of the church, the Haynes and the Stewarts, set about building the church for several years and they held tent services until they raised enough money. The occasional rock thrower disturbed these raucous tent services. The hallmark of the church was the worship, led by sisters Alpha and Omega Haynes. Alpha's husband, K.C. Stewart, played in the worship band as well. On occasion, Stewart fashioned a percussion section from washboards, tin cans, and baking pans that joined the church piano and tambourine as the church's only instruments. K.C. and Alpha Stewart raised all their five children in church. Evangelism was also a family affair; K.C. took his homemade instruments into the cotton and tomato fields of Denton and the family sang and played for the field workers.[8] K.C., according to his daughter Vaetta, played all manner of homemade instruments, especially the washboard, while Alpha played the guitar. Vaetta says that K.C.'s playing supported the family financially. When the children were older, they played local churches as well, standing on tables entertaining their fellow COGIC parishioners.[9] By all accounts, the Stewart family was close, the children active in church, and many, if not all, were imbued with a sense of COGIC tradition.

The family moved out west in the 1950s to take advantage of better economic prospects in the Bay Area. K.C. became a warehouse supervisor and Alpha continued her work as a housekeeper along with raising their children. The children excelled in local schools, with oldest son Sylvester ("Sly") taking an interest in forming musical groups beginning in middle school. Three of the Stewart children went into the music business. Vaetta joined a gospel group, "The Heavenly Tones," which included future gospel stars Elva Mouton, Mary McCreary, and Tramaine Hawkins.[10] The group began out of the Ephesians COGIC church in Berkeley, founded in 1937. Vaetta's brother Freddie began a band called "Freddie and the Stone Souls." Sly became a DJ in the Bay Area after a few years of being in bands in Vallejo. In the mid-1960s a multicultural band fronted by Sly, his brother's band, and sister's gospel group merged their talents into a new band, Sly and the Family Stone. The detour to discuss the Stewart family is intentional since this rather remarkable transmission of musical talent coming out of one Pentecostal denomination would not have been possible without the Great Migration, without African Americans looking for new places to call home. One need not repeat the entire rationale behind the Great Migration and the subsequent failure to find new homes in the Northeast, Midwest, and West that did not discriminate when it came to housing, employment, education, and most notably, the criminal justice system. Suffice to say, blacks in the Bay Area, while finding California more hospitable, soon found themselves in similar situations that confronted them in the South.

Perhaps it was the multicultural realities of the Bay Area that influenced Sly Stewart to form musical groups that included mixed-race line-ups, or his mother's gracious hospitality that fed and cared for diverse neighborhood children in Vallejo. And perhaps it was the mirage of multiculturalism that soon caused Sly to dispense with the sunny optimism of his early songs like "Everyday People," transitioning to the angry growls filtered through layers of distorted sound insisting he not be called the n-word in the song "Don't Call Me Nigger, Whitey." While Sly and the Family Stone wanted to proclaim feel-good notions of togetherness and racial reconciliation in most of their early music, their latter music displayed the harsh realities of the 1960s. Pentecostalism's imagining Azusa Street as a racial utopia operated in much the same way; wanting to proclaim racism over, at least spiritually, without dealing with the metastasis of race—power.

Power

When Pentecostals think of power, they think of spiritual power. For many, there is nothing the power of the Holy Spirit cannot overcome. This includes healing the historic and systemic ills of racism. When Azusa Street chronicler Frank Bartleman wrote that the "color line had been washed away in the blood,"[11] it is no wonder that for decades this became the quasi-official political view of many denominations. The racial diversity on display at Azusa Street somehow overcame the intractable racial divisions, and not only in Los Angeles from 1906 to 1909. This event transcended time and space to heal all manner of racial problems. The power exhibited at Azusa Street, to blend genders, races, ethnicities, and classes, is a power exhibited repeatedly, with the same result presumably because God, in this equation, is not a variable—God is unchanging. So, it follows God wrought this massive global outpouring in the twentieth-century United States' segregated society forty years after the Civil War. A final outpouring before the *eschaton* would be able to handle whatever problems the twentieth century offered up.

Nevertheless, sixty years after Azusa Street, at the end of the 1960s, Pentecostalism's power to effect racial harmony lay dormant under the weight of decades of conservative political stances that muted Pentecostalism's earliest progressive impulses. Most, if not all, white Pentecostal denominations viewed the civil rights movement with suspicion, believing it to be infiltrated by communists and therefore not worthy of support. Others ignored the movement entirely. Moreover, while some black Pentecostals were active in the movement, others, like Sly Stone, did not use the musical stage to preach politics. During the some of the most convulsive years of U.S. history, Sly and the Family Stone produced no songs about the civil rights movement, Vietnam, or racial strife. Yet, despite the band's seeming silence on the momentous events of the times, at least one observer of African American culture found Sly Stone to be a liberative force.

In a curious set of YouTube videos that chronicles the history of the group, theologian Cornel West, in full fan mode, gushes over Sly Stone and reminiscences about going to see the group in 1960s Sacramento. West said that he only "knew two free black men," in the 1960s: one was Richard Pryor, the other was Sly Stone. West continued that Stone seemed free of the constraints of white America; he wrote his own songs, chose his own band mates, produced his own music, and comported himself without deference to established constraints on black men that did not allow them to express their blackness in whatever forms they wished. West then referred to the popular song "Everyday People" that, for him, best expressed the early hope of Sly Stone's outlook towards race.[12] "Everyday People," if you don't know it or if you don't remember, is a mainstream pop song extolling the virtues of accepting people as they are, it was one of their most popular singles of the path-breaking 1969 album *Stand!* The title track extolled the virtues of self-determination in the face of oppression, and it became a Black Panther theme song. Even though Sly and the Family Stone wrote songs that did refer to the tumult of the 1960s, to self-determination and the struggle for freedom, the hard-hitting political songs, like "Don't Call me Nigger, Whitey," were rare.

It was not until the group was past its zenith that other kinds of songs, harkening to Mother Africa, became part of their catalog. Unfortunately, by this time Sly was in no shape mentally or physically to take advantage of this new Afrocentric consciousness. Stone's drug addictions turned into years of missed concert dates, and later decades of seclusion and homelessness. The multiracial composition of the group and the positivity placed on learning how to get along must have, for a time, made people believe that the Family Stone was onto something that "we are the same whatever we do." Stone's "religion," if you will, was a vague 1960s call for "brotherhood." By the time Stone went solo and started using terms like Mother Africa, his music and personal struggles with substance abuse made the hazy pop airiness of "Everyday People" seem distant and naive. When dealing with racial issues, American Pentecostals seemed stuck between the vagueness of brotherhood and an often less than satisfying call for reconciliation. A brief look at one of the latest attempts to deal with race demonstrates the point.

One of most well-known acts of racial reconciliation, the "Memphis Miracle," occurred in 1994 among members of the Pentecostal Fellowship of North America (PCNA) and COGIC. The coverage of that event reveals a lot about narrative power constructed through prisms of privilege.

To begin with, it is no accident that this event becomes a miracle narrative. Two prominent Assemblies of God theologians, Gregory Sutton and

Martin Mittelstadt, writing about how the Memphis Miracle demonstrates the love of God and love of neighbor, use the event to reiterate some common assumptions about racial power in U.S. Pentecostalism. They, like Bartleman, assume that multiracial/multiethnic diversity of early Pentecostalism was enough to sustain racial inclusiveness. They called the racial exclusion of African Americans from the PCNA and other historic racial incidents "misdeeds." The miracle itself consisted of a message in tongues spoken by an African American at a PCNA conference, subsequently interpreted by then–Foursquare leader Jack Hayford as meaning that it was time to bring the two streams, black and white, into one body. The church leaders at the meeting all washed each other's feet and asked forgiveness for past racial attitudes and deeds. The theologians conclude: ". . . much work remains."[13] In examining the interpretation of this event, what is missing from this event is reconciliation among other groups. Neither Latinos/as nor women, who have made up at least 50 percent of congregations in most, if not all, Pentecostal denominations are mentioned. Where is their Memphis Miracle? While the Pentecostal theological prism Sutton and Mittelstadt is not deficient for the faithful, neither is it sufficient since it does not address the role of power and privilege in shaping an event and its history.

Paradox

How can you lose your life and, in doing so, save it? How is it possible for there to be three different people in one transcendent God? These paradoxes have perplexed Christian thinkers for two millennia. In addition to these, Pentecostalism has its own conundrums. For Spirit-powered Pentecostals, how does a converted person live supernaturally, and yet live a life filled with perpetual temptation, struggle, sin, and failure? How does a faith rooted in a world-denying, high-tension hatred of this world, a movement that still brands itself as being part of the "last wave" before the end of time, become the global leader of a this-worldly, low-tension love of material wealth that enriches them upon prayerful request? We cannot begin to take each one of these paradoxes and explore them fully since each requires their own theological and philosophical treatment, both of which are gladly outside the scope of this book. In the waning pages of this book, what is left is to examine these paradoxes and where U.S. Pentecostalism has been and where it may be going. Pentecostalism, unlike its Holiness relatives, added a physical component to the certainty that once they knew they were "saved," they were regenerated people with a supernatural experience that made life easier to navigate. However, conversion comes first. Spirit baptism, for classical Pentecostals, is still hierarchical, the initial evidence of speaking in tongues being the first gift that makes the rest possible. Pentecostals, especially some denominations, are very meticulous about counting these categories. Keeping track of salvations, of recommitments, Spirit baptisms, and healings are still part of nearly every denomination's literature. Conversion is a singular event in which a person who would otherwise spend an eternity in the absence of God is transformed into one who will spend an eternity with God. Conversion is, thus, a totalizing event, possible through belief in Jesus. It does not, however, obviate moral failures. When these occur, repentance and regeneration are the answers. Public figures especially are subject to the need for a repentance narrative. This kind of choice works if the public figure's persona is useful for building the movement. Elvis, Marvin Gaye, Sly Stone, Katy Perry, Joe Jonas, and Axl Rose (to name a few) all have Pentecostal backgrounds. If they are not "living out their faith," they must show signs of struggle and contrition to come back to the fold. Elvis and Gaye did not use their talents in church, which is why their struggles remained outside the context of a redeeming narrative. Pentecostals know about these "celebrity" ex-Pentecostals, and they also know that they do not need to look to celebrities to understand the paradox of conversion. Conversion literally opens the gates of heaven; it directs the thousands of steps that redeemed people must take in trying to live that perfected life. Pentecostals have no use for bloodless conversion that does not immediately transform. Yet Pentecostals instinctively know that conversion is a process; it transforms unequally, and sometimes it does not transform at all.

That said, Pentecostalism's genius is that it takes on the character of the lands where it's planted. The movement's insistence on radical transformation of behavior and belief has not wavered in over one hundred years of missionary activity. Emphasis on healing, especially in areas of desperate need, focus on demonic exorcism in other areas—Pentecostalism offers both. But the most recent export, the prosperity gospel, may be its most popular brand yet. Indeed, Pentecostalism's zealousness, born out of a deep theological conviction that this was the prophesized "last wave" of the Spirit before the *eschaton*, makes it a world-denying faith. This faith rails continually against the loss of holiness in the world and the unhallowed prince unleashing his legions into this world.

But while this world is doomed, God has predetermined the ultimate victory, and in the interim, Pentecostals take advantage of other blessings summoned down from the heavens. These are not abstract: they include healing, material wealth, and the insistence that accumulating that wealth is fine. In addition to theological certainty and a bounty of spiritual gifts, people want healing from ailments, from diseases, and from poverty—when institutions and governments do not fulfill their roles, people look for other avenues. People want certainty, even if it is not terribly convincing to outsiders, and they want to believe. When it comes to the prosperity gospel, it works because people do not have to see any tangible results; all they have to do is believe that these results are coming, assuming they have faith. And because Pentecostalism offers both the avenue to faith and so much else to so many, it continues to grow.

I have conversed with Pentecostals for years. Most of them are of a different social, economic, and political stripe than your typical U.S. Pentecostal. Most Pentecostals I know are colleagues, highly educated, upper middle class, politically moderate to liberal, and personally their theologies veer from traditionally Pentecostal to more universalist than they admit or are comfortable with. So, when we discuss these issues, for me, there is an abstract quality to framing my questions and answers. The prosperity gospel, for me, is fascinating; it's awe-inspiring because of its estrangement from classic Christian theology, and yet it is one of the largest growth areas in global Christianity. For my Pentecostal colleagues, the prosperity gospel is a theological aberration, something that pains them. They wonder how a movement they have spent their lives in has fallen so far so fast away from the core tenets of historic Christianity. For my colleagues, the tangible working of the Holy Spirit is why they are still, in some fashion, affixed to the label, Pentecostal. Faith for them is not abstract, like most of the hundreds of people whom I have interviewed over twenty years; their Pentecostalism is rooted in family, church, worship, and social networks that maintain the core of their commitments for generations. These beliefs cause joy to some and pain to others who can no longer follow them. The rigor of holiness standards maintains people's steadfastness in this movement, and serves as a bulwark against those who have given themselves over to the "world." Those same standards have hurt people and ostracized others who have struggled through divorce and sat pained with their sexualities unreconciled. Certainly, Pentecostalism is not the only Christian movement with high-tension demands that may be too much for some and often viewed as unnecessary for others. There are subjects that this book barely touched upon that await more study, more ruminations, more talking to people about how this faith shapes their lives. Pentecostals tell great stories. I can't conclude this book by telling you I believe any or all of them, but I think after all these years, I understand why they work, why people believe them, and why a movement that has as many strands and strains as Pentecostalism does will continue to befuddle its detractors, fascinate its observers, and comfort its followers.

NOTES

Introduction

1. The Azusa Street Revival began in the spring of 1906 and ended in 1909. Headed by William J. Seymour, the revival is considered by adherents, a revival that launched the modern-day Pentecostal movement in the United States. The most striking characteristics of the revival—its multiracial/multiethnic make-up, its gender balance, and its catalytic spark of literally dozens of denominations and missions efforts—are all parts of events whose factual contents are not in question, but certainly what Azusa Street meant and means today are certainly up for contention.

2. Inspired by sociologists Peter Berger and Thomas Luckmann, I attempt to tackle something as fluid as prophecy as something I call a "prophetic imperative," meaning Pentecostals deploy and re-invent prophecy often based on predetermined vested interests. This is akin to the way Pentecostals tell and re-tell their stories, to best meet the interests of their intended audiences. In terms of beliefs, rather than spending a significant amount of time arguing over whether Pentecostals are evangelicals or not (there are arguments on both sides), it may suffice to say that however evangelicalism in America defines itself today it seems very similar to Pentecostalism, perhaps without as much supernatural activity and emphasis, without as much emphasis on things like the prosperity gospel, but certainly in terms of the emphasis on Biblicism, the exclusivity of Jesus as savior, and the urgency of evangelism. Pentecostals exhibit those traits and more. As such, I don't have problems in using charismatic Christians like Agnes Sanford, because her experiences with the Holy Spirit and her emphasis on healing fit the kinds of people I am including in this book. For more, please see Peter Berger and Thomas Luckmann, *The Social Construction of Reality: A Treatise in the Sociology of Knowledge* (New York: Anchor Books, 1967).

3. The historiography of the Holiness movement often suffers from the same kind of reliance on timelines and details about who founded particular churches at what particular time, when someone left to form another church, and so on. Many of the books are self-consciously confessional, including *The Holiness-Pentecostal Tradition* by noted Pentecostal historian Vinson Synan (Grand Rapids, Mich.: Eerdmans, 1997), which is typical of monographs that seek to trace the movement in purely theological terms and assume that theological lineages are straight lines from one pulpit to another. Other notable works such as Donald Dayton's *Theological Roots of Pentecostalism* (Ada, Mich.: Baker, 1991) and the collections of bibliographic information on the Holiness movement by Charles E. Jones are likewise not detached from the movement. But over the last twenty years, several scholars have published some of the most evocative and engaging histories of American Pentecostalism from vantage points that move the lens away from denominational history and hagiographic biography. Books such as Daniel Ramírez's *Migrating Faiths* (Chapel Hill: University of North Carolina Press, 2015), Leah Payne's *Gender and Revivalism* (New York: Palgrave Macmillan, 2015), Kate Bowler's *Blessed* (New York: Oxford University Press, 2013), and Angela Tarango's *Choosing the Jesus Way* (Chapel Hill: University of North Carolina Press, 2014) are reshaping the field and changing the way American religious history treats U.S. Pentecostalism.

4. The literature on Seymour by Pentecostals and scholars of the movement is vast. While Douglas Nelson was one of the first to compile Seymour's wide-ranging story from his Catholic baptism to his years in the Holiness movement to his eventual leadership of Azusa Street, others have followed a rather extensive paper trail on Seymour and seek to ensure that Seymour is not forgotten as the legitimate "founder" of the Azusa Street Mission. Others take a more scholarly tone. Of particular note are Gaston Espinosa's *William Seymour and the Origins of Global Pentecostalism* (Durham, N.C.: Duke University Press, 2014) and Justin Doran's dissertation on "The Heartfelt Spirit: Capitalism, Affect, and Pentecostal Modernity in the Americas" (University of Texas, Austin, 2016).

5. G. T. Haywood is a lesser known figure among the more dominant Trinitarian branches, but among Oneness followers he is legendary. Unfortunately, the same issue that plagues much of Pentecostal history is evident in the most comprehensive work on Haywood by Talmadge Leon French. While his dissertation "Early Oneness Pentecostalism, Garfield T. Haywood, and the Interracial Pentecostal Assemblies of the World, 1906–1931" (Birmingham University, 2011) has an astounding amount of information, it also goes in for some lionizing of Haywood. When French calls Haywood's achievements "staggering" (14) and explains that they contributed to the growth of African American Oneness traditions, he is writing in a genre in which the achievements of "founders" are often placed in the context of whether their brand of Pentecostalism grew or not. If it did, it was because God's hand was on the movement. Growth means people have been going to church; they have joined churches, and by extension, they have been "saved."

6. According to Apostolic Faith Church's (the denominations uses Apostolic Faith Mission and Church interchangeably) "History," Crawford had a revelation from God on a trip to Minnesota where God told her to go back to Portland. Crawford "gave up" her home in Los Angeles and moved back to Portland in 1908. The official history also discounts the case of the purloined mailing list, stating that "Azusa Street turned over the existing 22 copies of the mailing list and transferred responsibility to her of publishing the paper." The "paper" in question was Azusa Street's newspaper, *The Apostolic Faith*. For more, see "History," Apostolic Faith Mission (Portland, Ore.: Apostolic Faith Mission), 2005, http://apostolicfaith.org/Portals/0/Index/History%20Book/afchistorybook/index.html, 36–37.

7. Unless otherwise noted, the sources from the following section are all from: Apostolic Faith Mission, "History."

8. Tanya M. Luhrmann, *When God Talks Back: Understanding the American Evangelical Relationship with God* (New York: Alfred A. Knopf, 2012), loc. 2063.

9. See Chas. H. Barfoot, *Aimee Semple McPherson and the Making of Modern Pentecostalism, 1890–1926* (New York: Routledge, 2014), 139–40.

1. Pentecostal Faith and Practice

1. Folklorist Elaine Lawless's work in the late 1980s and early 1990s among Oneness Pentecostals in the Midwest is instrumental to my own understanding of how narratives not only of healing, but of conversion and spiritual growth work together to create what Lawless termed "spiritual life stores," which are pastiches of oral traditions, culturally conditioned responses, and often New Testament motifs, intermingled together with the experiential tangibles of Pentecostal practice to create the holistic version of one's faith story. Within that story, certain "events" cannot be empirically proven as having occurred or in the exact order that the adherent claims, and in fact, it is not important to verify such things. What is important is that spiritual life stories operate very much like a childhood game of "telephone." A narrative of healing then starts as one person's story, then becomes another person's testimony to the "truth" of the event, and so on, the point being to shore up adherents' belief that healing is possible. For more, please see Elaine J. Lawless, "Rescripting Their Lives and Their Narratives: The Spiritual Life Stories of Pentecostal Women Preachers," *Journal of Feminist Studies in Religion* 7, no. 1 (1991): 58.

2. "Spirit and Power—A 10-Country Survey of Pentecostals," Pew Research Center's Religion & Public Life Project, October 4, 2006, http://www.pewforum.org/2006/10/05/spirit-and-power/.

3. Benedict Carey, "A Neuroscientific Look at Speaking in Tongues," *New York Times*, November 11, 2006.

4. Douglas Jacobsen, *Thinking in the Spirit: The Theologies of the Early Pentecostal Movement* (Bloomington: University of Indiana Press, 2003), 49–50.

5. Charles F. Parham, "A Voice Crying in the Wilderness: Kol Kare Bomidbar," (Bishop's Waltham, U.K.: Revival Library, 2014), 29. Kindle.

6. Jacobsen, *Thinking in the Spirit*, 25.

7. Parham, "A Voice Crying in the Wilderness," 26.

8. Sarah Parham, *Life of Charles Parham* (Baxter Springs, Kans.: Apostolic Faith Bible College, 1930), 163.

9. Phil Jackson, *Sacred Hoops: Spiritual Lessons of a Hardwood Warrior* (New York: Hyperion, 1996), 29–30.

10. Tanya Luhrmann's work exploring charismatic evangelicals in the Vineyard denomination says much about how other charismatically oriented Christians approach the perpetually vexing question of theodicy. According to Luhrmann, they simply ignore it. In fact in many quarters, the subject of why healing does not occur never comes up. Luhrmann sums up the charismatic view: "When God is very close and very powerful and always very loving, there is no easy explanation when he does not deliver" (Tanya Luhrmann, *When God Talks Back: Understanding the American Evangelical Relationship with God* [New York: Alfred A. Knopf, 2012], Kindle loc. 5460).

11. In its early years, the Pentecostal Holiness Church did not allow its members to go to doctors, though the policy did later change. Recently, questions arose when members of televangelist Kenneth Copeland's Eagle Mountain Church in Texas refused measles vaccinations and an outbreak ensued. See Lauren Silverman, "Texas Megachurch at Center of Measles Outbreak," NPR, September 1, 2013, http://www.npr.org/2013/09/01/217746942/texas-megachurch-at-center-of-measles-outbreak. For more on the legal matters of the Church of the First Born, see Kyle Odegard, "Rossiters Set for Trials; Court Paperwork Details Faith-Healing Church," *Albany Democrat Herald*, February 20, 2014, accessed July 21, 2015, http://democratherald.com/news/local/crime-and-courts/rossiters-set-for-trials-court-paperwork-details-faith-healing-church/article_53bee87c-99cd-11e3-8321-0019bb2963f4.html.

12. Parham, A *Voice Crying in the Wilderness*, 41.

13. Stuart Blume and Ingrid Geesink, "A Brief History of Polio Vaccines," *Science* 288, no. 5471 (2000): 1593–94. doi:10.1126/science.288.5471.1593.

14. "A Failure of Faith in a Faith Healer," *Life*, March 5, 1956.

15. Information on Coe's arrest and trial from ibid. Coe's sermon, "Jack Coe, Practicing Medicine Without a License," can be viewed on YouTube at https://youtu.be/Bns7osifxao.

16. Websites run by Jack Coe's son do not mention his father's death, but in other websites physical exhaustion or overwork is a common rationale for the deaths of famous healing evangelists who do not receive healing. Coe, McPherson, Allen, and others' deaths are attributed to working too hard. For more, see http://www.jackcoe.org/.

17. Candy Gunther Brown, *Testing Prayer* (New York: Oxford University Press, 2012), 118.

18. Meredith B. McGuire, *Ritual Healing in Suburban America* (New Brunswick, N.J.: Rutgers University Press, 1998), 35.

19. Roland Barthes, *Mythologies* (New York: Hill and Wang, 1972), 117.

20. Joshua Rothman, "The Church of U2," *New Yorker*, September 16, 2014, http://www.newyorker.com/culture/cultural-comment/church-u2.

21. Matthew A. Sutton's *American Apocalypse* (Cambridge, Mass.: Harvard University Press, 2015) is the latest and more specific work on how evangelicals construct their various premillennial schemas throughout the twentieth century. Another important work is the classic by Paul Boyer, *When Time Shall Be No More* (Cambridge, Mass.: Harvard University Press, 2009).

22. Nils G. Holm, "Pentecostalism: Conversion and Charismata," *International Journal for the Psychology of Religion* 1, no. 2 (1991): 136–37, doi: http://dx.doi.org/10.1207/s15327582ijpr0103_1.

23. Ibid.

24. According to Berger and Luckmann, subjective reality is always depended upon specific plausibility structures, a specific social base, and social processes that maintain it. See Peter L. Berger and Thomas Luckmann, *The Social Construction of Reality: A Treatise in the Sociology of Knowledge* (New York: Anchor, 1967), 136.

2. Pentecostal Innovators

1. Kate Bowler, *Blessed: A History of the American Prosperity Gospel* (New York: Oxford University Press, 2013), 48.

2. "Zion Home of Hope for Erring Women," *Leaves of Healing* 6, no. 1 (October 28, 1899): 10.

3. "The Story of Zion," *Leaves of Healing* 6, no. 1 (October 28, 1899), 3.

4. J. A. Dowie, "The Flogging of Amos Dresser," *Leaves of Healing* 3, no. 42 (August 14, 1897): 657.

5. Ibid.

6. William D. Faupel, "Theological Influences on the Teachings and Practices of John Alexander Dowie," *Pneuma* 29, no. 2 (2007): 235, doi:10.1163/157007407 x237935.

7. Faupel, "Theological Influences," 235.

8. "The Masses Are Unfitted to Rule Themselves," *Leaves of Healing* 15, no. 26 (October 9, 1904): 895.

9. Faupel, "Theological Influences," 230.

10. Ibid., 502.

11. Grant Wacker, "Marching to Zion: Religion in a Modern Utopian Community," *Church History* 54, no. 4 (1985): 499, doi: 10.2307/3166516.

12. Quoted in Gordon P. Gardiner, "The Apostle of Divine Healing: The Story of John Alexander Dowie," www.hopefaithprayer.com/ . . . /Apostle%28Dowie%29ofDivineHealing-Gordon, 12.

13. Ibid., 9

14. Faupel, "Theological Influences," 238.

15. John Alexander Dowie, "What Should a Christian Do When Sick," *Leaves of Healing* 8, no. 39 (July 24, 1897): 617.

16. Quoted in Dennis Gordon Lindsay, *John Alexander Dowie: A Life Story of Trials, Tragedies, and Triumphs* (Dallas: Christ for the Nations, 1980), 74.

17. Ibid., 31.

18. Ibid.

19. Probably the most exhaustive history of Azusa Street is Mel Robeck's *Azusa Street Mission and Revival* (New York: Thomas Nelson, 2006). Though Robeck does not hide his affinity for Pentecostalism's religious goals (he is an Assemblies of God minister), for sheer information and primary source material Robeck's book is an invaluable contribution to the field. At the same time, Joe Creech's article casting doubt on the mythos surrounding Azusa Street is also an important and much-needed corrective. See Joe Creech, "Visions of Glory: The Place of the Azusa Street Revival in Pentecostal History," *Church History* 65, no. 3 (1996): 405–24, doi: 10.2307/3169938.

20. James Goff, *Fields White unto Harvest: Charles F. Parham and the Missionary Origins of Pentecostalism* (Fayetteville: University of Arkansas Press, 1988), 121.

21. Parham's racial views are well-known, as is his infamous quote calling Seymour a "big, buck, nigger." See Charles Parham, *Apostolic Faith*, December 1, 1912, 4–5.

22. The inductive method has roots in the late nineteenth-century's evangelical seminary culture, which in order to counter the influence of Higher Criticism, held that the Bible could be read by anyone, in "their own mother tongue" and discover the truth for themselves. As such, the inductive method accomplished two things: (1) it rendered the need to learn biblical languages moot and (2) it validated the supremacy of English as equally as effective in rendering the truth found in the Bible to both the educated seminary professor and common reader alike—a very important part of evangelicalism's democratizing process. For this insight into the inductive method, I am grateful to my colleague, Dr. Lynn Losie.

23. Historian Douglas Jacobsen's otherwise admirable book *Thinking in the Spirit* repeats Parham's biographical note on how he read the Bible as an entirely unbiased reader. Jacobsen does not take issue with this statement, and therefore fails to question how Parham's theological development, particularly his hermeneutical strategy, affected the initial evidence doctrine, and especially Parham's integration of British Israelism and white supremacy in his eschatological scheme. See Douglas Jacobsen, *Thinking in the Spirit* (Bloomington: Indiana University Press, 2002), 20.

24. Ibid., 49.

25. Ibid., 27.

26. Parham's racist invective against Seymour also had to do with the interracial nature of Azusa Street. Especially galling for Parham was that white women interacted too closely with African American men. See Charles Parham, *Apostolic Faith*, December 1, 1912, 4–5.

27. Scholars have noted that Parham was probably exposed to British Israelism at Frank Sandford's Holy Ghost and Us Bible School in Shiloh, Maine. According

to historian Leslie Callahan, Parham subscribed to the view that God created two different species of humanity, during two different epochs of creation. The first species was created on the sixth day, and on the eighth day, the Adamic race was formed from the dust; it was this latter race that fell victim to the Fall. This view answers the age-old question of where Cain got his first wife; that is, the first child of the eighth-day humans married a woman of the sixth-day humans in what amounted to the first intermarriage. For Parham, this serves as the real beginning of the Fall: "This be a woeful inter-marriage of races for which cause the flood was sent as punishment." See Leslie Callahan, "Redeemed or Destroyed: Re-evaluating the Social Dimensions of Bodily Destruction in the Thought of Charles Parham," *Pneuma* 28, no. 2 (2006): 203–27, doi: 10.1163/157007406778689951.

28. Parham, "A Voice Crying in the Wilderness: Kol Kare Bomidbar" (Bishop's Waltham, U.K.: Revival Library, 2014), 118. Kindle.

29. Ibid., 6.

30. Ibid., 103.

31. Ibid., 90.

32. Callahan, "Redeemed or Destroyed," 204.

33. Ibid., 227.

34. Parham, quoted in ibid., 211.

35. Parham, "A Voice Crying in the Wilderness," 28.

36. Ibid., 16.

37. Ibid., 126.

38. Charles F. Parham and Sarah E. Parham, *Selected Sermons of Charles F. Parham [and] Sarah E. Parham* (Baxter Springs, Kans.: Apostolic Faith Bible College, 1941), 2, 25.

39. Ibid., 48.

40. Goff, *Fields White unto Harvest*, 22.

41. Jarod Roll, "From Revolution to Reaction: Early Pentecostalism, Radicalism, and Race in Southeast Missouri, 1910–1930," *Radical History Review* 90, no. 1 (Fall 2004): 9.

42. Ibid., 10.

43. Historian Leah Payne suggests that by manipulating her public image, and adopting assertive preaching and worship styles, McPherson made herself acceptable to a male-dominated movement. For more, see Leah Payne, *Gender and Revivalism: Making a Female Ministry in the Early 20th Century* (New York: Palgrave Macmillan, 2015).

44. Gilbert González, *Culture of Empire: American Writers, Mexico, and Mexican Immigrants, 1880–1930* (Austin: University of Texas Press, 2003), 143.

45. Richard Rayner, *A Bright and Guilty Place: Murder, Corruption, and L.A.'s Scandalous Coming of Age* (New York: Anchor, 2009), 27.

46. Grant Wacker, *Heaven Below: Early Pentecostals and American Culture* (Cambridge, Mass.: Harvard University Press, 2001), 107.

47. Matthew A. Sutton, *Aimee Semple McPherson and the Resurrection of Christian America* (Cambridge, Mass.: Harvard University Press, 2009), 26–27.

48. Ibid., 75.

49. Rodney Stark and Roger Finke, in describing the church-sect theory set forth by Reinhold Niebuhr, posit the idea that high-tension faiths involve a certain "degree of distinctiveness, separation and antagonism between a religious group and the 'outside' world." Pentecostalism fits the definition of "high tension" because it offers "close relations with the supernatural and distinctive demands for membership without isolating individuals from the culture around them." For more, see Roger Finke and Rodney Stark, "The New Holy Clubs: Testing Church to Sect Propositions," *Sociology of Religion* 62, no. 2 (2001): 176, doi: 10.2307/3712454.

50. Collective representation, Durkheim's concept of how religious leaders often take on the task of representing the entire faith to the outside world, is useful here. Accordingly, their faith stories all are usable to promote the faith. For more, see Émile Durkheim, *Elementary Forms of Religious Life* (London: G. Allen & Unwin, 1976).

51. A. A. Allen and Lexie Allen, *The Life and Ministry of A.A. Allen*, ed. John W. Carver Jr. (Westminster, Md.: Faith Outreach International, 2010), 98–100.

52. "A. A. Allen's Life Story: The Early Years," *Early Life*, Miracle Valley Archives, accessed May 1, 2017, http://www.miraclevalleyarchives.org/gpage16.html.

53. Ronald L. Baker, "*Miracle* Magazine in the Sixties: Mass Media Narratives of Healings and Blessings," *Journal of American Folklore* 118, no. 468 (2005): 205–6.

54. The drunk driving event, like much else in Allen's controversial career, is filled with alternative "facts" about whether Allen's drink at dinner was spiked by envious ministers who wanted to see Allen taken down. Or, if one believes the skeleton of the story, Allen did drive under the influence and did jump bail rather than face investigation. Subsequently, Assemblies of God superintendent Ralph Riggs asked Allen to cease his ministry until the authorities completed an investigation of the matter. In response, Allen voluntarily turned in his ministerial license to the AG and was independently ordained by his own organization, the Miracle Revival Fellowship. Allen also resigned from Gordon Lindsay's organization, the Voice of Healing. That website published a sympathetic account of the event. For a small sample of the accounts of this event, see http://www.voiceofhealing.info/03healingrevival/overview.html; and Roberts Liardon, *God's Generals: Why They Succeeded and Why Some Failed* (Tulsa: Albury Publishing, 1997), 356–57.

55. Bowler, *Blessed*, 74.

56. Ibid., 208.

57. Ibid.

58. A. A. Allen, "Prosperity, The Cadillac," https://www.youtube.com/watch?v=8KILo5z3tsY&feature=em-share_video_user.

59. Baker, "*Miracle* Magazine in the Sixties," 208.

60. A. A. Allen, "One Body, Racism," https://www.youtube.com/watch?v=8ZtY86LVAvU&index=26&list=PLE6EEBBBC75FA39E4.

61. Baker, "*Miracle Magazine*," 213.

62. Allen's controversial death, like his life, did not escape a flurry of accusations of conspiracy. Many devout followers did not and still do not believe Allen died surrounded by pills and alcohol. The most intriguing flourish to the story is located in the electronic Miracle Valley Archive. A former student at the Miracle Valley Bible College supposedly sent a letter to the organization offering their testimony about Allen's death. Opening the mail one day, a worker discovered a check for $10,000 with a letter. The letter was allegedly from the coroner who examined Allen. Dr. Henry Turkel, coroner for San Francisco, wrote to ask for forgiveness because he stated that Allen died of cirrhosis of the liver attributed to acute alcoholism. Before the organization could arrange a meeting with Dr. Turkel, he committed suicide. "To Whom It May Concern," Miracle Valley Archives Department, http://www.miraclevalleyarchives.org/gpage2.html.

63. Robert Anglen, "Don Stewart: A Life In Pursuit of God's Reward," AZCentral.com, May 4, 2009, http://archive.azcentral.com/news/articles/2009/05/04/20090504charities-stewart0504.html.

64. On the other end of the transgressive spectrum is performance artist and former Pentecostal Ron Athey, who has disavowed his religious upbringing, mocks Pentecostal practices such as speaking in tongues, and engages in sadomasochistic acts. On the other hand, the behavior of other transgressive "performers" such as Ted Haggard, Jimmy Swaggart, and gospel singer Donnie McClurkin, who are all still avowed Christians, can be used as a way to build the ongoing redemption narratives that Pentecostals rely on to demonstrate the need for repentance and the certainty of their faith.

3. Gender, Sexualities, and Pentecostalism

1. Women's ordination, as sociologist Margaret Poloma demonstrates in her work on the Assemblies of God, is still problematic since the role of senior pastor is often beyond their reach. See Margaret M. Poloma, *Assemblies of God at the Crossroads: Charisma and Institutional Dilemmas* (Knoxville: University of Tennessee Press, 1989).

2. To recap, McPherson was accused of having an affair with a radio engineer and fabricating her kidnapping to cover it up. Parham was arrested in 1907 on sodomy charges after being found in a red-light district area of San Antonio, Texas, with a younger male. See chapter 2 for discussion of both.

3. A quick perusal at of Amazon's Christian book section shows that there are over four thousand titles on sexuality and over three thousand under the "Marriage and Sex" category. The majority of these books focus on heterosexual married

relationships and sex within those relationships. Those books that concern single people emphasize the ideal of chastity.

4. See Arlene M. Sánchez Walsh, *Latino Pentecostal Identity* (New York: Columbia University Press, 2003).

5. Amy DeRogatis's excellent work does an exceptional job of tracing the evolution of evangelical purity culture from youth to young adult. For more, please see Amy DeRogatis, *Saving Sex: Sexuality and Salvation in American Evangelicalism* (New York: Oxford University Press, 2014), Kindle.

6. *Emmanuel College Student Handbook 2016–2017* (Franklin Springs, Ga.: Emmanuel College), http://www.ec.edu/life/student-handbook-0.

7. Ibid.

8. In the last five to ten years alone, over three thousand books discussing dating and prohibitions against dating have been published, most of them focusing on staying pure while you search for your perfect mate.

9. *Elim Bible Institute and College Student Handbook* (Lima, N.Y.: Elim Bible Institute), http://www.elim.edu/connect/student-resources/.

10. Ibid.

11. Roger Finke and Rodney Stark, *Churching of America, 1776–2005: Winners and Losers in American Religious Economy* (New Brunswick, N.J.: Rutgers University Press, 2008), chaps. 3–5.

12. Sociologist Phil Zuckerman supports what several surveys have found—namely, that New England, the Pacific Northwest, and some of the Rocky Mountain states are the most irreligious in this country. Specifically, Zuckerman found that Oregon, Washington, Colorado, Idaho, Wyoming, Montana, Vermont, New Hampshire, and California contained significant numbers of people who considered themselves irreligious. Phil Zuckerman, "Atheism, Secularity, and Well-Being: How the Findings of Social Science Counter Negative Stereotypes and Assumptions," *Sociology Compass* 3, no. 6 (2009): 952, doi: 10.1111/j.1751-9020.2009.00247.x.

13. Gordon Conwell Theological Seminary, "Fall 2017 Census," accessed December 30, 2017, www.gordonconwell.org.

14. All descriptions are from the *Life Pacific College Student Handbook* (San Dimas, Calif.: Life Pacific College, August 2015).

15. This is taken from the *Evangel University Student Handbook 2017–2018*, Office of Student Development, July 1, 2017. There are many stories about students realizing that these moral and behavioral codes are simply too onerous to bear. In one anecdote, a group of dorm mates established a kind of infraction fund kept in a jar—just in case.

16. According to the U.S. Census of 2010 and a 2010 study by the National Center for Health Statistics, the number of married couples fell below 50 percent for the first time that year (it was 48 percent). In addition, 40 percent of women have never been married, those who do choose to are delaying marriage, and many

are foregoing it all together by cohabitating. See Sabrina Tavernise, "Married Couples Are No Longer a Majority," *New York Times*, May 26, 2011, and Sharon Jayson "Nearly 40% of Women Today Have Never Been Married," *USA Today*, March 22, 2012.

17. Millennials are the first generation to see a distinction between parenting and marriage—probably because of their own social realities with divorced parents. Only 22 percent of millennials are married (though upwards of 70 percent want to be married with children eventually); 51 percent of out-of-wedlock births occur among the millennial demographic. See "For Millennials, Parenthood Trumps Marriage," Pew Research Center, Social and Demographic Trends, March 9, 2011, http://pewsocialtrends.org/files/2011/03/millennials-marriage.pdf.

18. Taking a cue from Benedict Anderson's "imagined communities," I am suggesting that what most Pentecostals believe to be an unchanging stable institution called marriage is in fact culled from their reliance on reading the Bible a certain way—namely, through a literalist hermeneutic that privileges their present ideological conditioning over historical and sociocultural analysis of particular texts. Marriage imaginaries then work like imaginary numbers do in mathematics. They allow the construction of an imagined ideal time when marriage was so sacred that discussions of it as a passé institution were heretical—and like mathematics, the essential concrete application of marriage imaginaries is used to construct as many pathways as possible to marriage as the culmination of one's adult life. See Benedict Anderson, *Imagined Communities: Reflections on the Origins and Spread of Nationalism* (London: Verso, 2016).

19. Here is just a sampling of verses, first from the Old Testament: Gen. 2:24, Exod. 21: 7–11, Deut. 21: 10–14, Deut. 24: 1–2 Neh. 13: 23–30; and from the New Testament: Matt. 5: 31–32, Matt. 19: 3–9, Mark 10: 2–12, Luke 16: 18, 1 Cor. 7: 10–17. The Mark passage is often referred to as the one passage where Jesus seems to forbid divorce in all instances, and thus it is one of the most referred to by denominations that support that position.

20. Religious studies scholar Sean McCloud calls this type of activity "spiritual housecleaning." Though the church in question was an Assemblies of God church, it seems that the belief that demons inhabit objects transferred over from the neo-Pentecostal Third Wave adherents, who became very popular with charismatics and Pentecostals beginning in the 1970s. For more on Third Wave charismatics and demonic possession, see McCloud's *American Possessions: Fighting Demons in Contemporary U.S.* (New York: Oxford University Press, 2015), 10. Kindle.

21. Elim Fellowship, "Statement Concerning Divorce and Remarriage," in Elim Fellowship, Constitution, By-Laws and Policies, www.elimfellowship.org/ef/wp-content/uploads/2015/10/Elim-Fellowship-CBL.pdf.

22. In an age when family values are under severe attack and the traditional foundation of the family seems to be cumbling, the Assemblies of God recognizes the

need for strong teaching on the biblical view of marriage and the family. To read the entire statement on marriage, please see "Marriage," General Council of the Assemblies of God, https://ag.org/Beliefs/Topics-Index/Marriage.

23. "Spirit and Power: A 10-Country Survey of Pentecostals," Pew Research Center, Religion and Public Life Project, October 5, 2006, http://www.pewforum.org/2006/10/05/spirit-and-power/.

24. Quotations taken from both Elim Fellowship's statement on marriage and Assemblies of God's statement on marriage. See elim.fellowship.org/ef-constitution-a-by-laws and ag.org/top/beliefs/relations.

25. Andrew J. Cherlin, "American Marriage in the Early Twenty-First Century," *Future of Children* 15, no. 2 (2005): 33–55. doi: 10.1353/foc.2005.0015.

26. Charles W. Conn, *Where the Saints Have Trod: A History of Church of God Missions* (Cleveland, Tenn.: Pathway Press, 1959), quoted in "Making of a Saint," Church of God, Cleveland, Tenn., www.cogwm.org.

27. Ibid.

28. Hector Avalos, "Maria Atkinson and the Rise of Pentecostalism in the U.S. Mexico Borderlands," *Journal of Religion and Society* 3 (2001): 3–4.

29. Mary I. O'Conner, "Evangelicals in the Lower Mayo Valley," in *Holy Saints and Fiery Preachers: The Anthropology of Protestantism in Mexico*, ed. James W. Dow and Alan Sandstrom (New York: Praeger, 2001).

30. Avalos, "Maria Atkinson," 5.

31. Ibid., 8.

32. Ibid., 8–10.

33. Lerone Martin, *Preaching on Wax: The Phonograph and the Shaping of Modern African American Religion* (New York: New York University Press, 2014), 109–10, 112. Kindle.

34. Gayle F. Wald, "From Spirituals to Swing: Sister Rosetta Tharpe and Gospel Crossover," *American Quarterly* 55, no. 3 (2003): 409–10.

35. I am grateful for the communication about Sister Tharpe from Dr. Gayle Wald, whose *Shout, Sister, Shout! The Untold Story of Rock-and-Roll Trailblazer Sister Rosetta Tharpe* (Boston: Beacon Press, 2007) was instrumental in reframing my ideas about Tharpe and whose hours of interviews with Tharpe's friends provide what little information there is available on how Tharpe viewed her marriages. Email communication, Gayle F. Wald, April 26, 2012.

36. Wald, "From Spirituals to Swing," 411.

37. Ibid., 393.

38. Wald, "The Bride Played Guitar," *Washingtonian*, March 1, 2007, https://www.washingtonian.com/2007/03/01/the-bride-played-guitar-1/.

39. Mick Csaky, dir., "Sister Rosetta Tharpe: The Godmother of Rock and Roll," in *American Masters*, PBS, February 2013.

40. Monique Moultrie, "After the Thrill Is Gone: Married to the Holy Spirit but Still Sleeping Alone," *Pneuma* 33, no. 2 (2011): 243, doi: 10.1163/027209611x575032.

41. Ibid.
42. Quoted in ibid., 241.
43. DeRogatis, *Saving Sex*, 135, 137.
44. "Weddings of the Year," *Ebony*, February 2004, 57.
45. Ibid.
46. Moultrie, *After the Thrill Is Gone*, 255.
47. Gayle Haggard with Angela Elwell Hunt, *Why I Stayed: The Choices I Made In My Darkest Hour* (Carol Stream, Ill.: Tyndale House Publishing, 2010). Haggard's narrative of the early years of their engagement and marriage shows that as a woman raised in a conservative Christian home, she was predisposed to sacrificing her needs to make their marriage work. The first chapter of the book highlights her waitressing job, as she "dreamed" about their wedding while Ted was away on a missions trip. She did not finish her degree at Louisiana State; instead, she went with Ted back to the mission field. She says that she "trusted his discernment."
48. Martha Nussbaum, *From Disgust to Humanity: Sexual Orientation and Constitutional Law* (New York: Oxford University Press, 2010), 148. Kindle.

4. Pentecostalism and Popular Culture

1. Peter Guralnick, *Last Train to Memphis: The Rise of Elvis Presley* (Boston: Little, Brown, 1994), 67.
2. Ibid.
3. Ibid., 68.
4. Ibid., 39.
5. The life story of Elvis's rise to stardom as a singer with Sun Records is very well known, but among the best recollections of his story is the exhaustive two-volume work by Peter Guralnick and the work by music and cultural critic, Greil Marcus, *Mystery Train: Images of America in Rock 'n' Roll Music* (New York: Penguin, 2008). Specifically, see chapters for Elvis's biographical information.
6. Bill C. Malone, *Don't Get above Your Raisin': Country Music and the Southern Working Class* (Champaign: University of Illinois Press, 2002), 90.
7. Gail Sweeney, "The King of White Trash: Elvis Presley and the Aesthetics of Excess," in *White Trash: Race and Class in America*, eds. Matt Wray and Annalee Newitz (New York: Routledge, 1997), 253.
8. Michael T. Bertrand, *Race, Rock and Elvis* (Champaign: University of Illinois Press, 2000), 103.
9. Ibid., 217.
10. Paul Harvey, *Freedom's Coming: Religious Culture and the Shaping of the South from the Civil War through the Civil Rights Era* (Chapel Hill: University of North Carolina Press, 2005), 167.
11. It has only been relatively recently that classical Pentecostalism has credited its African American roots—and most of that came from being pushed to do so by the

influential work of German historian Walter Hollenweger, who challenged the prevailing conceit that Charles Parham was the "founder" of American Pentecostalism.

12. Bertrand, *Race, Rock and Elvis*, 115.
13. Guralnick, *Last Train to Memphis*, 358–59.
14. Ibid., 376.
15. Bertrand, *Race, Rock and Elvis*, 153.
16. Guralnick, *Last Train to Memphis*, 320.
17. Marcus, *Mystery Train*, 157.
18. Ibid., 140.
19. Guralnick, *Last Train to Memphis*, 331.
20. Ibid.
21. Betty Friedan, *The Feminine Mystique* (New York: Norton, 2001), 267. Kindle.
22. Agnes Sanford, *Sealed Orders* (Plainfield, N.J.: Logos International, 1972), 87.
23. Ibid., 89.
24. Ibid., 96.
25. Ibid., 91.
26. Ibid., 94.
27. Pavel Hejzlar, *Two Paradigms for Divine Healing: Fred F. Bosworth, Kenneth E. Hagin, Agnes Sanford, and Francis MacNutt in Dialogue* (Leiden: Brill, 2010), http://o-site.ebrary.com.patris.apu.edu/id/10439305.
28. Ibid, 103.
29. Ibid., 247.
30. Ibid., 249.
31. Agnes Sanford, *The Healing Light*, rev. ed. (New York: Ballantine Books, 1983), 110.
32. Charles Zeiders, "The Anthropological and Scientific Case for Psycho-Energetic Healing," *International Journal of Healing and Caring* 3, no. 1 (January 2003): 13.
33. Agnes Sanford, *Behold Your God* (St. Paul, Minn.: Macalester Park, 1958), 34.
34. Sanford, *Healing Light*, 30.
35. Ibid., 36.
36. Ibid., 44.
37. Ibid., 19.
38. Ibid., 115.
39. Gaye's denomination was founded by Bishop Rufus Abraham Reed Johnson, son of a slave. Johnson was born in 1863, raised Methodist, and started what eventually became the House of God as a group called the "Commandment Keepers" in 1914. In 1918, Johnson founded the House of God in Washington, D.C. In an interesting admixture of influences, the House of God incorporated Jewish rituals such as keeping kosher and observing the Sabbath, and did not observe Christian holi-

days such as Christmas or Easter. The House of God is a Oneness denomination of Pentecostalism, meaning that they do not accept the Trinity and baptize members in the name of Jesus only. For more on the origins of this group, see Jacob Dorman, *Chosen People* (New York: Oxford University Press, 2013). Kindle.

40. David Ritz, *Divided Soul: The Life of Marvin Gaye* (New York: McGraw-Hill, 1985), 12.

41. Ibid., 4.

42. Michael Eric Dyson, *Mercy, Mercy Me: The Art, Loves and Demons of Marvin Gaye* (New York: Basic Civitas), 14.

43. Ritz, *Divided Soul*, 23.

44. Ibid., 5.

45. Ibid., 14.

46. Ibid., 132.

47. Ibid., 123.

48. Ibid.

49. Ibid., 30.

50. Dyson, *Mercy, Mercy Me*, 146.

51. Ritz, *Divided Soul*, 151.

52. Ibid, xv.

53. Dyson, *Mercy, Mercy Me*, 80.

54. Ibid.

55. Ritz, *Divided Soul*, 17.

56. Ibid., xv.

57. Marvin Gaye and Ed Townsend, "Let's Get It On," recorded 1973, in *Let's Get It On*, Marvin Gaye, Tamla Records, CD.

58. Marvin Gaye, *Marvin Gaye Says Goodbye* (Soul Immortal, 2009), CD.

59. Marvin Gaye, "The World Is X-Rated," recorded in 1972, in *Motown Remembers Marvin Gaye: Never Before Released Masters*, released 1986, CD.

60. Philip Sinitiere, *Salvation with a Smile: Joel Osteen, Lakewood Church, and American Christianity* (New York: New York University Press, 2015) 39.

61. Edward Wyatt, "Religious Broadcaster Gets Rich Contract for Next Book," *New York Times*, March 15, 2006, http://www.nytimes.com/2006/03/15/business/media/religious-broadcaster-gets-rich-contract-for-next-book.html.

62. Ibid.

63. Charles Brown, "Selling Faith: Marketing Christian Popular Culture to Christian and Non-Christian Audiences," *Journal of Religion and Popular Culture* 24, no. 1 (2012): 124–26, doi: 10.1353/rpc.2012.0001.

64. Christine Miller and Nathan Carlin, "Joel Osteen as Cultural Self-Object: Meeting the Needs of the Group Self and Its Individual Members in and from the Largest Church in America," *Pastoral Psychology* 59, no. 1 (2010): 31, doi: 10.1007/s11089-009-0197-7.

65. Ibid., 39.
66. Ibid.
67. Ibid., 41.

5. Race, Ethnicity, and the Construction of an American Pentecostal Identity

1. Jacob S. Dorman, *Chosen People: The Rise of American Black Israelite Religions* (New York: Oxford University Press, 2013), 98. Kindle.

2. Julie Courtwright, "A Slave to Yellow Peril: The 1886 Chinese Ouster Attempt in Wichita, Kansas," *Great Plains Quarterly* 22, no. 1 (Winter 2002): 23, http://digitalcommons.unl.edu/greatplainsquarterly/2351/. Courtwright writes that in keeping with the general anti-Chinese tenor of the times, and led by the Knights of Labor and the Women's Industrial League, both groups initiated "driving out time."

3. Angela Tarango, *Choosing the Jesus Way: American Indian Pentecostals and the Fight for the Indigenous Principle* (Chapel Hill: University of North Carolina Press, 2014), 8.

4. Ibid., 101.

5. Walter J. Hollenweger, *Pentecostalism: Origins and Development Worldwide* (Peabody, Mass.: Hendrickson, 1997), 23. Additionally there are at least a dozen major works that capture African American Pentecostal history from many perspectives. One that makes a further case for the African roots of African American Pentecostalism is Iain MacRobert's *Black Roots and White Racism of Early Pentecostalism in the United States* (Basingstoke, U.K.: Macmillan, 1988).

6. Jacob S. Dorman's excellent work *Chosen People* is a must-read for anyone interested in these diverse branches of the African American Pentecostal tree; see especially chap. 3.

7. Leonard Lovett, "Perspectives on the Black Origins of the Contemporary Pentecostal Movement," *Journal of the Interdenominational Theological Seminary*, no. 1 (1973): 42.

8. Anthea Butler, *Women in the Church of God in Christ: Making a Sanctified World* (Chapel Hill: University of North Carolina Press, 2007), 20.

9. Estrelda Alexander, *Black Fire: One Hundred Years of African American Pentecostalism* (Downers Grove, Ill.: IVP Academic, 2011), Kindle loc. 3286–313. Alexander's work is a useful contribution to the general understudied field of African American Pentecostalism. Though it veers towards the confessional side, it nevertheless is work that is needed for its vast amounts of information about the subject.

10. H. Norton Browne, "Elder Rosa Horn, Radio Exhorter, Believes in Witchcraft and that She Can Raise the Dead," *Afro American*, October 20, 1934, 5, https://news.google.com/newspapers?nid=UBnQDr5gPskC&dat=19341020&printsec=frontpage&hl=en.

11. Ibid.

12. Ibid.

13. Ibid.

14. Mark Ellis, *Race War and Surveillance: African Americans and the United States Government During World War I* (Bloomington: Indiana University Press, 2001), 66–67. Mississippi draft board workers wanted Mason prosecuted for interfering with the draft, and offered a conspiracy theory that COGIC was funding some of their church building with German backing. When Cowdry's Philadelphia church members who were eligible for the draft refused, the U.S. government seized the church's publications and membership lists.

15. Henry C. Ball, "Work among the Mexicanos in the War Zone," *Pentecostal Evangel*, May 22, 1915, 4.

16. F. C. Hale, "Kingsville," *Pentecostal Evangel*, May 22, 1915, 9.

17. F. C. Hale, "Mexican Work at Ricardo, Tex.," *Pentecostal Evangel*, February 12, 1916, 12.

18. Henry C. Ball, "Missionary Reports," *Latter Rain Evangel*, October 1917, 18.

19. Henry C. Ball, "Untitled," *Weekly Evangel*, March 11, 1916, 12.

20. Alice E. Luce, "Untitled," *Pentecostal Evangel*, October 21, 1916. 13

21. Francisco Olazábal, "Our Near Neighbors," *Latter Rain Evangel*, October 1921, 23.

22. Ibid.

23. For further explanation of the racial dynamics of the home missions work of the AG with Mexicans and Mexicanos, see my *Latino Pentecostal Identity* (New York: Columbia University Press, 2003), chaps. 2–3.

24. Henry C. Ball, "Great Blessing at Latin American Council," *Pentecostal Evangel*, February 13, 1932, 11.

25. Henry C. Ball, "Visit among Our Latin American Brethren," *Pentecostal Evangel*, July 13, 1935, 9.

26. "Anti-Religion in Mexico," *Pentecostal Evangel*, November 10, 1934, 6.

27. Otto Klink, "Otto-Graphs," *Christ's Ambassadors Herald*, June 1935, 16.

28. "Bolshevistic Mexico," *Pentecostal Evangel*, June 22, 1935, 5.

29. "Untitled," *Pentecostal Evangel*, July 16, 1935, 5.

30. "Communism, the Scourge of God," *Bridegroom's Messenger*, May 1936, 7.

31. Historically, Mexico underwent a couple of decades of anti-Catholic sentiment, first under the regime of Plutárco Calles (1924–1926), when churches were closed and Protestant missionaries were forced to leave the country. The Cristero War (1926–1929), in which Mexican Catholics fought back against the government's anti-Catholic policies, is rarely if ever mentioned when Pentecostal magazines write about religious persecution and link it to communism. But perhaps the most virulent anti-Catholicism came from the Lázaro Cárdenas regime, which banned religious instruction from schools, imposed limitations on priests, and set other policies culminating in the killing of over five thousand Catholic laity and priests. Because of the Pentecostal authors' fear of atheism coupled with communism, one suspects

that the Cárdenas regime's land reforms and other redistributive programs would have alarmed them as much as his anti-church policies. For more, see Deborah J. Baldwin, *Protestants and the Mexican Revolution: Missionaries, Ministers, and Social Change* (Champaign: University of Illinois Press, 1990).

32. Ibid.

33. A. A. Allen, "Did God Call the Apostle Paul to Preach to the Black Man?" (MusicXpress, n.d.), MP3.

34. Howard Elinson, "The Implications of Pentecostal Religion for Intellectualism, Politics and Race Relations," *American Journal of Sociology* 70, no. 4 (1965): 406. doi: 10.1086/223874.

35. Ibid.

36. Ibid., 415.

37. Ibid.

38. Urbane Leindecker, "Vision on Miracle Valley," MiracleValley.com, accessed July 12, 2012.

39. John J. Lyon, "The Christ Miracle Healing Center and Church: Racial Crises in Arizona, 1980–1982" (master's thesis, Arizona State University, 2002), 87, 93.

40. Thomas Javier Castillo, dir., *Gun Shot Valley* (incomplete), documentary film (Arizona State University, 2008–2010), miraclevalleydoc.blogspot.com.

41. Lyon, "The Christ Miracle Healing Center and Church," 61.

42. Ibid., 36.

43. Ibid., 146.

44. Ibid. See Lyon, 10, also all of chapter 7 of Lyon's thesis, which is dedicated to a meticulous account of the shoot-out and the events leading up to it.

45. Ben Bradlee Jr., "Church's Dream of Building Oasis Dries Up," *Arizona Courier*, December 19, 1982, https://news.google.com/newspapers?nid=892&dat=19821219&id=NphOAAAAIBAJ&sjid=pUwDAAAAIBAJ&pg=6732,2958477.

46. Ibid.

47. Michael Wilten, quoted in ibid.

48. Quoted in ibid.

49. Melvin Harter, "Shoot-Out in Miracle Valley," MiracleValley.com, accessed July 13, 2013.

50. Ibid.

51. Lyon, "The Christ Miracle Healing Center," 135.

52. Michael O. Emerson with Rodney M. Woo, *People of the Dream: Multiracial Congregations in the U.S.* (Princeton, N.J.: Princeton University Press, 2006). Chapter 6 captures the pitfalls of multicultural church building and the problems with communicating past issues of power.

53. Arlene M. Sánchez Walsh, "Fieldnotes," July 2004, Pasadena Foursquare Church.

54. Duncan Campbell, "Temple Awaits Another Miracle," *Guardian*, July 17, 2000, accessed June 13, 2013.

55. Ibid.

56. Kurt Streeter, "Angelus Temple Will Keep Historic Interior," *Los Angeles Times*, October 15, 2001, accessed June 13, 2013.

57. All the numbers for this section are from the International Church of the Foursquare Gospel's website, www.foursquare.org, accessed May 26, 2016.

6. Outliers in American Pentecostalism

1. There are few works on Kuhlman that do not have an overt confessional bent. An exception is Amy Artman, " 'The Miracle Lady': Kathryn Kuhlman and the Gentrification of Charismatic Christianity in Twentieth-Century America" (Ph.D. diss., University of Chicago, 2009), 24–25.

2. Ibid., 57–58, 62.

3. Artman notes that Kuhlman made charismatic Christianity respectable to a broad audience. I agree and would add that it was not simply Baptists like Kuhlman who popularized the charismatic movement, but Episcopalians like Agnes Sanford who made the movement popular within liturgical movements.

4. "Lonnie Frisbee on Kathryn Kuhlman Show," YouTube, February 10, 2011, https://www.youtube.com/watch?v=U2Ujlhwt9d8

5. Artman, " 'The Miracle Lady,' " 157.

6. Ibid., 243–44. Very much in keeping with future televangelists, Kuhlman's life became subject to the tabloid press, particularly a piece in *People* magazine that alleged that Kartsonakis was Kuhlman's escort and that she became possessive of him. Unethical use of finances earmarked for ministry were also part of the story. See Lois Armstrong, "Kathryn Kuhlman Is Accused of Not Keeping the Faith," *People*, August 11, 1975, http://www.people.com/people/archive/article/0,,20065526,00.html.

7. Joyce Meyer, "List of Confessions," 2008, https://secure.joycemeyer.org/content/articles/ea/list_of_confessions_by_joyce_meyer/listofconfessionsbyjoycemeyer.pdf.

8. Heather Cole, "Meyer's 57 Million Dollar Evangelism Empire," *St. Louis Business Journal*, June 22, 2003. "https://www.bizjournals.com/stlouis/stories/2003/06/23/story2.html.

9. In 2009, Meyer's head of security, Chris Coleman, killed his family to be with his mistress. The ministry soon became embroiled in the murder, with Coleman's in-laws filing a lawsuit against the ministry for not notifying their daughter Sheri of Chris's affair and for possibly knowing that Chris was plotting the murders by sending false email threats to Sheri via work emails. Meyer testified at a closed hearing that she had no knowledge of Chris's affair and suspected nothing awry about Chris's behavior, except that he called in sick the day he killed his family. For more see Joel Christie, "Court Upholds Life Sentence, Televangelism's Bodyguard Strangled Family to Death," *Daily Mail*, January 3, 2015, http://www.dailymail.co.uk/news/article-2895728/Court-upholds-life-sentence-televangelist-s-bodyguard-strangled-family-death-slept-starting-affair-wife-s-childhood-friend.html.

10. Jennifer Heller, "The Search for Something More: Evangelical Women, Middle-Class Marriage, and the 'Problem That Has No Name,' in Popular Advice Books of the 1970s" (Ph.D. diss., University of Kansas, 2007), https://search.proquest.com/docview/304859517/5BD982700E864C34PQ/1?accountid=10226, 2.

11. Carlton Pearson, *The Gospel of Inclusion: Reaching Beyond Religious Fundamentalism to the True Love of God and Self* (New York: Atria, 2014), 73.

12. Two of the most prominent outlets to report on Pearson's story were *Dateline* and *This American Life*. See *Dateline*, "To Hell and Back," featuring Keith Morrison, aired August 13, 2006, on NBC, http://www.nbcnews.com/id/14337492/ns/dateline_nbc/t/hell-back/; and "Heretics," *This American Life*, December 16, 2005, https://www.thisamericanlife.org/radio-archives/episode/304/heretics/.

13. Margaret Ramirez, "Some Christ Universal Temple Members Oppose Rev. Carlton Pearson's Appointment," *Chicago Tribune*, May 11, 2009, http://articles.chicagotribune.com/2009-05-11/news/0905100192_1_new-thought-church-new-storm.

14. Darnise C. Martin, *Beyond Christianity: African Americans in a New Thought Church* (New York: New York University Press, 2005), 41–42.

15. Carleton Pearson, *God Is Not a Christian, nor a Jew, Muslim, Hindu—: God Dwells with Us, in Us, around Us, as Us* (New York: Atria, 2010), 191.

16. Ibid., 57.

17. Carlton Pearson interview with Dr. Michael Beckwith, https://www.youtube.com/watch?v=PsjkDP-yZkM. Also "Neale Donald Walsch, Michael Bernard Beckwith Carlton Pearson & Dr. Marissa," YouTube, February 2, 2016, https://www.youtube.com/watch?v=1goWjrGTAjk.

18. Pearson, *Gospel*, 71.

19. Ibid., 265–66.

20. "Bishop George Bloomer Interviews Bishop Carlton Pearson," YouTube, https://www.youtube.com/watch?v=xoFqIlt1nTg.

21. Jay Bakker, *Son of a Preacher Man: My Search for Grace in the Shadows* (New York: Harper Collins, 2002), 20.

22. Ibid., 35.

23. Ibid., 36.

24. Ibid., xix.

25. Ibid., 37–38.

26. Ibid., 40.

27. Jay Bakker with Martin Edlund, *Fall to Grace: A Revolution of God, Self & Society* (New York: FaithWords, 2014), 104–5.

28. Ibid., 106.

29. Jay Bakker, *Faith, Doubt, and Other Lines I've Crossed: Walking with the Unknown God* (Nashville: Jericho Books, 2013), 119.

30. Max Weber, *On Charisma and Institution Building*, ed. S. N. Eisenstadt (Chicago: University of Chicago Press, 1968), 57–58.

Epilogue

1. Joseph Liu, "Christian Movements and Denominations," Pew Research Center, Religion & Public Life Project, December 18, 2011, http://www.pewforum.org/2011/12/19/global-christianity-movements-and-denominations/.
2. Ibid.
3. Ibid.
4. Candy Gunther Brown, ed., *Global Pentecostal and Charismatic Healing* (New York: Oxford University Press, 2011).
5. The figures for the Assemblies of God are from the following: https://ag.org/About/Statistics. The figures for the Church of God, Cleveland, Tennessee and the Church of God in Christ are from the following: Pew Research Center, Religion and Public Life, "Religious Landscape Survey: Members of the Church of God (Cleveland, Tennessee)," http://www.pewforum.org/religious-landscape-study/religious-denomination/church-of-god-cleveland-tennessee/; and Pew Research Center, Religion and Public Life, "Religious Landscape Study: Racial and Ethnic Composition among Members of the Church of God in Christ," http://www.pewforum.org/religious-landscape-study/religious-denomination/church-of-god-in-christ/racial-and-ethnic-composition/.
6. Marilynn S. Johnson, *The Second Gold Rush: Oakland and the East Bay in World War II* (Berkeley: University of California Press, 1996), 133–34.
7. Ibid.
8. Jeff Kaliss, *I Want to Take You Higher: The Life and Times of Sly and the Family Stone* (Milwaukee: Backbeat, 2008), 2.
9. "Small Talk about Sly, part 2: Vet Stone & Cynthia Robinson, Documentary on Sly and the Family Stone," YouTube, January 25, 2016, https://www.youtube.com/watch?v=6CqK8EEC6Fc.
10. "Sly's Lil Sis," accessed April 29, 2017, http://www.slyslilsis.com/index1.cfm.
11. Frank Bartleman, *How Pentecost Came to Los Angeles* (Grand Rapids, Mich.: Christian Classics Ethereal Library, 1925), 54, https://www.ccel.org/ccel/bartleman/los.html.
12. "Small Talk about Sly, part 1: Cornel West, Sly & the Family Stone Documentary," YouTube, January 23, 2016, https://www.youtube.com/watch?v=iBh9D3BGo3g.
13. Geoffrey W. Sutton and Martin W. Mittelstadt, "Loving God and Loving Others: Learning About Love From Psychological Science and Pentecostal Perspectives," *Journal of Psychology and Christianity* 31, no. 2 (2012): 160–61.

BIBLIOGRAPHY

Articles and Essays

"A. A. Allen's Life Story: The Early Years." *Early Life*. Accessed May 1, 2017. http://www.miraclevalleyarchives.org/gpage16.html.

"AG USA Adherents by Race 2001–2016." Assemblies of God. Springfield, MO.: Assemblies of God, 2016. https://ag.org/About/Statistics.

Anglen, Robert. "Don Stewart: A Life in Pursuit of God's Reward." AZCentral .com, May 4, 2009. http://archive.azcentral.com/news/articles/2009/05/04/20090504charities-stewart0504.html.

"Anti-Religion in Mexico." *Pentecostal Evangel*, November 10, 1934, 6.

Armstrong, Lois. "Kathryn Kuhlman Is Accused of Not Keeping the Faith." *People*, August 11, 1975. http://people.com/archive/kathryn-kuhlman-is-accused-of-not-keeping-the-faith-vol-4-no-6/.

"Asa Alonso Allen." *The Voice of Healing*. 2011. http://www.voiceofhealing .info/05otherministries/allen.html.

Avalos, Hector. "Maria Atkinson and the Rise of Pentecostalism in the U.S. Mexico Borderlands." *Journal of Religion and Society* 3 (January 1, 2001): 1–20. https://works.bepress.com/hector_avalos/1/.

Baker, Ronald L. "*Miracle Magazine* in the Sixties: Mass Media Narratives of Healings and Blessings." *Journal of American Folklore* 118, no. 468 (2005): 204–18. doi: 10.1353/jaf.2005.0014.

Ball, Henry C. "Missionary Reports." *Latter Rain Evangel*, October 1917, 18.

———. "Present Condition in the Lower Mexican Work." *Pentecostal Evangel*, October 20, 1917, 9.

———. "Untitled." *Weekly Evangel*, March 11, 1916, 12.

———. "Visit among Our Latin American Brethren." *Pentecostal Evangel*, July 13, 1935, 9.

———. "Work among Mexicanos in the War Zone." *Pentecostal Evangel*, May 22, 1915, 4.

Bennett Kinnon, Joy. "Weddings of the Year." *Ebony*, February 2004.

Blume, Stuart, and Ingrid Geesink. "A Brief History of Polio Vaccines." *Science* 288, no. 5471 (2000): 1593–94. doi: 10.1126/science.288.5471.15931594.

"Bolshevistic Mexico." *Pentecostal Evangel*, June 22, 1935, 5.

Bradlee, Ben, Jr. "Church's Dream of Building Oasis Dries Up." *Arizona Courier*, December 19, 1982. https://news.google.com/newspapers?nid=892&dat=19821219&id=NphOAAAAIBAJ&sjid=pUwDAAAAIBAJ&pg=6732,2958477.

"Breaking News: Carlton Pearson Steps Down from Christ Universal." *Gospel Today*, January 10, 2011. http://www.gospeltoday.com/blog/2011/01/10/breaking-news-carlton-pearson-steps-down-from-christ-universal.

Brown, Charles. "Selling Faith: Marketing Christian Popular Culture to Christian and Non-Christian Audiences." *Journal of Religion and Popular Culture* 24, no. 1 (2012): 113–29. doi: 10.1353/rpc.2012.0001.

Browne, H. Norton. "Elder Rosa Horn, Radio Exhorter, Believes in Witchcraft and that She Can Raise the Dead." *Afro American*, October 20, 1934. https://news.google.com/newspapers?nid=UBnQDr5gPskC&dat=19341020&printsec=frontpage&hl=en.

Callahan, Leslie. "Redeemed or Destroyed: Re-evaluating the Social Dimensions of Bodily Destiny in the Thought of Charles Parham." *Pneuma* 28, no. 2 (2006): 203–27. doi: 10.1163/157007406778689951.

Campbell, Duncan. "Temple Awaits Another Miracle." *Guardian*, July 17, 2000.

Carey, Benedict. "A Neuroscientific Look at Speaking in Tongues." *New York Times*, November 6, 2006. http://www.nytimes.com/2006/11/07/health/07brain.html.

Cherlin, Andrew J. "American Marriage in the Early Twenty-First Century." *Future of Children* 15, no. 2 (2005): 33–55. doi: 10.1353/foc.2005.0015.

Christie, Joel. "Court Upholds Life Sentence for Televangelist's Bodyguard Who Strangled His Family to Death While They Slept After Starting an Affair With His Wife's Childhood Friend." *Daily Mail*, January 3, 2015. www.dailymail.co.uk/news/article-2895728/Court-upholds-life-sentence-televangelist-s-bodyguard-strangled-family-death-slept-starting-affair-wife-s-childhood-friend.html.

Cole, Heather. "Meyer's 57 Million Evangelism Empire." *St. Louis Business Journal*, June 22, 2003. https://www.bizjournals.com/stlouis/stories/2003/06/23/story2.html.

"Communism, the Scourge of God." *Bridegroom's Messenger*, May 1936.

Courtwright, Julie. "A Slave to Yellow Peril: The 1886 Chinese Ouster Attempt in Wichita, Kansas." *Great Plaines Quarterly* 22, no. 1 (Winter 2002): 23–33. http://digitalcommons.unl.edu/greatplainsquarterly/2351/.

Creech, Joe. "Visions of Glory: The Place of the Azusa Street Revival in Pentecostal History." *Church History* 65, no. 3 (1996): 405–24. doi: 10.2307/3169938.
Dowie, John A. "The Flogging of Amos Dresser." *Leaves of Healing*, August 14, 1897, 657.
———. "What Should a Christian Do When Sick." *Leaves of Healing* 8, no. 39 (July 24, 1897): 617.
Elim Fellowship, "Statement Concerning Divorce and Remarriage." In Elim Fellowship, Constitution, By-Laws and Policies. www.elimfellowship.org/ef/wp-content/uploads/2015/10/Elim-Fellowship-CBL.pdf.
Elinson, Howard. "The Implications of Pentecostal Religion for Intellectualism, Politics, and Race Relations." *American Journal of Sociology* 70, no. 4 (1965): 403–15. doi: 10.1086/223874.
"A Failure of Faith in a Faith Healer." *Life*, March 5, 1956.
Faupel, William. "Theological Influences on the Teachings and Practices of John Alexander Dowie." *Pneuma* 29, no. 2 (2007): 226–53. doi: 10.1163/157007407X237935.
Finke, Roger, and Rodney Stark. "The New Holy Clubs: Testing Church-to-Sect Propositions." *Sociology of Religion* 62, no. 2 (2001): 175–89. doi: 10.2307/3712454.
"For Millennials, Parenthood Trumps Marriage." Pew Research Center, Social and Demographic Trends, March 9, 2011. http://www.pewsocialtrends.org/files/2011/03/millennials-marriage.pdf.
Gardiner, Gordon. "The Life, Ministry and Message of John Alexander Dowie." Accessed May 1, 2017. https://sites.google.com/site/leavesofhealing/leavesofhealingthelifegardiner.
General Council of the Assemblies of God. "Marriage." https://ag.org/Beliefs/Topics-Index/Marriage.
Hale, F. C. "Kingsville." *Pentecostal Evangel*, May 22, 1915, 9.
———. "Mexican Work at Ricardo, Texas." *Pentecostal Evangel*, February 12, 1916, 12.
Harter, Melvin. "1982 Gun Fight." MiracleValley.net. Accessed May 3, 2017. http://www.miraclevalley.net/subpage39.html.
Holm, Nils G. "Pentecostalism: Conversion and Charismata." *International Journal for the Psychology of Religion* 1, no. 2 (1991): 135–51. doi: http://dx.doi.org/10.1207/s15327582ijpr0103_1.
Jayson, Sharon. "Nearly 40% of Women Today Have Never Been Married." *USA Today*, March 22, 2012. https://usatoday30.usatoday.com/news/health/wellness/story/2012-03-22/Nearly-40-of-women-today-have-never-been-married/53697418/1.
Klink, Otto. "Otto-Graphs: Keeping Up With the Times." *Christ Ambassadors Herald*, June 1935, 16.

Lawless, Elaine J. "Rescripting Their Lives and Narratives: Spiritual Life Stories of Pentecostal Women Preachers." *Journal of Feminist Studies in Religion* 7, no. 1 (1991): 53–71. http://www.jstor.org/stable/25002145.

Leindecker, Urbane. "Vision on Miracle Valley." MiracleValley.com. www.miraclevalley.com.

Liu, Joseph. "Christian Movements and Denominations." Pew Research Center, Religion and Public Life Project, December 18, 2011. http://www.pewforum.org/2011/12/19/global-christianity-movements-and-denominations/.

Lovett, Leonard. "Perspective on the Black Origins of the Contemporary Pentecostal Movement." *Journal of the Interdenominational Theological Center* 1 (1973): 36–49.

Luce, Alice E. "Untitled." *Pentecostal Evangel*, October 21, 1916, 13.

"The Masses Unfitted To Rule Themselves." *Leaves of Healing* 15, no. 26 (October 15, 1904): 895.

Miller, Christine, and Nathan Carlin. "Joel Osteen as Cultural Selfobject: Meeting the Needs of the Group Self and Its Individual Members in and from the Largest Church in America." *Pastoral Psychology* 59, no. 1 (2009): 27-51. doi:10.1007/s11089-009-0197-7.

Moultrie, Monique. "After the Thrill Is Gone: Married to the Holy Spirit but Still Sleeping Alone." *Pneuma* 33, no. 2 (2011): 237–53. doi: 10.1163/027209611x575032.

O'Conner, Mary I. "Evangelicals in the Lower Mayo Valley." In *Holy Saints and Fiery Preachers: The Anthropology of Protestantism in Mexico*, edited by James W. Dow and Alan Sandstrom, 25–39. New York: Praeger, 2001.

Odegard, Kyle. "Rossiters Set for Trials; Court Paperwork Details Faith-Healing Church." *Albany Democrat Herald*, February 20, 2014. http://democratherald.com/news/local/crime-and-courts/rossiters-set-for-trials-court-paperwork-details-faith-healing-church/article_53bee87c-99cd-11e3-8321-0019bb2963f4.html.

Olazábal, Francisco. "Our Near Neighbors." *Latter Rain Evangel*, October 1921, 23.

Parham, Charles. "Free Love." *Apostolic Faith*, December 1, 1912, 4–5.

Ramirez, Margaret. "Some Christ Universal Temple Members Oppose Rev. Carlton Pearson's Appointment." *Chicago Tribune*, May 11, 2009. http://articles.chicagotribune.com/2009-05-11/news/0905100192_1_new-thought-church-new-storm.

"Religious Landscape Study." Pew Research Center, Religion and Public Life Project, May 11, 2015. http://www.pewforum.org/religious-landscape-study/.

Roll, Jarod H. "From Revolution to Reaction: Early Pentecostalism, Radicalism, and Race in South East Missouri, 1910–1930." *Radical History Review*, no. 90 (Fall 2004): 5–29.

Rothman, Joshua. "Church of U2." *New Yorker*, September 16, 2014. http://www.newyorker.com/culture/cultural-comment/church-u2.

Silverman, Lauren. "Texas Megachurch at Center of Measles Outbreak." *Weekend Edition Sunday*, National Public Radio, September 1, 2013. http://www.npr.org/2013/09/01/217746942/texas-megachurch-at-center-of-measles-outbreak.

"Spirit and Power: A 10-Country Survey of Pentecostals." Pew Research Center, Religion, Public Life Project, October 4, 2006. http://www.pewforum.org/2006/10/05/spirit-and-power/.

"The Story of Zion." *Leaves of Healing* 16, no. 1 (October 28, 1899): 3.

Streeter, Kurt. "Angelus Temple Will Keep Historic Interior." *Los Angeles Times*, October 15, 2001.

Sutton, Geoffrey W., and Martin W. Mittlestadt. "Loving God and Loving Others: Learning about Love from Psychological, Science, and Pentecostal Perspectives." *Journal of Psychology and Christianity* 31, no. 2 (2012): 161.

Sweeney, Gail. "The King of White Trash: Elvis Presley and the Aesthetics of Excess." In *White Trash: Race and Class in America*, edited by Matt Wray and Annalee Newitz (New York: Routledge, 1997), 249–67.

Tavernise, Sabrina. "Married Couples are No Longer a Majority." *New York Times*, May 26, 2011.

"To Whom It May Concern." Antioch-Jubilee.net. Accessed December 31, 2017. http://www.antioch-jubilee.net/miracle-valley-archive--aaallens-deathuntitled.html.

"To Whom It May Concern." *Miracle Valley Archives*. Accessed June 17, 2010. http://www.miraclevalleyarchives.org/gpage2.html.

"Untitled." *Bridegroom's Messenger*, May 1936, 7.

"Untitled." *Pentecostal Evangel*, July 16, 1935.

"Vet's Page." *Sly's Lil Sis*. Accessed December 31, 2017. http://www.slyslilsis.com/index1.cfm.%7BAU.

Wacker, Grant. "Marching to Zion: Religion in a Modern Utopian Community." *Church History* 54, no. 4 (1985): 496–511. doi: 10.2307/3166516.

Wald, Gayle. "The Bride Played Guitar." *Washingtonian*, March 1, 2007. https://www.washingtonian.com/2007/03/01/the-bride-played-guitar-1/.

———. "From Spirituals to Swing: Sister Rosetta Tharpe and Gospel Crossover." *American Quarterly* 55, no. 3 (2003): 387–416. doi: 10.1353/aq.2003.0031.

Wyatt, Edward. "Religious Broadcaster Gets Rich Contract for Next Book." *New York Times*, March 15, 2006. http://www.nytimes.com/2006/03/15/business/media/religious-broadcaster-gets-rich-contract-for-next-book.html.

Zeiders, Charles. "The Anthropological and Scientific Case for Psycho-Energetic Healing." *International Journal of Healing and Caring* 31, no. 1 (January 2003): 1–32.

"Zion Home of Hope for Erring Women." *Leaves of Healing* 6, no. 1 (October 28, 1899): 10.
Zuckerman, Phil. "Atheism, Secularity, and Well-Being: How the Findings of Social Science Counter Negative Stereotypes and Assumptions." *Sociology Compass* 3, no. 6 (2009): 949–71. doi: 10.1111/j.1751-9020.2009.00247.x.

Dissertations and Theses

Artman, Amy Collier. " 'The Miracle Lady': Kathryn Kuhlman and the Gentrification of Charismatic Christianity in Twentieth-Century America." Ph.D. dissertation, University of Chicago, 2009.
Doran, Justin. "The Heartfelt Spirit: Capitalism, Affect and Pentecostal Modernity in the Americas." Ph.D. dissertation, University of Texas–Austin, 2016.
French, Talmadge Leon. "Early Oneness Pentecostalism, Garfield Thomas Haywood and the Interracial Pentecostal Assemblies of the World, 1906–1931." Ph.D. dissertation, Birmingham University, 2011.
Heller, Jennifer L. "The Search for Something More: Evangelical Women, Middle-Class Marriage, and the 'Problem that Has No Name' in Popular Advice Books of the 1970s.'" Ph.D. dissertation, University of Kansas, 2007.
Lyon, John J. "The Christ Miracle Healing Center and Church: Racial Crisis in Arizona, 1980–1982." M.A. thesis, Arizona State University, 2002.
Nelson, Douglas J. "For Such a Time as This: The Story of Bishop William J. Seymour and the Azusa Street Revival; A Search For Penteecostal/Charismatic Roots." Ph.D. dissertation, University of Birmingham, 1981.

Books

Alexander, Estrelda. *Black Fire: One Hundred Years of African American Pentecostalism*. Downers Grove, Ill.: IVP Academic, 2011. Kindle.
Allen, A. A., and Lexie Allen. *The Life and Ministry of A.A. Allen*. Edited by John W. Carver Jr. Westminster, Md.: Faith Outreach International, 2010.
Anderson, Benedict. *Imagined Communities: Reflections on the Origin and Spread of Nationalism*. London: Verso, 2006.
Apostolic Faith Church. *The Apostolic Faith History, Doctrine and Purpose*. 2005. http://apostolicfaith.org/library/historical. E-book.
Bakker, Jay. *Faith, Doubt, and Other Lines I've Crossed: Walking with the Unknown God*. Nashville: Jericho Books, 2013.
———. *Son of a Preacher Man: My Search for Grace in the Shadows*. New York: Harper Collins, 2002.
Bakker, Jay, and Martin Edlund. *Fall to Grace: A Revolution of God, Self & Society*. New York: FaithWords, 2014.

BIBLIOGRAPHY

Baldwin, Deborah J. *Protestants and the Mexican Revolution: Missionaries, Ministers, and Social Change.* Champaign: University of Illinois Press, 1990.

Barfoot, Chas. H. *Aimee Semple McPherson and the Making of Modern Pentecostalism, 1890–1926.* New York: Routledge, 2014.

Bartleman, Frank. *How Pentecost Came to Los Angeles.* Grand Rapids, Mich.: Christian Classics Ethereal Library, 1925. https://www.ccel.org/ccel/bartleman/los.html.

Barthes, Roland. *Mythologies.* New York: Hill and Wang, 1972.

Berger, Peter L., and Thomas Luckmann. *The Social Construction of Reality: A Treatise in the Sociology of Knowledge.* New York: Anchor, 1967.

Bertrand, Michael T. *Race, Rock, and Elvis.* Champaign: University of Illinois Press, 2005.

Bowler, Kate. *Blessed: A History of the American Prosperity Gospel.* New York: Oxford University Press, 2013.

Boyer, Paul. *When Time Shall Be No More: Prophecy Belief in Modern American Culture.* Cambridge, Mass.: Harvard University Press, 2009.

Brown, Candy Gunther, ed. *Global Pentecostal and Charismatic Healing.* New York: Oxford University Press, 2011.

———. *Testing Prayer: Science and Healing.* Cambridge, Mass.: Harvard University Press, 2012. Kindle.

Butler, Anthea D. *Women in the Church of God in Christ: Making a Sanctified World.* Chapel Hill: University of North Carolina Press, 2007.

Conn, Charles W. *Where the Saints Have Trod: A History of Church of God Missions.* Cleveland, Tenn.: Pathway Press, 1959.

Dayton, Donald. *Theological Roots of Pentecostalism.* Ada, Mich.: Baker, 1991.

DeRogatis, Amy. *Saving Sex: Sexuality and Salvation in American Evangelicalism.* New York: Oxford University Press, 2014. Kindle.

Dorman, Jacob S. *Chosen People: The Rise of American Black Israelite Religions.* New York: Oxford University Press, 2013. Kindle.

Durkheim, Émile. *The Elementary Forms of the Religious Life.* London: G. Allen & Unwin, 1976.

Dyson, Michael Eric. *Mercy, Mercy Me: The Art, Loves, and Demons of Marvin Gaye.* New York: Basic Civitas, 2004.

Ellis, Mark. *Race, War, and Surveillance: African Americans and the United States Government during World War I.* Bloomington: Indiana University Press, 2001.

Emerson, Michael O., and Rodney M. Woo. *People of the Dream: Multiracial Congregations in the United States.* Princeton, N.J.: Princeton University Press, 2010.

Espinosa, Gaston. *William Seymour and the Origins of Global Pentecostalism.* Durham, N.C.: Duke University Press, 2014.

Finke, Roger, and Rodney Stark. *The Churching of America, 1776–2005: Winners and Losers in Our Religious Economy*. New Brunswick, N.J.: Rutgers University Press, 2008.

Friedan, Betty. *The Feminine Mystique*. New York: Norton, 2001. Kindle.

Gardiner, Gordon P. *The Story of John Alexander Dowie*.

Goff, James R. *Fields White unto Harvest: Charles F. Parham and the Missionary Origins of Pentecostalism*. Fayetteville: University of Arkansas Press, 1988.

González, Gilbert G. *Culture of Empire: American Writers, Mexico, and Mexican Immigrants, 1880–1930*. Austin: University of Texas Press, 2004.

Guralnick, Peter. *Last Train to Memphis: The Rise of Elvis Presley*. Boston: Little, Brown, 1994.

Haggard, Gayle, with Angela Elwell Hunt. *Why I Stayed: The Choices I Made in My Darkest Hour*. Carol Stream, Ill.: Tyndale House Publishers, 2010.

Harvey, Paul. *Freedom's Coming: Religious Culture and the Shaping of the South from the Civil War through the Civil Rights Era*. Chapel Hill: University of North Carolina Press, 2005.

Hejzlar, Pavel. *Two Paradigms for Divine Healing: Fred F. Bosworth, Kenneth E. Hagin, Agnes Sanford, and Francis MacNutt in Dialogue*. Leiden: Brill, 2010.

Hollenweger, Walter J. *Pentecostalism: Origins and Developments Worldwide*. Peabody, Mass.: Hendrickson, 1997.

Jackson, Phil, and Hugh Delehanty. *Sacred Hoops: Spiritual Lessons of a Hardwood Warrior*. New York: Hyperion, 1996.

Jacobsen, Douglas G. *Thinking in the Spirit: Theologies of the Early Pentecostal Movement*. Bloomington: Indiana University Press, 2003.

Johnson, Marilynn S. *The Second Gold Rush: Oakland and the East Bay in World War II*. Berkeley: University of California Press, 1996.

Jones, Charles E. *The Holiness-Pentecostal Movement: A Comprehensive Guide*. Lanham, Md.: Scarecrow Press, 2008.

Kaliss, Jeff. *I Want to Take You Higher: The Life and Times of Sly & the Family Stone*. Milwaukee: Backbeat, 2008.

Liardon, Roberts. *God's Generals: Why They Succeeded and Why Some Failed*. New Kensington, Penn.: Whitaker House, 2003. Kindle.

Lindsay, Dennis Gordon. *John Alexander Dowie: A Life Story of Trials, Tragedies and Triumphs*. Dallas: Christ for the Nations, 1980.

Luhrmann, Tanya M. *When God Talks Back: Understanding the American Evangelical Relationship with God*. New York: Alfred A. Knopf, 2012. Kindle.

MacRobert, Iain. *The Black Roots and White Racism of Early Pentecostalism in the USA*. Basingstoke, U.K.: Macmillan, 1988.

Malone, Bill C. *Don't Get above Your Raisin': Country Music and the Southern Working Class*. Champaign: University of Illinois Press, 2002.

Marcus, Greil. *Mystery Train: Images of America in Rock 'n' Roll Music*. New York: Penguin, 2008.

Martin, Darnise C. *Beyond Christianity: African Americans in a New Thought Church.* New York: New York University Press, 2005.
Martin, Lerone A. *Preaching on Wax: The Phonograph and the Shaping of Modern African American Religion.* New York: New York University Press, 2014. Kindle.
McCloud, Sean. *American Possessions: Fighting Demons in the Contemporary United States.* New York: Oxford University Press, 2015. Kindle.
McGuire, Meredith B., and Debra Kantor. *Ritual Healing in Suburban America.* New Brunswick, N.J.: Rutgers University Press, 1998.
Nussbaum, Martha Craven. *From Disgust to Humanity: Sexual Orientation and Constitutional Law.* Oxford: Oxford University Press, 2010. Kindle.
Parham, Charles F. "A Voice Crying in the Wilderness: Kol Kare Bomidbar." Bishop's Waltham, U.K.: Revival Library, 2014. Kindle.
Parham, Charles F., and Sarah E. Parham. *Selected Sermons of Charles F. Parham [and] Sarah E. Parham.* Baxter Springs, Kans.: Apostolic Faith Bible College, 1941.
Parham, Sarah E. *The Life of Charles F. Parham, Founder of the Apostolic Faith Movement.* Joplin, Mo.: Hunter Printing Company, 1930, Second Printing, 1969.
Payne, Leah. *Gender and Revivalism: Making a Female Ministry in the Early 20th Century.* New York: Palgrave Macmillan, 2015.
Pearson, Carlton. *God Is Not a Christian, nor a Jew, Muslim, Hindu—: God Dwells with Us, in Us, around Us, as Us.* New York: Atria, 2010.
———. *The Gospel of Inclusion: Reaching Beyond Religious Fundamentalism to the True Love of God and Self.* New York: Atria, 2014.
Poloma, Margaret M. *The Assemblies of God at the Crossroads: Charisma and Institutional Dilemmas.* Knoxville: University of Tennessee Press, 1989.
Ramírez, Daniel. *Migrating Faiths.* Chapel Hill: University of North Carolina Press, 2015.
Rayner, Richard. *A Bright and Guilty Place: Murder, Corruption, and L.A.'s Scandalous Coming of Age.* New York: Anchor, 2009.
Ritz, David. *Divided Soul: The Life of Marvin Gaye.* New York: McGraw-Hill, 1985.
Robeck, Mel. *Azusa Street Mission and Revival.* New York: Thomas Nelson, 2006.
Sánchez Walsh, Arlene M. *Latino Pentecostal Identity.* New York: Columbia University Press, 2003.
Sanford, Agnes Mary White. *Behold Your God.* St. Paul, Minn.: Macalester Park, 1958.
———. *The Healing Light.* New York: Ballantine Books, rev. ed. 1983.
———. *Sealed Orders.* Plainfield, N.J.: Logos International, 1972.
Sinitiere, Phillip Luke. *Salvation with a Smile: Joel Osteen, Lakewood Church, and American Christianity.* New York: New York University Press, 2015.
Sutton, Matthew A. *Aimee Semple McPherson and the Resurrection of Christian America.* Cambridge, Mass.: Harvard University Press, 2009.

———. *American Apocalypse: A History of Modern Evangelicalism*. Cambridge, Mass: Harvard University Press, 2015.
Synan, Vinson. *The Holiness-Pentecostal Tradition*. Grand Rapids, Mich.: Eerdmans, 1997.
Tarango, Angela. *Choosing the Jesus Way: American Indian Pentecostals and the Fight for the Indigenous Principle*. Chapel Hill: University of North Carolina Press, 2014.
Wacker, Grant. *Heaven Below: Early Pentecostals and American Culture*. Cambridge, Mass.: Harvard University Press, 2001.
Wald, Gayle Freda. *Shout, Sister, Shout! The Untold Story of Rock-and-Roll Trailblazer Sister Rosetta Tharpe*. Boston: Beacon Press, 2007.
Weber, Max. *On Charisma and Institution Building*. Edited by S. N. Eisenstadt. Chicago: University of Chicago Press, 1968.

Miscellaneous

Allen, A. A. *Did God Call the Apostle Paul to Preach to the Black Man?*, Music-Xpress, n.d. MP3.
Elim Bible Institute and College Student Handbook. Lima, N.Y.: Elim Bible Institute.
Emmanuel College Student Handbook 2016–17. Franklin Springs, Ga.: Emmanuel College.
Evangel University Student Handbook 2017–2018. The Office of Student Development, July 1, 2017.
"Fall 2017 Census." Gordon Conwell Theological Seminary. 2016. http://www.gordonconwell.edu/hamilton/future/FAQs.cfm.
Gaye, Marvin. "Marvin Gaye Says Goodbye." Soul Immortal. Allegro Corporation. 2010.
Gaye, Marvin, and Ed Townsend, writers. "Let's Get It On," recorded 1973, on Marvin Gaye, *Let's Get In On*, Tamla Records, 2002. CD.
"Heretics." *This American Life*, December 16, 2005. https://www.thisamericanlife.org/radio-archives/episode/304/heretics/.
Life Pacific College Student Handbook. San Dimas, Calif.: Life Pacific College, August 2015. http://lpc-docs.s3.amazonaws.com/lpc_student_handbook.pdf.
Meyer, Joyce. "List of Confessions." Joyce Meyer Ministries, 2008. https://secure.joycemeyer.org/content/articles/ea/list_of_confessions_by_joyce_meyer/listofconfessionsbyjoycemeyer.pdf.
NorthPoint Bible College Student Handbook. Haverhill, Mass.: NorthPoint Bible College and Graduate School, 2017.
Sánchez Walsh, Arlene M. *Fieldnotes*. Pasadena Foursquare Church, Pasadena, Calif. July 2004.

Videos

"A. A. Allen, One Body, Racism." YouTube, February 12, 2011. https://www.youtube.com/watch?v=8ZtY86LVAvU.

"A. A. Allen, Prosperity the Cadillac." YouTube, February 12, 2011. https://www.youtube.com/watch?v=8KIL05z3tsY.

"Bishop George Bloomer Interviews Bishop Carlton Pearson." YouTube, February 28, 2013. https://www.youtube.com/watch?v=xoFqIlt1nTg.

"Carlton Pearson Interview with Dr. Michael Beckwith." YouTube, June 25, 2009. https://www.youtube.com/watch?v=PsjkDP-yZkM.

Castillo, Thomas J. "Miracle Valley National News Stories." YouTube, September 10, 2008. https://www.youtube.com/watch?v=K8dIbIzeVoI.

Csaky, Mick, dir. "Sister Rosetta Tharpe: The Godmother of Rock and Roll." In *American Masters*. PBS. February 2013. http://www.pbs.org/wnet/americanmasters/sister-rosetta-tharpe-full-episode/2516/.

"Jack Coe Practicing Medicine Without a License." YouTube, February 16, 2011. https://www.youtube.com/watch?v=Bns7osifxao.

"Lonnie Frisbee on Kathryn Kuhlman Show." YouTube, February 10, 2011. https://www.youtube.com/watch?v=U2Ujlhwt9d8.

"Neale Donald Walsch Michael Bernard Beckwith Carlton Pearson & Dr. Marissa." YouTube, February 2, 2016. https://www.youtube.com/watch?v=1goWjrGTAjk.

"Small Talk about Sly part 1: Cornel West, Sly & the Family Stone Documentary." YouTube, January 23, 2016. https://www.youtube.com/watch?v=iBh9D3BG03g.

"Small Talk about Sly, part 2: Vet Stone & Cynthia Robinson, Documentary on Sly and the Family Stone." YouTube, January 25, 2016. https://www.youtube.com/watch?v=6CqK8EEC6Fc.

"To Hell and Back." *Dateline*, August 13, 2006. www.nbcnews.com

INDEX

A. A. Allen Revivals, 30
abortion, 36, 38
adultery, 44
AFC. *See* Apostolic Faith Church
Africa, Pentecostal statistics for, 103
African Americans, xxiv, 16–17, 94; Bay Area migration of, 105, 106–7; increased numbers of Pentecostal, 104; musicians influence on Presley, 53, 54, 55; Pentecostalism as started by, 70–71, 126n11, 125–126n11, 128n5, 128n9; racism against CMHCC, 76–81; tongues and, 5, 67
African Methodist Episcopal (AME) Church, xxii
AG. *See* Assemblies of God
Allen, Asa Alonzo, 15, 28–33, 120n54, 121n62; Miracle Valley land envisioned by, 77–78; racial integration efforts of, 16, 70, 76–77
allopathic medicine, opposition to, 8, 14, 16, 18–19
AME. *See* African Methodist Episcopal
American Christianity, racism in, xxii–xxiii

American exceptionalism, 23
Angelus Temple, 25, 27, 83–84
anti-Catholicism, 73, 74, 75, 129n31
anti-Semitism, 75
Apostolic Faith, xxiii, xxiii, xxvii
Apostolic Faith Church (AFC), xxvi–xxviii, 115n6
Assemblies of God (AG), 15, 38; anti-Catholicism in Mexican mission work of, 73, 74, 75, 129n31; deliverance ministry of, 52; indigenous principle in missions of, 69–70; on marriage, 40–41, 123n22; Mexican border missions of, 72–76, 129n31; Presley and, 53, 55; racial integration feared by, 54
assimilationist drive, 43–44, 69
Athey, Ron, 121n64
Atkinson, Maria, 42–44
Azusa Street Revival, xiv, 113n1 xviii, 118n19; Crawford and, xxiii, xxvi–xxix; imagined pasts of, 108; mailing list, xxiii, xxvi; Parham attempted takeover of, 20;

Azusa Street Revival (*continued*)
race and ethnicity, 107, 118*n*26; racism and, xx; Seymour's vision and, xx, xxiii, 114*n*4; speaking in tongues, 4–5; women in narratives on, 34

Bakker, Jay, 87, 88, 97–101
Bakker, Jim, 88, 98–99
Bakker, Tammy Faye, 88, 98, 100
Ball, Henry, 72–76
baptism, fire, xx. *See also* Spirit baptism
Barnett, Tommy, 49
Bay Area, African American migration to, 105, 106–107
bible colleges and universities: behavior and dress code handbooks, 35–39; geographic isolation and, 37–38, 122*n*12
bibles, sale of, 67
biblicism, 1, 7; divorce and, 123*n*19; evangelical bible reading and, 21, 118*nn*22–23
black Holiness Pentecostal denominations, xx–xxi
black New Thought churches, 95–96
Bloomer, George, 96
Bradford College, 38
Brazilian Pentecostal churches, 104
British Israelism, 22–23, 118*n*27
Buddhism, xv–xvi
bulbar polio, 9
Bynum, Juanita, 46–48, 50

calling out tactic, in healing, 90–91
Camps Farthest Out, 58
Cárdenas, Lázaro, 75, 129*n*31
Castillo, Thomas Javier, 78
Catholicism, 16; anti-, 73, 74, 75, 129*n*31; hell and, 96
celibacy, xxviii

charismatics and charismatic Christianity: anti-Pentecostal bias of, 59; Gaye's healing aesthetic and, 60–64, 126–127*n*39; Kuhlman's influence on view of, 89, 131*n*3; Osteen and, 65–68; populism and, 53–68; Presley's life and, 53–57; publicity problem of, 66; Sanford and, 58–60; successors and, 101
Chinese language, tongues in, 4, 20, 69, 128*n*2
Chinese ouster, 69, 128*n*2
Christ Miracle Healing Center and Church (CMHCC), 76–81
Christian Catholic Apostolic Church, 16
Church of God in Christ (COGIC), xvii, xxv, 44–47, 94, 108–9; Bay Area migration and, 105; first, 105; speaking in tongues in Chicago, 2, 6; St. Andrews, 105–6; women in, 70
church-sect theory, 120*n*49
civil rights movement, 77, 107
Clark, Glenn, 58
The Clash, 52
CMHCC. *See* Christ Miracle Healing Center and Church
Cochise County, Arizona. *See* Miracle Valley Ministerial Association; shoot-out, at Miracle Valley
Coe, Jack, 8–9, 16, 30
COGIC. *See* Church of God in Christ
Coleman, Chris, 131*n*9
collective representation, 29, 120*n*50
Collins, Dorothy, 78
competition, xiii, xiv, xvii, 105
confessions, xii, 2, 49, 63, 92–93, 114*n*3
conscientization, 83
conversion, 44; paradox of, 110
Copeland, Kenneth, 116*n*11
corporate takeover, of PTL, 99
Cotton Club, 44
country music, 54

Cowdry, William S., 71–72, 129*n*14
Crawford, Florence, xxiii, xxvi–xxix
Cristero War, 129*n*31
crossover artists, 45, 88

dancing, xxv, 36, 38, 39
dating, 37, 122*n*8
deliverance ministry, 52
demographics, 37–38, 83, 122*n*12; Latino/Latina population growth and, 84–85; marriage, 39, 122*n*16
demons, 40, 52, 64, 65, 123*n*20
denominations: black Holiness Pentecostal, xx–xxi; founded by women, xxi, 25; largest U.S., 104. *See also* white denominations; *specific denominations*
Denton, Texas, 105
depression, 58, 62
disputes, over origins, xvii. *See also* theological disputes
divorce, xxv, 38, 43–48, 50; bible and, 123*n*19; demonic rabbits blamed for, 40; destigmatization, 41–42
domestic violence, 48
Dowie, John Alexander, 8, 14, 16–19
draft, World War II, 71–72, 129*n*14
dress codes, 36, 37, 38, 39, 45
Duran, Elaine, 81
Duran, Eli, 79

Eastern religion, 62
Elim Bible Institute, 37
Emmanuel College, 36–37
emotionality, in Pentecostal broadcasting, 66
entertainment, Pentecostalism as, 15, 24
eschaton (return of Jesus), xiv, xv, xx, xxi, 110; Ethiopians and, 16, 17; Mexicans as signal of, 75; tongues and, 21
Ethiopians, 16, 17

ethnicity. *See* race and ethnicity
Evangel University, Assembly of God, 38–39
evangelism, xviii, 1, 21, 68, 113*n*2, 118*n*22; spiritual primogeniture in, 97. *See also* televangelists
"Everyday People" (Sly and the Family Stone), 106, 108
exile, Pearson's, 97
exorcism, 52

faith and practices, overview of, xvii. *See also specific practices*
Falwell, Jerry, 98–99
"Finished Work" controversy, xxvii–xxviii
Fire Baptized Holiness Church (Iowa), xx
forgiveness, Bakker, Jay on, 99, 100
founders, xi, xvii, 125–126*n*11; women, xxi
Foursquare denomination, 25–28, 81, 83–85, 119*n*43
Fox, Emmet, 58, 59–60
Friedan, Betty, 57
Frisbee, Lonnie, 89–90
Full Gospel Businessmen's Association, 65

Gay, Marvin, Sr., 60, 61, 63, 64
Gaye, Marvin, xviii, 60–64, 110, 126–127*n*39
gender and sexuality, xviii, 35–38, 46, 49–50, 88, 121*nn*2–3; Gaye and, 60, 62, 63; gender inequalities, xiii, 34, 121*n*1, 125*n*47; Presley's sexual aesthetic, 56; sexual purity ideal, 46–47; women's submission and, 92, 93
genocide, 82
geography, migration and, 104–105
glossolalia, 3

Golden Age, of Pentecostalism, xxi
Gordon-Conwell Seminary, 38
gospel of inclusivity, Pearson's, 94, 97
gospel singers, 76, 121. *See also* Tharpe, Rosetta
Great Depression, 15–16, 26, 27, 54
Great Migration, rationale behind, 106

Haggard, Gayle, 50, 125*n*47
Haggard, Ted, 48–50
hagiography, xv
Hahn, Jessica, 98
Hale, F. C., 72
Harter, Melvin, 78, 80. *See also* shoot-out, at Miracle Valley
Haynes, Alpha, 105, 106
Haynes, Omega, 105
Haywood, Garfield T., xxiv–xxvi, 70, 114*n*5
healing, 6–9, 7, 42–43, 116*n*10; calling out tactic, 90–91; Gaye's aesthetic of, 60–64, 126–127*n*39; narratives, 17–18, 57; in popular culture, 52–53; of poverty, 30–31; Sanford ministry of, xviii–xix, 57–60; therapeutic failure in, 10
hell, 94, 96, 100
hereditary charisma, 101
heretics, 87, 95
Heritage USA, 98
heterosexuality, 48, 49–50
Higher Dimensions Ministries, 94, 95
high-tension faith, 28, 37, 42, 120*n*49
historians, religious, xii, xiii, xvii
historiography, xii, xvi–xvii, xx, 114*n*3
Holiness movement: historiography of, 114*n*3; Pentecostalism ties to, xx–xxii
Hollywood, 26–28
Holm, Nils, 12
Holy Rollers, Presley and, 55–56
homosexuality, 36, 38, 49–50

Horn, Rosa A., 71–72
House of God, 62, 126–127*n*39
Hutton, David, 26

I Believe in Miracles (tv show), 89
ill health, Pentecostal view of, 8
indigenous principle, AG missions, 69–70
inductive method, of bible reading, 21, 118*n*22
innovators: narratives ignoring flaws of, 19; overview of Pentecostal, 14–16
International Divine Healing Association, 16
International Pentecostal Holiness, 36–37
interracial ministries, 31–32
interracial relations, 14; marriage, xxiv–xxv
interracial worship, racism not solved by, xx
invincibility narratives, 93
Irwin, Benjamin, xx

Jewish rituals, in House of God, 126–127*n*39
Jones, Charles P., xx–xxi
Jonestown, 78

kidnapping, McPherson, A., alleged, 25–26, 122*n*2
Kuhlman, Kathryn, 9, 87–91, 131*n*3, 131*n*6

Lakewood church, 65–67
Larson, Bob, 52
Latinos/Latinas, 84–85, 104, 109
Leiendecker, Urbane, 78
LGBT people, 88, 97–98, 100, 101
Life Bible Institute. *See* Life Pacific College
Life Pacific College, 38

INDEX

Lindsay, Gordon, 17, 19
Leaves of Healing, 16–17
Locke, Dixie, 53, 57
Luce, Alice E., 73
Luckmann, Thomas, xxiii, 113n2, 117n24
Luhrmann, Tanya, xiii, xxviii, 116n10
Lum, Clara, xxiii, xxvi–xxvii
Lyon, John J., 79

MacRobert, Iain, xxv–xxvi
malaria, 25
Malone, Bill C., 54
marriage, xxiv–xxv, xxviii–xxix, 36; AG on biblical view of, 40–41, 123n22; binary of divorce and, 46; choosing Spirit over, 47; crisis of, 51; demographics, 39, 122n16; Foursquare denomination bylaws on, 26; ideal and real, 39–42, 51, 122n16; imaginaries, 39, 48, 123n18; interracial, xxiv–xxv; millennials attitude towards, 123n17; ministry chosen above, 43; public Pentecostal examples of, 42–50, 125n47; same-sex, 88; statistics, 122n16
Martin, Gene, 31–32, 76
Mason, Charles Harrison, xx–xxi, 70, 71
McGlothen Temple Church of God, 105
McPherson, Aimee Semple, 15, 25–28, 84, 119n43; Kuhlman and, 90. *See also* Foursquare denomination
McPherson, Harold Stewart, 25
measles, refused vaccinations for, 116n11
Memphis Miracle, 108–109
Mexican Americans, 96
Mexican Pentecostal churches, 104
Mexican Revolution, 72
Mexicans: AG borderland missions and, 72–76, 129n31; anti-Catholicism periods, 129n31

Meyer, Joyce, 87, 88, 91–93, 131n9
migration: African American Bay Area, 105, 106–7; Horn's ministry and, 72; Mexican border missions and, 72–76, 129n31; three major streams of, 72; urban, 76–81; within U.S., 104–7
ministries: Bakker's puppet, 98; marriage and, 43; women in, 34, 71, 89, 90, 121n1
Miracle magazine, 31, 121n59, 121n61
miracle narratives, 109; smallpox healing and, xxvii
Miracle Revival Fellowship, 30
Miracle Valley Ministerial Association, 28–33; shoot-out, 76–81
miracle water, 30
miscegenation, 17; religious and musical, 54, 55, 56
missions and missionaries, 15; AG Mexican border, 72–76; assimilation goal of, 43–44; indigenous principle, 69–70; Parham attempted takeover of other, 20; tongues as aid to, 4–5, 21–22, 69
Moore, Jenny, xxiii
Morrison, Russell, 45
Murcutt, Florence, 73, 74
murder, Meyer scandal involving, 93, 131n9
music, 36, 44–47, 52, 105; Presley influenced by African American, 53, 54, 55; race and, 106–8

narratives: healing, 17–18, 57; invincibility, 93; miracle, xxviii, 109; power and, 108–9; repentance, 110; transgression spectrum and redemptive, 121n64; transgressions ignored in, 19, 28–29; women in Azusa Street, 34. *See also* stories

Native Americans, 29, 69–71, 104
New Life Church, 48–49
New Thought, 58, 59–60, 95–96
Niebuhr, Reinhold, 120n49
No More Sheets tour, 47
NorthPoint Bible College and Graduate School, 37–38
Nubin, Katie Bell, 44

Oakland Federal Council of Churches (OFCC), 105
Olazábal, Francisco, 73–74
Old Testament, prophecy and, 11–12
Oneness denomination, xxiv–xxvi, 70, 114n5, 126–127n39; largest African American, xxiv; reason for break from Trinitarian branch, 1
Oral Roberts University (ORU), 66, 94
orthodoxy, outliers and, 87–88, 100
ORU. *See* Oral Roberts University
Osteen, Joel, xviii, 64–68
Osteen, John, 65
outliers: definition of, 87; heretics as, 87, 95; orthodoxy and, 87–88, 100; polarizing effect of, 91; public figures as, xviii–xix. *See also specific people*
Ozman, Agnes, 4, 20, 69

pacifism, African American, 17, 57, 71
Palestine, xvi
paradox, 109; Pentecostalism future and, 110–11
Parham, Charles, xx, 8, 19, 23–25, 118nn22–23; AFC timeline and, xxvi–xxvii; challenge to founder status of, 125–126n11; influence of, 15; interracial worship opposed by, 5; Seymour and, 4, 20, 118n26; on Spirit baptism, xxii–xxiii; tongues ideas of, 4–5, 21–22, 69

PAW. *See* Pentecostal Assemblies of the World
PCNA. *See* Pentecostal Fellowship of North America
PE. *See Pentecostal Evangel*
Pearson, Carlton, 87, 93–97, 101
Pentecostal Assemblies of the World (PAW), xxiv, xxv
Pentecostal Evangel (PE), 72, 73, 75
Pentecostal Fellowship of North America (PCNA), 108–9
Pentecostalism: African American roots of, 70–71, 125–126n11, 128n5, 128n9; branches, 1, 70; definition difficulty for, 85–86; enduring characteristic of, xiii–xv; entrepreneurial spirit of, 14–16; evangelism compared to, 1; founders/pioneers most revered in, xi; future of, 110–11; gender inequalities in, xiii, 34, 121n1; geographic centers of origin, xxi; geography, of U.S., 104; Golden Age of, xxi; growth of, 103–4; hagiography, xv; as high-tension faith, 28, 37, 41–42, 120n49; history of origin stories, xx–xxv; number of adherents, xiii; pioneer focus of, xix; polarization of early, 24–25; racial groups comprising U.S., 104; revival launching modern-day, 113n1; statistics, 103; suburban, 81–86; timeline and spiritual lineage notions in, xvi–xvii. *See also specific denominations; specific topics*
performance artists, on transgression spectrum, 121n64
polio, 8–9
populism, xviii–xix, 15, 24, 30–31, 52; charismatics and, 53–68
poverty, healing of. *See* prosperity gospel
power, race and, 85, 107–9

INDEX

Praise the Lord (PTL) network, 98, 99
prayer rugs, 30
premillennialism, xxv
Presley, Elvis, xviii–xix, 53–57, 110
prophecy, 1–2, 10, 47–48, 75; prophetic imperative, xix, 72, 113*n*2; subjective reality and, 12, 117*n*24; types, 11–13
prosperity cloths, 32
prosperity gospel, 15–16, 30–32, 66, 68; Meyer known for, 87; paradox of, 111; Pentecostalism synonymous with, 103; popularity of, 111; word of faith, 92, 103
Protestants, U.S., percentage of Pentecostals among, 103
PTL. *See* Praise the Lord network

rabbits, divorce and, 40
race and ethnicity: AG indigenous principle and, 69–70; anti-Semitism, 75; assimilation and, 43–44, 69; Azusa Street, 5, 107, 118*n*26; diversity as racial integration, 82, 83–85, 109; divisions over, xx, 113*n*1; divisiveness over, xiii; ethnic identity in white Pentecostalism, 82–83; geographic regions of migration by, 104–5; Mexican migration and, 72–76, 129*n*31; Miracle Valley shoot-out and, 76–81; mirage of multiculturalism, 106; multiracial narratives, xvi; power and, 85, 107–9; Presley's racial interchange, 53–57; racial inequality, xxvi; Seymour's vision for harmony of, xx, xxiii, 114*n*4
racial integration, 29; Allen's belief in, 16, 70, 76–77; Presley's AG fear of, 54

racism, xi, xx, xxviii–xxix; in American Christianity, xxii; British Israelism and, 22–23, 118*n*27; against CMHCC African Americans, 76–81; Great Migration and, 106; interracial worship and, xx; mission work and, 15; Parham, 20, 22, 24; in PAW, xxv
Radio Chapel, 89
redemptive narratives, 121*n*64
religious historians, xii, xiii, xvii
religious miscegenation, 54, 55, 56
repentance narrative, 110
"Rev. E.," 95
revivals: A. A. Allen Revivals, 30; Miracle Revival Fellowship, 30. *See also* Azusa Street Revival
riots, Mansfield, Ohio, 18
Roberts, Oral, 30
Robertson, Pat, 11–12
Robinson, Lizzie, 70
rock music, 52
Roll, Jarod, 24
RuPaul drag show, 100
rural populism, 24

sacred sites, of Pentecostalism origins, xvii
same-sex marriage, 88
sanctification, xxi–xxii, xxiv, 70; repurposing of, 63–64
Sanford, Agnes, xviii–xix, 57–60
Satan, 65
satanic attacks, depression as, 58
scandal, 15, 34–35, 101, 121*nn*2–3; murder and, 93, 131*n*9. *See also specific ministers*
Scandinavian Pentecostal churches, 104
School of Pastoral Care, 58–59
segregation, xxv, 24–25, 81, 105
Semple, Robert James, 25

sexuality. *See* gender and sexuality
Seymour, William J., xx, xxiii, 70, 113*n*1, 114*n*4; Crawford and, xxvi–xxiii; Parham and, 4, 20, 118*n*26. *See also* Azusa Street Revival
shoot-out, at Miracle Valley, 76–81. *See also* Miracle Valley Ministerial Association
sin and temptation, psychology term for, 49
Sly and the Family Stone, 106–8
smallpox healing, xxvii
speaking in tongues, xxi–xxii, 2, 96, 109; actual language requirement of, 22; African Americans and, 5, 67; in Chinese language, 4, 20, 69, 128*n*2; emotional experience of, 6; *eschaton* link with, 21; faking, 6; as mission aid, 4–5, 21–22, 69; number of practitioners of, 3; parts of brain involved in, 3; pressure to participate in, 6; prophecy function compared with, 13; as Spirit baptism evidence, 3, 4, 21; waning practice of, 5; xenoglossic idea behind, 4
Spirit baptism, xxi, xxii–xxiii, xxiv, 65; tongues as evidence of, 3, 4, 21
spiritual gifts: hierarchy, 65; synonyms, 1–2. *See also* healing; prophecy; speaking in tongues
spiritual housecleaning, 123*n*20
spiritual imperialism, 23
spiritual life stories, 1, 9–10, 19, 66, 115*n*1
spiritual primogeniture, 97
St. Andrews COGIC, 105–6
Stanton, Ed, 84
Stanton, Ivy, 83–84
Stewart, K. C., 105–6
Stewart, Sly (Sly Stone), 106–8
Stewart family, in Bay Area, 105–6

stories, xi, xiii, xiv, 9; diversity of, xvi; history of origin, xx–xxv; shaping and re-purposing of, xxix. *See also* narratives; spiritual life stories
sub-Saharan Africa, 103
suburban Pentecostalism, 81–86
successors, 97, 101
Swaggart, Donny, 101
Swaggart, Jimmy, 98, 99, 101

tarrying, 61
TBN. *See* Trinity Broadcasting Network
televangelists, 66, 67–68, 88–92, 131*n*6; scandals common to, 101
testimonies. *See* stories
Tharpe, Rosetta, 44–47, 50, 54
thematic approach, to Pentecostalism study, xii–xiii, xvii
theodicy, 7, 116*n*10
theological disputes: Azusa Street break-up and, xxiii; in early African American Pentecostalism, 70; "Finished Work" controversy as, xxvii–xxviii; Holiness advocates and, xxii; over tongues, xxi–xxii; Spirit baptism-sanctification, xxiv
Thomas, Frances, 76, 78, 79, 80. *See also* shoot-out, at Miracle Valley
Thomas, William, Jr., 79. *See also* shoot-out, at Miracle Valley
Thorpe, Thomas J., 44
tongues. *See* speaking in tongues
transgressions, 28, 32–33, 121*n*62, 121*n*64. *See also specific ministers*
Trials of Ted Haggard, The, 48
Trinitarian branches, 1, 70, 114*n*5
Trinity Broadcasting Network (TBN), 47

U2, 11
United States (U.S.): largest denominations and racial groups in, 104; Pentecostal Protestants in, 103; Pentecostals migration within, 104–7
universalism, 96, 100
Urshan, Andrew, xxv
U.S. *See* United States

vaccinations, 116n11
violence, 29, 48, 60, 61, 62. *See also* shoot-out, at Miracle Valley
visions, 88, 94, 101
visualization, 59

Waltrip, Burroughs, A., Sr., 89
Weeks, Thomas, 46–48
white denominations, 82–83; civil rights movement viewed by, 107; largest U.S., 104
women: in Azusa Street narratives, 34; COGIC, 70; denominations founded by, xxi, 25; divorce choice by ministerial, xxv; in early African American Pentecostalism, 70–71; founders, xxi; isolated lives of 1940s, 57–58; Memphis Miracle and, 109; Meyer emphasis on submission by, 93; in ministries, 34, 71, 89, 90, 121n1
word of faith, 92, 103. *See also* prosperity gospel
word of knowledge, 12, 13
words of wisdom, 2, 13
World War II, 55, 71–72, 129n14
world-denying faith, 110–111

xenoglossic idea, speaking in tongues, 4

Yeomans, Lillian, 17–18

Zion Bible College. *See* NorthPoint Bible College and Graduate School
Zion City, Illinois, 16, 17, 18, 20

GPSR Authorized Representative: Easy Access System Europe, Mustamäe tee
50, 10621 Tallinn, Estonia, gpsr.requests@easproject.com

www.ingramcontent.com/pod-product-compliance
Lightning Source LLC
Chambersburg PA
CBHW021950290426
44108CB00012B/1009